Dawn Rayborn
20583 SW Anna Ct, Beaverton OR 97006
DAWN C. RAYBORN

THE LAST DAYS

TEACHINGS OF THE MODERN PROPHETS

VOLUME I

WITH COMMENTARY BY

DANIEL C. PETERSON

ASPEN BOOKS

The Last Days
Teachings of the Modern Prophets

© 1998
Aspen Books

Library of Congress Cataloging-in-Publication Data
The last days: teachings of the modern prophets / with commentary by Daniel C. Peterson
p.   cm.
Includes bibliographical references and index.
ISBN 1-56236-062-0 (v. 1 : hard cover)
1. Church of Jesus Christ of Latter-day Saints—Doctrines. 2. Mormon Church—Doctrines.   I. Peterson, Daniel C.
BX8635.5.L37   1997   97-18818
236'.9—dc21   CIP

Printed in the United States of America

Cover photograph of the Angel Moroni
by Craig W. Dimond
© The Church of Jesus Christ of Latter-day Saints
Used by permission.

To my father, Carl P. Peterson—
an Israelite indeed, in whom there is no guile.

LIST OF ABBREVIATIONS

AF	*The Articles of Faith*
AL	*The Abundant Life*
CD	*Collected Discourses*
CR	*Conference Report*
DBY	*Discourses of Brigham Young*
DNTC	*Doctrinal New Testament Commentary*
DS	*Doctrines of Salvation*
DWW	*The Discourses of Wilford Woodruff*
ER	*Evidences and Reconciliations*
FPM	*Faith Precedes the Miracle*
GG	*The Government of God*
GK	*The Gospel Kingdom*
HC	*History of the Church*
IE	*Improvement Era*
JD	*Journal of Discourses*
LF	*Lectures on Faith*
MD	*Mormon Doctrine*
MFP	*Messages of the First Presidency*
MiM	*The Millennial Messiah*
MoM	*The Mortal Messiah*
MWW	*A Marvelous Work and Wonder*
NWAF	*A New Witness for the Articles of Faith*
SGO	*Sharing the Gospel with Others*
SYHP	*Stand Ye in Holy Places*
TETB	*Teachings of Ezra Taft Benson*
TLS	*Teachings of Lorenzo Snow*
TPJS	*Teachings of the Prophet Joseph Smith*
TSWK	*The Teachings of Spencer W. Kimball*
VM	*The Vitality of Mormonism*
WP	*The Way to Perfection*

CONTENTS

CHAPTER 1

THE DISPENSATION OF THE FULNESS OF TIMES

The Lord has declared, by his own voice and by revelation to his servants, the prophets, that we are living in the last days. When we speak of the last days, we do not mean that this is the end of the earth, that it shall cease presently to exist. We mean that we are living in that period of time known as the dispensation of the fulness of times, in which the Father has promised to gather all things together in Christ, both which are in heaven and which are on earth. We mean we are living in the day when unrighteousness shall cease, when wickedness shall no longer be found on the face of the earth, when this earth shall be turned over, according to the promise the Lord made to Daniel the Prophet, to the saints of the Most High, who shall possess it forever and ever.[1]

Since the beginning of the Restoration, Latter-day prophets and apostles have described human history as a series of dispensations. God has called prophets and revealed the gospel unto them; the truth has been taught to others, and then, repeatedly, the inhabitants of the earth have rejected both the prophets and the truth they brought with them. Revelation or restoration has been followed by apostasy, and then the process has begun again. David W. Patten, the first president of the Quorum of the Twelve in the history of The Church of Jesus Christ of Latter-day Saints, spoke of this theme in a way that has been standard ever since:

Unto Adam first was given a dispensation. It is well known that God spake to him with His own voice in the garden, and gave him the promise of the Messiah. And unto Noah also was a dispensation given . . . And from Noah to Abraham, and from Abraham to Moses, and from Moses to Elias [Elijah], and from Elias [Elijah] to John the Baptist, and from then to

---

[1] Joseph Fielding Smith, DS, 3:14.

Jesus Christ, and from Jesus Christ to Peter, James, and John, the Apostles —all received in their time a dispensation by revelation from God.[2]

Unlike other Christian theologians, however, many of whom have interpreted the biblical record and the history it presents in much the same way, Latter-day Saint theologians teach that the revelations and dispensations of God are not confined to the ancient world. Indeed, the culminating dispensation began with the appearance of God the Father and God the Son to a young farmboy in a grove of trees near Palmyra, New York, in the spring of 1820. That young boy, Joseph Smith, became the founding prophet of this latest dispensation. He testified from deep personal knowledge and experience:

> God purposed in Himself that there should not be an eternal fullness until every dispensation should be fulfilled and gathered together in one, and that all things whatsoever, that should be gathered together in one in those dispensations unto the same fullness and eternal glory, should be in Christ Jesus; therefore He set the ordinances to be the same forever and ever, and set Adam to watch over them, to reveal them from heaven to man, or to send angels to reveal them. . . . These angels are under the direction of Michael or Adam, who acts under the direction of the Lord.[3]

Adam, as the founding prophet of the very first dispensation, the first man, and the father of all succeeding prophets and, indeed, of all men and women on the earth, holds the keys to his own dispensation and to all others. Under the Lord himself, he is responsible for them, and bears authority over them. Similarly, each founding prophet holds the keys for his own dispensation and, as declared by modern seers, exercises authority over whatever prophets and apostles may be called to succeed him in that dispensation. "Thus," said Brigham Young, the successor to Joseph Smith,

> the Lord found him [Joseph Smith Jr.], and called him to be a Prophet, and made him a successful instrument in laying the foundation of His kingdom for the last time. This people

---

2 David W. Patten, HC, 3:51.
3 Joseph Smith Jr., TPJS, 168.

never professed that Joseph Smith was anything more than a Prophet given to them of the Lord; and to whom the Lord gave the keys of this last dispensation, which were not to be taken from him in time, neither will they be in eternity.[4]

Fulfillment of the Hopes of All Previous Dispensations

But Latter-day Saint teachings present Joseph Smith's position in the divine plan as somewhat different from that of other founding prophets, for, just as Adam held and holds the keys to all succeeding dispensations, Joseph Smith was to preside over a dispensation in which all the authority and all the truths of all previous dispensations were to be restored. David W. Patten, who was not only the first president of the Quorum of the Twelve Apostles in this dispensation but also its the first martyr, taught that "the dispensation of the fullness of times is made up of all the dispensations that ever have been given since the world began, until this time." Throughout all of history, he said, God was moving "to accomplish the great scheme of restitution, spoken of by all the holy prophets since the world began; the end of which is the dispensation of the fullness of times, in the which all things shall be fulfilled that have been spoken of since the earth was made."[5] In so teaching, Elder Patten was passing on the doctrine that had been taught him by Joseph Smith, who, speaking of God, said,

> Now the purpose in Himself in the winding up scene of the last dispensation is that all things pertaining to that dispensation should be conducted precisely in accordance with the preceding dispensations.[6]

President John Taylor taught about this in great and explicit detail. "We have had," he explained,

> in the different ages various dispensations; for instance what may be called the Adamic dispensation, the dispensation of Noah, the dispensation of Abraham, the dispensation of

---

[4] Brigham Young, JD, 2.127.
[5] David W. Patten, HC, 3:51.
[6] Joseph Smith Jr., TPJS, 168.

Moses and of the prophets who were associated with that dispensation; the dispensation of Jesus Christ, when he came to take away the sins of the world by the sacrifice of himself, and in and through those various dispensations, certain principles, powers, privileges and priesthoods have been developed. But in the dispensation of the fulness of times a combination or a fulness, a completeness of all those dispensations was to be introduced among the human family. If there was anything pertaining to the Adamic, (or what we may term more particularly the Patriarchal) dispensation, it would be made manifest in the last days. If there was anything associated with Enoch and his city, and the gathering together of his people, or of the translation of his city, it would be manifested in the last days. If there was anything associated with the Melchizedek priesthood in all its forms, powers, privileges and blessings at any time or in any part of the earth, it would be restored in the last days. If there was anything connected with the Aaronic priesthood, that also would be developed in the last times. If there was anything associated with the apostleship and presidency that existed on this continent, it would be developed in the last times, for this is the dispensation of the fulness of times, embracing all other times, all principles, all powers, all manifestations, all priesthoods and the powers thereof that have existed in any age, in any part of the world. For, "those things which never have been revealed from the foundation of the world, but have been kept hid from the wise and prudent, shall be revealed unto babes and sucklings in this, the dispensation of the fulness of times." (D&C 128:18.)[7]

According to official declaration, the process of restoration is not yet complete. Some things, perhaps many things, remain to be brought back. "We believe all that God has revealed, all that He does now reveal, and we believe that He will yet reveal many great and important things pertaining to the Kingdom of God."[8] However, authorities of the Church have clearly taught that much has been done and that the saving essentials are here. John Taylor testified that

---

[7] John Taylor, GK, 101-2.
[8] Article of Faith 9.

God has ordained his holy priesthood upon the earth with presidents, apostles, bishops, high councils, seventies, high priests, and the order and organization of the church and kingdom of God in its fulness and completeness, more complete, perhaps, than it ever was since the world was framed. Why? Because it is the dispensation of the fulness of times, embracing all other times that have ever existed since the world was, and he has gathered us together for that purpose.[9]

President Wilford Woodruff, likewise, wished to impress upon us the immense significance of this time and of our assignment to it. "We live," he said,

in one of the most important dispensations that God ever gave to man, namely, the great and last dispensation of all dispensations, and the one in which the whole flood of prophecy in the holy Bible will be fulfilled, for most all of the prophecies contained in the sacred volume, from Adam to John the revelator, point to the great work of God in the last days, the days in which the God of heaven would set up a kingdom that should be an everlasting kingdom, and to whose dominion there should be no end, and the kingdom and the greatness of the kingdom under the whole heavens should be given into the hands of the Saints of the Most High God, and they are to possess it for ever and ever. I wish to have the Latter-day Saints understand their appointment, position, and responsibility before the God of heaven, and their responsibilities to both Jew and Gentile, living and dead, on this and the other side of the vail. . . . There never was a generation of the inhabitants of the earth in any age of the world who had greater events awaiting them than the present. As I before remarked, the fulfillment of this whole volume of revelation points to our day. The building up of the kingdom of God, the building up of the Zion of God, in the mountains of Israel, the erection of a standard for the Gentiles to flee unto, the warning of the nations of the earth to prepare them for the great judgments of our God, the building up of the Church, the sanctifying of the people, the building of Temples to the Most High God, that his servants may enter therein and become saviors on Mount Zion, redeeming both the living and the dead, all

---

[9] John Taylor, GK, 130.

these things are to be performed in our day. And an age fraught with greater interest to the children of men than the one in which we live never dawned since the creation of the world.[10]

Again, John Taylor, Wilford Woodruff's immediate predecessor in the presidency of the Church, sought to emphasize the seriousness of the mission of this dispensation. He explained:

We are living in a very important day and age of the world, in a time which is pregnant with greater events than in any other period that we know of, or in any other dispensation that has existed upon the earth. It is called "the dispensation of the fulness of times," when God "will gather together in one all things in Christ, both which are in heaven, and which are on earth"; for the heavens, the Gods in the eternal worlds, the holy priesthood that has existed upon the earth, the living that live upon the face of the earth, and the dead that have departed this life, are all interested in the work in which we are engaged. Consequently, it is of the greatest importance that everything we do, that every ordinance we administer, that every principle we believe in, should be strictly in accordance with the mind and word, the will and law of God.[11]

It was, however, not only God who looked forward to and worked toward this final dispensation. Wilford Woodruff, fourth president of The Church of Jesus Christ of Latter-day Saints, taught that "all inspired men, from the days of father Adam to the days of Jesus, had a view, more or less, of the great and last dispensation of the fulness of times, when the Lord would set his hand to prepare the earth and a people for the coming of the Son of Man and a reign of righteousness."[12] Orson Pratt agreed, and explained one of the reasons for the great interest that earlier prophets have taken in this dispensation. For this great time will see not only the restoration of principles linking the various dispensations together, but the establishment of links between the actual prophets and saints of the ancient and modern churches. The ancient saints, Elder Pratt taught, will be literal participants in the events of these latter days.

---

10 Wilford Woodruff, JD, 18:110–11.
11 John Taylor, GK, 20.
12 Wilford Woodruff, JD, 17:244–45.

When Adam, and Enoch, and his Zion, and all the righteous men before the flood, and all the holy patriarchs and Prophets of the eastern and western Continents, men who lived on the earth as strangers and pilgrims, but who through the eye of faith were permitted to behold, that in the dispensation of the fullness of times, all things would be gathered in one that were in Christ, even all things which are in heaven and which are on the earth; I say that when all these receive their inheritances, this will be an organization that takes hold of eternity, that takes hold of the children of God in all ages, that unites all dispensations in one, that brings all the kingdoms, and authorities, and powers, of all other dispensations, and unites them in one; and upon whom knowledge like a flood will be poured out even upon the vast congregations of the Church of the First Born, the living and the dead, for the dead will then be living.[13]

THE LAST DAYS A TIME OF GATHERING

Prophets and righteous men and women throughout history have looked forward, specifically, to this dispensation, and Church leaders have taught that there are a number of characteristics which set this dispensation apart from all others. One of the differences between our time and previous dispensations will be the literal, physical gathering of Christ's people, as Orson Pratt observed:

The dispensation that was introduced in the days of the apostles was not a dispensation of gathering. When the apostles went forth to build up the Church of Christ at Corinth or at Ephesus, in Galatia or any other part of the earth, the Christians all remained where they received the Gospel except those who were driven into the mountains by the persecutions of their enemies. But in the last dispensation there is to be one feature characterizing it that did not characterize the dispensation established by the ancient apostles, namely the gathering together of the people—all that are in Christ from the ends of the earth. When that dispensation is introduced Zion will be introduced again, the Lord will bring again Zion.[14]

---

[13] Orson Pratt, JD, 19:19.
[14] Orson Pratt, JD, 14:348.

NEVER AGAIN TO BE TAKEN FROM THE EARTH

The physical gathering of the Saints to the valleys of the American West was, in fact, a unique characteristic of the restored Church well into the twentieth century. But the prophets teach that there is, perhaps, an even more fundamental and important difference. Earlier dispensations failed. This one will not. Joseph Smith contrasted the dispensation in which we live with those led by earlier prophets:

> This is why Adam blessed his posterity; he wanted to bring them into the presence of God. They looked for a city, etc., ["whose builder and maker is God."—Hebrews 11:10]. Moses sought to bring the children of Israel into the presence of God, through the power of the Priesthood, but he could not. In the first ages of the world they tried to establish the same thing; and there were Eliases raised up who tried to restore these very glories, but did not obtain them; but they prophesied of a day when this glory would be revealed. Paul spoke of the dispensation of the fullness of times, when God would gather together all things in one, etc.; and those men to whom these keys have been given, will have to be there; and they without us cannot be made perfect.[15]

Wilford Woodruff declared that

> this is the only dispensation that God has ever established that was foreordained, before the world was made, not to be overcome by wicked men and devils. All other dispensations have been made war upon by the inhabitants of the earth, and the servants and Saints of God have been martyred. This was the case with Jesus and the Apostles in their day.[16]

On another occasion, President Woodruff reflected:

> It is true that other dispensations have had their Prophets and Apostles, but they never enjoyed the privilege that we do of having the kingdom of God continue upon the earth until it triumphs over all other kingdoms upon the face of the earth

---

[15] Joseph Smith Jr., HC, 3:388.
[16] Wilford Woodruff, JD, 17:245.

and stands forever. Former Apostles and Prophets had the unpleasant reflection that the Church which they had built up would fall away, or be overcome by the power of the Devil and wicked men, and that when they passed off the earth and went behind the vail, they would have to take the priesthood with them, because there would be none living worthy to receive it from under their hands. They will be crowned with the Saviour according to the promises, but in their lifetime they never had the opportunity of planting on the earth a kingdom that should remain until Jesus should reign as King of kings and Lord of lords.[17]

The "Great Apostasy," as Latter-day Saints often and with entire justice term the destruction of the early church and the period of relative darkness that ensued, meant real suffering to real, faithful people. But, to our immense blessing, we have the divine promise that this will not happen again, not to us. Ezra Taft Benson, thirteenth president of the Church, made much the same point that President Woodruff did. "This is," he said,

> the last and great dispensation in which the great consummation of God's purposes will be made, the only dispensation in which the Lord has promised that sin will not prevail. The Church will not be taken from the earth again. It is here to stay. The Lord has promised it and you are a part of that Church and kingdom—the nucleus around which will be builded the great kingdom of God on the earth. The kingdom of heaven and the kingdom of God on the earth will be combined together at Christ's coming—and that time is not far distant.[18]

A TIME OF JUDGMENT AND SEPARATION

However, not everything, and not everybody, will be "combined together at Christ's coming." The prophets have taught that the last days will also be a time of separation—between good and evil, between the righteous and the unrighteous. "It seems that this is a

---

[17] Wilford Woodruff, JD, 9:162.
[18] Ezra Taft Benson, TETB, 19.

dispensation peculiar in its nature, differing from former dispensations," said Orson Pratt.

> It is a dispensation of mercy and of judgment—of mercy to those who receive the message of mercy, but of judgment to those who reject that message. In other words it is a dispensation in which the Gospel has been revealed from heaven, the servants of God called to labor in the vineyard for the last time, and in which the Lord intends to pour out great and terrible judgments upon the nations of the wicked after they have been warned by the sound of the everlasting Gospel. . . . It seems that the dispensation in which the Angel should fly was to be characterized as a dispensation of judgment. Immediately after the Angel brought the Gospel judgment was to be poured out on the nations of the earth. In the 8th verse [Revelation 14] we read, "And there followed another Angel, saying, 'Babylon is fallen, is fallen, that great city, because she made all nations drink of the wine of the wrath of her fornication.' And a third Angel followed, saying with a loud voice, "If any man worship the beast and his image, and receive his mark in his forehead or in his hand, the same shall drink of the wine of the wrath of God, which is poured out without mixture into the cup of his indignation and he shall be tormented with fire and brimstone in the presence of the holy Angels and in the presence of the Lamb.'" (Revelation 14:9-10.)[19]

"There is a parable concerning this gathering dispensation," Elder Pratt said on another occasion.

> You recollect the Savior, in speaking of the end of the wicked world, in a parable, calls it a time of harvest. Before the time of harvest, there seemed to be a gathering together, and by and by, after this gathering, the tares were plucked out from among the wheat, and cast out in bundles, ready to be burned; but those that were not tares, those that were really wheat, were the ones that were prepared to enter in and partake of the blessing of the Lord. This was spoken, not concerning the former dispensation, but that dispensation immediately preceding the end of the world.[20]

---

[19] Orson Pratt, JD, 15:329, 336.
[20] Orson Pratt, JD, 21:279.

The prophets have taught that for the righteous, however, for those who love truth and goodness and God, this will be a glorious time of restitution and reconciliation between peoples, between the living and the dead, between God and his children. Perhaps Joseph Smith caught something of the excitement of it when he declared:

> The building up of Zion is a cause that has interested the people of God in every age; it is a theme upon which prophets, priests and kings have dwelt with peculiar delight; they have looked forward with joyful anticipation to the day in which we live; and fired with heavenly and joyful anticipations they have sung and written and prophesied of this our day; but they died without the sight; we are the favored people that God has made choice of to bring about the Latter-day glory; it is left for us to see, participate in and help to roll forward the Latter-day glory, "the dispensation of the fullness of times, when God will gather together all things that are in heaven, and all things that are upon the earth, "even in one," when the Saints of God will be gathered in one from every nation, and kindred, and people, and tongue, when the Jews will be gathered together into one, the wicked will also be gathered together to be destroyed, as spoken of by the prophets.[21]

---

[21] Joseph Smith, Jr., HC, 4:609–10.

CHAPTER 2

THE RESTORATION OF THE GOSPEL

AN ANGEL SENT FROM HEAVEN

From the beginning, the apostles and prophets of this dispensation have associated the restoration of the gospel with the prophecy of John the Revelator, according to which an angel would "fly in the midst of heaven, having the everlasting gospel to preach to them that dwell on the earth, and to every nation, and kindred, and tongue, and people, saying with a loud voice, Fear God, and give glory to him; for the hour of his judgment is come."[1] There were, of course, other "restorationists" in early nineteenth-century America, and perhaps elsewhere. And, very possibly, there were others who also expected that restoration to be effected by angelic means. Where The Church of Jesus Christ of Latter-day Saints differed, and differed gloriously, with such people was in its claim that this restoration had already occurred. John Taylor summarized the claims of the Restoration as follows:

> Now, then, an event like this was to transpire; the everlasting Gospel was again to be introduced to man upon the earth. Joseph Smith came forward telling us that an angel had administered to him, and had revealed unto him the principles of the Gospel as they existed in former days, and that God was going to set his hand to work in these last days to accomplish his purposes and build up his kingdom, to introduce correct principles, to overturn error, evil, and corruption, and to establish his Church and kingdom upon the earth.[2]

Orson Pratt, who knew Joseph Smith well and was associated with the Church from its earliest years, was forthright in his declaration. "Now we have this important message to testify," he declared,

---

1 Revelation 14:6. See, for instance, John Taylor, JD, 14:364-65.
2 John Taylor, JD, 14:365.

and we testify it in all boldness, we testify it before the heavens, we testify it before the earth, we testify it in the name of
the Lord God who has sent us, in the name of Jesus Christ
who has redeemed us, that that angel has already come, that
the 19th century is the favored century in which God has fulfilled this ancient prediction, uttered by the mouth of his
ancient servant. God has indeed sent that angel, and when he
came he revealed the everlasting gospel.[3]

This was earthshaking news, and Elder Pratt knew it. "God," he
said,

who is in yonder heavens, has spoken in our day . . . he has
sent forth angels, messengers from heaven, who have appeared
to men here on the earth, and have conversed with them. . . .
God, by angels, and by his own voice, has sent forth messengers again unto the human family with an important message,
a message more important, in one sense of the word, than any
which has before been delivered to man—a message to prepare the way before the face and coming of his Son from the
heavens.[4]

The Prophet Joseph Smith, to whom the angel had initially
come, also testified of that visit and of its importance to us. He tried
to warn us how much depends upon whether or not we accept the
message delivered by the angel and the testimony of those chosen to
convey it to us.

The scripture is ready to be fulfilled when great wars, famines,
pestilence, great distress, judgments, etc., are ready to be
poured out on the inhabitants of the earth. John saw the angel
having the holy Priesthood, who should preach the everlasting
Gospel to all nations. God had an angel—a special messen-
ger—ordained and prepared for that purpose in the last days.
Woe, woe be to that man or set of men who lift up their hands
against God and His witness in these last days: for they shall
deceive almost the very chosen ones![5]

---

3 Orson Pratt, JD, 14:258.
4 Orson Pratt, JD, 14:256.
5 Joseph Smith Jr., TPJS, 365.

Orson Pratt suggested a reason why an angel was necessary to restore the gospel. If an angel was required, Elder Pratt reasoned, it could only be because, prior to the angel's appearance, the true gospel was not on the earth.

> Here then, we perceive the nature of the preparatory work for the coming of the Son of Man sitting upon a cloud. The Gospel is to be preached to all nations, and that Gospel, when it is restored to the earth, must be restored by an angel from heaven... What does this indirectly prove? It proves that there was no nation, no people, no kindred, no tongue, upon the face of the whole earth that had the everlasting Gospel when the angel should come; because, if there had been any people, however obscure they might be, however distant they might be from what are termed civilized nations, if there had been any people, on the earth who had the Gospel, they would have a Christian Church, with Apostles and Prophets and all the gifts of the spirit therein. But inasmuch as every nation, kindred, tongue and people on the whole earth was completely destitute of the Gospel, and of the Church as organized in ancient days, it was necessary to restore it anew from heaven, and it is predicted that that should be done by an angel.[6]

THE SPREAD OF THE GOSPEL

The work of the latter days was, of course, not completed by the revelations to Joseph Smith. Much remained, and remains, to be done. Brigham Young, who succeeded the great founding prophet of this dispensation in the presidency of the Church, knew this as well as anybody. "Joseph Smith," he testified,

> has laid the foundation of the kingdom of God in the last days; others will rear the super structure. Its laws and ordinances, its blessings and privileges have been laid before all people who would hear; the testimony of God's servants has sounded like the voice of a trumpet from nation to nation, and from people to people, warning the honest and meek of the earth to flee from Babylon to the chambers in the mountains for safety

---

6 Orson Pratt, JD, 18:173.

until the indignation shall be past. If all the inhabitants of the earth had been as diligent in searching out the truth and as willing to receive it as hundreds in this congregation have been, the world would have been converted long ago. But few people, compared with the masses, have ever received and lived the Gospel of Jesus Christ, in any age of the world in which it has been preached.[7]

Knowing that the gospel message would meet resistance and faithlessness, President Young nevertheless hoped that the work would be completed in his day and that he would live to see the final outcome. He was well aware, though, that this might not be the case.

I may say that this Gospel is to spread to the nations of the earth. Israel is to be gathered, Zion redeemed, and the land of Joseph, which is the land of Zion, is to be in the possession of the Saints, if the Lord Almighty lets me live; and if I go behind the veil somebody else must see to it. My brethren must bear it off shoulder to shoulder.[8]

For prophets such as President Young, there was and is no doubt whatsoever about how things will end, for God, who does not fail, is in command of the whole process.

By and by the world will be overturned according to the words of the prophet, and we will see the reign of righteousness enter in, and sin and iniquity will have to walk off. But the power and principles of evil, if they can be called principles, will never yield one particle to the righteous march of the Savior, only as they are beaten back inch by inch, and we have got to take the ground by force. Yes, by the mental force of faith, and by good works, the march forth of the Gospel will increase, spread, grow and prosper, until the nations of the earth will feel that Jesus has the right to rule King of nations as he does King of Saints.[9]

Brother Brigham's confidence rested on the rock of personal testimony. He and his brethren of the Council of the Twelve had

7 Brigham Young, JD, 9:364-65.
8 Brigham Young, DBY, 322.
9 Brigham Young, DBY, 113.

declared this testimony in a statement issued in the dark days just after the murder of their leader, the Prophet Joseph Smith.

> [God] has revealed the fulness of the gospel, with its gifts, blessings, and ordinances.—And we know it. He has commanded us to bear witness of it, first to the Gentiles and then to the remnants of Israel and the Jews.—And we know it.[10]

THE PURPOSE OF THE RESTORATION

The purpose of the Restoration is, of course, to save us. This is the purpose of every action undertaken by God, who is a being of unlimited goodness. "For behold," he says, "this is my work and my glory—to bring to pass the immortality and eternal life of man."[11] And modern prophets have explained that those goals cannot be attained except on the basis of revelation and the ordinances of the priesthood. John Taylor understood this and taught it clearly:

> God has restored the gospel for the purpose of bringing life and immortality to light; and without the knowledge of the gospel there is no knowledge of life and immortality; for men cannot comprehend these principles only as they are made known unto them, and they cannot be revealed only through the medium of the gospel, and through obedience to the laws of salvation associated therewith. . . . Hence when the heavens were opened and the Father and Son appeared and revealed unto Joseph the principles of the gospel, and when the holy priesthood was restored and the Church and kingdom of God established upon the earth, there were the greatest blessings bestowed upon this generation which it was possible for man to receive. If they could comprehend it, it was the greatest blessing which God could confer upon humanity. Then he sent his servants forth to proclaim this gospel to the nations of the earth, and he is now sending them forth to preach the gospel of the Son of God, to deliver the testimony that he has given unto us. And, speaking for the priesthood, have we done it? We have, and we have done it in the name of Israel's God; and he has been with us and I know it.[12]

10 The Twelve Apostles, MFP, 1:263.
11 Moses 1:39.
12 John Taylor, GK, 123.

Because of the Restoration, we can approach God upon the same basis as the Saints and believers of ancient history. And, modern Church authorities such as President Taylor have affirmed, we have precisely the same hope of salvation and exaltation that was made available to them.

> Now this is the position; it is just the same as they had in former days. The Gospel that they had in any age of the world was to lead men to God; the Gospel that we have, and that we have taught to you, is to lead you to God, to righteousness, to virtue, purity, integrity, to honor, to revelation, to a knowledge of the ways of God, and of his purposes pertaining to you and your families, to your progenitors and your posterity; pertaining to this world and that which is to come. It is a revelation adapted peculiarly to the position that we occupy in these last days.[13]

Some may wonder why it is that the records of the believers of former days would not be enough for us. Do we not have the accounts of the ancient Saints, and the teachings of the ancient prophets, in the Bible? Joseph Smith knew and taught that the ordinances of the gospel were not to be obtained from the study of old books alone, valuable and helpful though those are.

> Though we cannot claim [the] promises which were made to the ancients for they are not our property, merely because they were made to the ancient Saints, yet if we are the children of the Most High, and are called with the same calling with which they were called, and embrace the same covenant that they embraced, and are faithful to the testimony of our Lord as they were, we can approach the Father in the name of Christ as they approached Him, and for ourselves obtain the same promises. These promises, when obtained, if ever by us, will not be because Peter, John, and the other Apostles, with the churches at Sardis, Pergamos, Philadelphia, and elsewhere, walked in the fear of God, and had power and faith to reveal and obtain them; but it will be because we, ourselves, have faith and approach God in the name of His Son Jesus Christ, even as they did; and when these promises are obtained, they

13 John Taylor, JD, 14:366.

will be promises directly to us, or they will do us no good. They will be commandments and walking uprightly before Him. If not, to what end serves the Gospel of our Lord Jesus Christ, and why was it ever communicated to us?[14]

WORKING TOWARD A BETTER WORLD

But our individual salvation is not the only aim of the restoration of the gospel. That Restoration, and its spread and acceptance throughout the world, will also reform the societies in which we live. Our relations with our fellow human beings will be improved, just as our relationship with our Father in heaven will be. This, too, was the dream of the Quorum of the Twelve when they issued their proclamation to the world not long after the assassination of the Prophet Joseph Smith. Though they may have underestimated the time and difficulty that remained before the return of the Savior—would they have been able to bear the burden so well, if they had known at the first how long it would rest upon them and their posterity?—their statement shows beyond doubt that their attention was focused not only on salvation in another world. No, they hoped for, and intended to help build, a better world in the here and now as well.

Have you not the same interest in it that we have? Is it not sent forth to renovate the world—to enlighten the nations—to cover the earth with light, knowledge, truth, union, peace and love? And thus usher in the great millennium, or sabbath of rest, so long expected and sought for by all good men? We bear testimony that it is. And the fulfillment of our words will establish their truth, to millions yet unborn: while there are those now living upon the earth who will live to see the consummation.[15]

This concern for earthly society as well as for the eternal individual has remained characteristic of the teachings of the prophets and apostles of The Church of Jesus Christ of Latter-day Saints. While some in the Christian world opt for an individualistic pietism that ignores social issues and concentrates only upon personal salvation,

14 Joseph Smith Jr., TPJS, 66.
15 The Twelve Apostles, MFP, 1:256.

and some others hold that true Christianity is to be expressed in liberation theologies that often downplay hopes for a world beyond this one, the restored gospel insists both on the celestial kingdom and the building of Zion. It perfectly blends this-worldliness, sanctified, with other-worldliness. Our prophets have long taught us to serve in both the temples and on the welfare farms, to pray and to work hard, to value both the spirit and the body, to recognize that nothing, not even the most humble or seemingly mundane aspect of life, is fully secular or wholly temporal.[16] "This is a time," said David O. McKay,

> when mankind should turn their thoughts to the teachings of Christ, our Lord and Savior, and in larger numbers than the world has heretofore witnessed conform thereto their attitudes and actions. Unless multitudes of men and women so change their hearts and lives, the world will continue to be in turmoil, and our present civilization be threatened with disintegration.[17]

Earlier, President McKay had explained that

> we believe firmly that the basis upon which world peace may be permanently obtained is not by sowing seeds of distrust and suspicion in people's minds; not by engendering enmity and hatred in human hearts; not by individuals or nations arrogating to themselves the claim of possessing all wisdom, or the only culture worth having; not by war with resulting suffering and death from submarines, poison gas, or explosions of nuclear bombs. No! The peace that will be permanent must be founded upon the principles of righteousness as taught and exemplified by the Prince of Peace, our Lord and Savior, Jesus Christ, ". . . for there is none other name under heaven given among men, whereby we must be saved." (Acts 4:12.)[18]

It is by means of this combination of the temporal and the eternal, the glorious and the mundane, out of a constant effort of prayer and work and study and service and receiving the ordinances of the priesthood that we will grow—with the indispensable help of our Father in Heaven and through the atonement of his Son Jesus

---

16 See, for instance, Doctrine and Covenants 29:34.
17 David O. McKay, CR, April 1969, 5.
18 David O. McKay, CR, April 1955, 24.

Christ—toward Godlikeness, which is our goal. No factor alone, whether it be work or prayer or study or service or ordinances, will suffice for the full, embodied, glorious exaltation that we have been promised if we are faithful. And, since life in the celestial world is social, organized in families, it is fitting that the gospel taught by the Church here on earth emphasizes not only personal piety but our life together as Saints and our being in (but not of) the world.

There is, of course, a long way to go. None of us, not the president of the Church nor the most recent convert, has learned and mastered all there is to know and do. It can easily seem overwhelming. But the prophets remind us that there is no cause for concern or despair, so long as we are on the right path. The atonement of Christ, by assuring us that we need not be perfect to qualify as candidates for exaltation, has given us all the time not merely in the world but in the eternities. As Joseph Smith taught,

> When you climb up a ladder, you must begin at the bottom, and ascend step by step, until you arrive at the top; and so it is with the principles of the gospel—you must begin with the first, and go on until you learn all the principles of exaltation. But it will be a great while after you have passed through the veil before you will have learned them. It is not all to be comprehended in this world; it will be a great work to learn our salvation and exaltation even beyond the grave.[19]

TO THE GENTILES FIRST, THEN TO THE JEWS

Modern prophets and apostles have few if any illusions about how difficult it will be to reform the world, or to take the gospel to each and every child of God. They know that there are some who, for whatever reason, simply will not accept it. Brigham Young, ever the realist, saw this clearly:

> Enoch possessed intelligence and wisdom from God that few men ever enjoyed, walking and talking with God for many years; yet, according to the history written by Moses, he was a great length of time in establishing his kingdom among men. The few that followed him enjoyed the fulness of the

---

19 Joseph Smith Jr., MFP, 1:214.

Gospel, and the rest of the world rejected it. Enoch and his party were taken from the earth, and the world continued to ripen in iniquity until they were overthrown by the great flood in the days of Noah; and, "as it was in the days of Noah, so shall it be in the days of the coming of the Son of Man."[20]

Having foreseen this, God himself has decreed the order in which the gospel will be taken to the inhabitants of the earth. "We have been laboring now for forty-five years in preaching the Gospel of Christ throughout the Gentile nations," said Wilford Woodruff in 1875.

We say Gentiles, because the Gospel goes to the Gentiles first, that the first may be last and the last first. Anciently the Jews were first in having the Gospel sent unto them, but they rejected it, and they were broken off through unbelief, and hence the Gospel turned to the Gentiles; and, as Paul says—"Ye Gentiles, take heed and fear, lest ye fall through the same example of unbelief, for if God spared not the natural branches, take heed also lest he spare not ye." The Gentiles are fallen through the same example of unbelief as did the Jews. They have put to death every Prophet, Apostle, and inspired man since the days of Jesus Christ, and the Church went into the wilderness, and the face of a Prophet, Apostle or inspired man, called of God to administer the ordinances of the Gospel, had not been seen for some eighteen hundred years, until the Lord raised up a Prophet in the day and age in which we live. Therefore the Gospel brought forth in the last days has to go to the Gentiles first.[21]

The preaching of the gospel to the Gentiles and then to the Jews was also a favorite theme of Orson Pratt. "The Lord," he said,

also told them that when the fullness of the Gentiles had come, when their times were fulfilled, then his servants should be sent to all the scattered remnants of the house of Israel, who should be grafted in again; but first, the fullness of the Gentiles must come in. You know that Scripture which says—"The first shall be last, and the last shall be first." Now the Gospel, when it was preached in ancient times, was preached first to the Jews,

---

20 Brigham Young, JD, 9:365.
21 Wilford Woodruff, JD, 18:112.

the house of Israel, to those of Israelitish origin, and when they counted themselves unworthy of eternal life, and rejected that Gospel, "Lo" says Paul, "we turn unto the Gentiles.". . . But in the last days, when the angel brings the Gospel, it is reversed, and it is preached first to the Gentiles, to bring in their fullness, and to fulfill their times, and then it will be sent to the house of Israel. . . . The great object of the angel in restoring the Gospel was, in the first place, to fulfill the times of the Gentiles. Inquires one—"What do you mean by that?" I mean that God will send this Gospel, restored by an angel, to every nation, kindred, people, and tongue in the Gentile world before he will permit his servants to go to the scattered remnants of Israel; and they will labor with, preach to and declare the work of God to the Gentile nations, and seek to bring them to a knowledge of the ancient Gospel, and to organize a Church among them, so far as they will hearken to and receive their testimony. Then, when the Gentile nations shall reject this Gospel and count themselves unworthy of eternal life, as the Jews did before them, the Lord will say—"It is enough, come away from them, my servants, I will give you a new commission, you shall go to the scattered remnants of the house of Israel. I will gather them in from the four quarters of the earth, and bring them again into their own lands. They shall build Jerusalem on its own heap; they shall rear a Temple on the appointed place in Palestine, and they shall be grafted in again." Now that, in short, is the nature of the great latter-day preparatory work for the coming of the Son of Man.[22]

"By and by," predicted Wilford Woodruff, sounding the same prophetic theme,

the testimony of the Gospel will be sealed among the Gentiles, and the Gospel will turn to the whole house of Israel, and the judgments of God will back up the testimony of the Elders of this Church, and the Lord will send messengers who will go forth and reap down the earth. The unbeliever may say that what we term judgments have always prevailed more or less among the nations, and that God has nothing to do with them, they are all natural. Well, if they have always prevailed, they will

---

22 Orson Pratt, JD, 18:176-77.

prevail to a greater extent in these last days than ever before, until everything that God has spoken shall come to pass.[23]

THE BIBLE AND THE BOOK OF MORMON

How will this be done? Again, Orson Pratt, explained the process by which the Lord, through his servants, will bear witness to the nations.

> The question is, How will he bring about the fulfillment of the times of the Gentiles? I answered, by sending forth to them the stick of Joseph, written upon for Joseph, in connection with the Bible, by his servants who go forth to the nations of the earth. They will proclaim to all people, nations and tongues, to the Gentiles first, the fullness of the Gospel of the Son of God, contained in these two records. The testimony of two nations running together and growing into one is stronger than the testimony of one nation; and when the Lord makes the ancient continent of America bear record to the same great truths; when he unites the Bible of the Western hemisphere, with the Bible of the East, and sends it forth to the nations of the earth, it will be a witness, and evidence and a testimony sufficient to bring about what is termed the fullness of the Gentiles, or to fulfill their times.[24]

This process is well under way even now. Millions on every continent have accepted the Book of Mormon, and found through it renewed committment to Jesus Christ. But more, much more, remains to be accomplished. Considering the magnitude of the task that still lies before us, members of the Church would do well to join in the prayer of President Ezra Taft Benson:

> God bless us as Latter-day Saints who have been given the custody of the gospel of salvation, and who will have the responsibility of carrying it not only to Judah but to all the world. God bless us that we may discharge that obligation honorably and faithfully and do all those things which the Lord requires at our hands.[25]

---

23 Wilford Woodruff, JD, 18:38.
24 Orson Pratt, JD, 15:190.
25 Ezra Taft Benson, TETB, 108.

CHAPTER 3

THE RESTORED CHURCH OF JESUS CHRIST

The story of the dispensation of the fulness of times begins in the United States of America, and the prophets and apostles of the modern Church have testified that this was not the result of mere chance. "It was the Lord," declared Ezra Taft Benson,

> who created an atmosphere of freedom here in America so that his Church could be restored in its fullness for the blessing of all mankind. Here in these United States the Lord has established his base of operations in these last days. He selected America. That is why I love the United States of America in a special manner.[1]

THE STONE OUT OF THE MOUNTAIN

From this base, the Church has spread around the world. The Lord and his servants knew from the start, of course, that this would happen. One of the most popular passages from the Old Testament among early Latter-day Saints was the prophecy of Daniel, from which we learn that "in the days of [certain latter-day rulers of whom the prophet had already spoken] shall the God of heaven set up a kingdom, which shall never be destroyed: and the kingdom shall not be left to other people, but it shall break in pieces and consume all these kingdoms, and it shall stand for ever." Daniel compared that kingdom to a "stone . . . cut out of the mountain without hands."[2] In our own dispensation, inspired commentators have linked the fulfillment of Daniel's prophecy with the rise and growth of The Church of Jesus Christ of Latter-day Saints. "Out of this Church," testified Brigham Young,

> will grow the Kingdom which Daniel saw. This is the very people that Daniel saw would continue to grow and spread

---

1 Ezra Taft Benson, CR, October 1965, 122.
2 See Daniel 2:34, 44-45.

and prosper; and if we are not faithful, others will take our places, for this is the Church and people that will possess the Kingdom for ever and ever.[3]

James E. Talmage offered an important explanation of the terms involved in consideration of this prophecy, pointing out that

the Kingdom of God and the Church of Christ are virtually synonymous terms. We do not pray that this organization shall come; for it is now existent. We pray and strive for its growth and development, for the spread of its saving principles, and for their acceptance by all mankind. But the Kingdom of Heaven is greater than the Church as the latter exists today, and when fully established will be seen to be a development thereof. Its advent is yet to be prayed for.[4]

Though much remains to be prayed for and to be done, a great deal has been accomplished. Since the commencement of the history of the Church with a poor, young, uneducated farmer on the New York frontier, the progress of the restored gospel has been nothing short of astonishing. As Spencer W. Kimball noted,

With ever greater speed the stone that Daniel saw cut out of the mountain without hands is rolling forth to fill the whole earth. From a church whose membership was for the first hundred years largely confined to the white nations of America and Europe, we have grown to a worldwide force, embracing men of all colors and cultures. And we must learn the lesson that our fellowship is as universal as God's love for all men.[5]

GROWING AS A MUSTARD SEED

Another favorite scriptural image to which modern apostles and prophets have commonly alluded as they discuss the remarkable growth of the kingdom in the latter days is that of the mustard seed, compared by the Savior himself to the community of those who had

---

[3] Brigham Young, DBY, 438.
[4] James E. Talmage, VM, 180.
[5] Spencer W. Kimball, FPM, 293-94.

covenanted to follow him. "The kingdom of heaven," he said, "is like to a grain of mustard seed, which a man took, and sowed in his field: which indeed is the least of all seeds: but when it is grown, it is the greatest among herbs, and becometh a tree, so that the birds of the air come and lodge in the branches thereof."[6] The Prophet Joseph Smith, for instance, identified this image as "having an allusion to the Kingdom that should be set up, just previous to or at the time of the harvest. . . . Now we can discover plainly that this figure is given to represent the Church as it shall come forth in the last days."[7] And a better symbol could scarcely be found for the latter-day Church, which has emerged from the obscurity of a handful of poor and uneducated people on the early nineteenth century New York frontier to worldwide prominence, embracing members in every region of the earth, from Latin America to Japan, from Central Asia to Iceland, from East Africa to India to New Zealand.

NOT WITHOUT OPPOSITION

Images like that of the rolling stone, cut from the mountain without hands, or of the tiny mustard seed growing into a substantial plant should not lull us into thinking that such growth, or such rapid forward progress, will be achieved without obstacles. Joseph Smith knew this well.

> The Kingdom of heaven is like unto a mustard seed. Behold, then is not this the Kingdom of heaven that is raising its head in the last days in the majesty of its God, even the Church of the Latter-day Saints, like an impenetrable, immovable rock in the midst of the mighty deep, exposed to the storms and tempests of Satan, but has, thus far, remained steadfast, and is still braving the mountain waves of opposition, which are driven by the tempestuous winds of sinking crafts, which have [dashed] and are still dashing with tremendous foam across its triumphant brow; urged onward with redoubled fury by the enemy of righteousness? . . . The above clouds of darkness have long been beating like mountain waves upon the immovable rock of the Church of the Latter-day Saints;

---

6 Matthew 13:31-32; compare Mark 4:30-32, Luke 13:18-19.
7 Joseph Smith Jr., TPJS, 98.

and notwithstanding all this, the mustard seed is still tower-
ing its lofty branches, higher and higher, and extending itself
wider and wider; and the chariot wheels of the Kingdom are
still rolling on, impelled by the mighty arm of Jehovah; and
in spite of all opposition, will still roll on, until His words are
all fulfilled.[8]

While scriptures and the prophets assure us that the Church as a
body will never be destroyed in this last dispensation, there is no guar-
antee that we as individuals cannot lose our path and fall away. "The
Lord," taught Ezra Taft Benson, "has stated that His Church will never
again be taken from the earth because of apostasy (see D&C 138:44)."

But He has also stated that some members of His Church will
fall away. There has been individual apostasy in the past; it is
going on now, and there will be an ever-increasing amount in
the future. While we cannot save all the flock from being
deceived, we should, without compromising our doctrine,
strive to save as many as we can. For, as President J. Reuben
Clark, Jr., said, "We are in the midst of the greatest exhibition
of propaganda that the world has ever seen." Do not believe
all you hear. . . . We are assured that the Church will remain
on the earth until the Lord comes again—but at what price?
The Saints in the early days were assured that Zion would be
established in Jackson County, but look at what their unfaith-
fulness cost them in bloodshed and delay.[9]

"The Church is under attack," observed Spencer W. Kimball. He
was referring not merely to the avowed enemies of the Church, with
their books and pamphlets and slickly dishonest movies. More than
those, and perhaps more even than the overt attacks of those who are
infuriated by the Church's positions on moral and family issues, he
had in mind the infinitely subtler assaults of immorality and materialism, of ethical rot, of indiscipline and the lust for immediate grati-
fication.

The Church and its agencies and institutions constitute a little island in a great ocean. If we cannot hold the line and keep

---

[8] Joseph Smith Jr., MFP, 1:65, 66–67.
[9] Ezra Taft Benson, TETB, 90, 107.

the floods of error and sin from entangling us and engulfing us, there is little hope for the world. Tidal waves of corruption, evil, deceit, and dishonor are pounding our shores constantly. Unless we can build breakwaters and solid walls to hold them back, the sea will engulf us and destroy us also.[10]

SECURITY IN PRIESTHOOD LEADERSHIP

Where amidst all these challenges, are we to find security? We are to find it as the ancient Saints found it, in the living oracles and revelations of God, as well as in the precious records of the prophets and Saints of former times. It is in this way, and only in this way, that we will come to unity in the faith. John Taylor declared this in the nineteenth century.

Here then, God was desirous of introducing his kingdom upon the earth, and he had, in the first place, to organize his church to organize the people that he had scattered among the nations and to bring them together, that there might be one fold and one shepherd, and one Lord, one faith, and one baptism, and one God, who should be in all and through all, and by which all should be governed. To facilitate this object, he organized his holy priesthood as it existed in the heavens, and he gave a pattern of these things, just as much as he did in the days of Moses, only more so.[11]

Ezra Taft Benson reaffirmed the same truth in the twentieth century.

It was predicted in scripture that the Lord would restore His Church in these latter days prior to His second coming. Like the former-day Church, His restored Church was to have Apostles, prophets, and current revelation which added new scripture. We declare that this prophecy has come to pass. Through the Prophet Joseph Smith the Lord has established His Church again on earth.[12]

---

[10] Spencer W. Kimball, TSWK, 438.
[11] John Taylor, GK, 208–9.
[12] Ezra Taft Benson, TETB, 111.

But unity and security do not come simply because ecclesiastical institutions or organization have been made to resemble or imitate the institutions of biblical times. Such resemblance is necessary, but it would not be sufficient. The same animating force that gave life to those ancient models must vivify the modern Church as well. And, thankfully, it does. Real priesthood authority functions today, led and guided, as it was anciently, by literal inspiration from God. The apostles and prophets of this dispensation have, therefore, taught since its earliest years that members of the Church can trust securely in the Lord's guidance of its leaders. "The Lord Almighty leads this Church," said Brigham Young,

> and he will never suffer you to be led astray if you are found doing your duty. You may go home and sleep as sweetly as a babe in its mother's arms, as to any danger of your leaders leading you astray, for if they should try to do so the Lord would quickly sweep them from the earth. Your leaders are trying to live their religion as far as they are capable of doing so.[13]

"We are safe as long as we do our duty," testified President Wilford Woodruff, whose long career put him in close contact with every prophet and apostle of the nineteenth century.

> No matter what trials or tribulations we may be called to go through the hand of God will be with us and sustain us. I ask my Heavenly Father to pour out his spirit upon me, as his servant, that in my advanced age, and during the few days I have to spend here in the flesh, I may be led by his inspiration. I say to Israel, the Lord will never permit me or any other man who stands as president of this Church to lead you astray. It is not in the program. It is not in the mind of God. If I were to attempt that the Lord would remove me out of my place, and so he will any other man who attempts to lead the children of men astray from the oracles of God and from their duty. God bless you. Amen.[14]

Spencer W. Kimball gave similar counsel, noting that

---

13 Brigham Young, DBY, 137.
14 Wilford Woodruff, DWW, 212–13.

Paul . . . warned us against the deceivers who would come even before his departing. And they have continued to come, and they are among us today. The authorities which the Lord has placed in his Church constitute for the people of the Church a harbor, a place of refuge, a hitching post, as it were. No one in this Church will ever go far astray who ties himself securely to the Church Authorities whom the Lord has placed in his Church. This Church will never go astray; the Quorum of the Twelve will never lead you into bypaths: it never has and never will. There could be individuals who would falter; there will never be a majority of the Council of the Twelve on the wrong side at any time.[15]

Even more recently, President Gordon B. Hinckley has offered the same testimony:

His Church will not be misled. Never fear that. If there were any dispostion on the part of its leaders to do so, He could remove them.[16]

Notice that there is no claim here of infallibility, and certainly no claim that individual leaders of the Church, even General Authorities, are protected against all error. They are imperfect, mortal human beings, and have never claimed to be anything else. Nonetheless, their callings are from God, and Elder Kimball rightly affirmed that

those people who stand close to them will be safe. And conversely, whenever one begins to go his own way in opposition to authority, he is in grave danger. I would not say that those leaders whom the Lord chooses are necessarily the most brilliant, nor the most highly trained, but they are the chosen, and when chosen of the Lord they are his recognized authority, and the people who stay close to them have safety.[17]

Joseph Fielding Smith, who served for many decades as historian of the Church, as well as an apostle and a prophet, reflected that

---

[15] Spencer W. Kimball, CR, April 1951, 104.
[16] Gordon B. Hinkley, Ensign, May 1997, 83,
[17] Spencer W. Kimball, CR, April 1951, 104.

No man ever went astray by following the counsel of the authorities of the Church. No man who ever followed the teachings or took advice or counsel from one who stands as the representative of the Lord ever went astray; but men who refused to accept counsel have gone astray and into forbidden paths, and in some instances have even denied the faith. Others who went astray because they failed to understand and to heed the counsels that were given unto them for their eternal good, have humbled themselves and come back to the Church acknowledging their error.[18]

No one, however, will be compelled to obey. Coercion has no part in The Church of Jesus Christ of Latter-day Saints. The prophets have taught that even when the gospel has gone forth to all the nations and every person has had the chance to hear it, there will always be those who will choose, for whatever reasons, not to accept it. As Brigham Young said,

If the Latter-day Saints think, when the Kingdom of God is established on the earth, that all the inhabitants of the earth will join the Church called Latter-day Saints, they are mistaken. I presume there will be as many sects and parties then as now. Still, when the Kingdom of God triumphs, every knee shall bow and every tongue confess that Jesus is the Christ, to the glory of the Father. Even the Jews will do it then; but will the Jews and Gentiles be obliged to belong to the Church of Jesus Christ of Latter-day Saints? No; not by any means.[19]

PURIFICATION OF THE CHURCH

There will, in the days before the coming of the Savior, even be those who have nominally accepted the gospel, members of the Church, who nonetheless do not live their lives according to the principles revealed from heaven. With these people, too, the prophets have counseled patience as well as loving service that attempts to recall them to their covenants. "I am not for cutting people off from the Church that worship their property instead of their God," said Brigham Young with his characteristic twinkle of humor,

---

[18] Joseph Fielding Smith, DS, 1:243.
[19] Brigham Young, DBY, 439

but for bearing with them until they shall gain light and knowledge so as to see their errors and turn to the God of truth. I would say to idolaters, "If you have faith in an idol, have a little more; and if you have faith enough the Lord may work upon your minds so that you can understand the blessings he has in store for his people."[20]

President John Taylor knew that, fundamentally, purification and reform in the Church had to come from recommittment in the lives of its members. It could not be imposed, somehow, from the top down, and Church leaders have never sought to do so. "We talk about a Church," said its third president,

> that is to be built up and purified. If it is ever built up and purified, it will be under the influence of the gift of the Holy Ghost, the power of God manifested among his people, whereby iniquity will be rooted out, righteousness sustained, the principles of truth advanced, honor, integrity, truth, and virtue maintained, and hypocrisy, evil, crime, and corruption of every kind be rooted out. That will have to be done by the aid and under the guidance of the Almighty. There is no man living in and of himself, can guide the ship of Zion or regulate the affairs of the Church and kingdom of God unaided by the Spirit of God, and hence he has organized the Church as he has with all the various quorums and organizations as they exist today.[21]

The Prophet Joseph Smith, however, referring to the parable of the wheat and the tares reported in the gospel of Matthew, reminded us that the Lord would not always permit the two to grow together in the Church.[22] There will come a time when he will divide them, thrusting the tares into the flames of everlasting punishment and misery.

> Now we learn by this parable, not only the setting up of the Kingdom in the days of the Savior, which is represented by the good seed, which produced fruit, but also the corruptions of

---

[20] Brigham Young, JD, 6:196.
[21] John Taylor, GK, 38.
[22] See Matthew 13:24–30, 36–43.

the Church, which are represented by the tares, which were sown by the enemy, which His disciples would fain have plucked up, or cleansed the Church of, if their views had been favored by the Savior. But He, knowing all things, says, Not so. As much as to say, your views are not correct, the Church is in its infancy, and if you take this rash step, you will destroy the wheat, or the Church, with the tares; therefore it is better to let them grow together until the harvest, or the end of the world, which means the destruction of the wicked.[23]

If we wish, therefore, to be a part of the progress of the kingdom in the latter days, it is up to us to conform our lives to the counsel of God's prophets, and to freely choose the path of obedience and service marked out by the Savior himself. In this respect, though much has been done, our leaders have emphasized that much more could yet be done to hasten the establishment of the Kingdom of Heaven. "If we were fully united as a people in our missionary work," Harold B. Lee declared,

we would rapidly hasten the day when the gospel would be preached to all people without and within the boundaries of the organized stakes of Zion. If we are not united, we will lose that which has been the lifeblood and which has fed and stimulated this Church for a generation.[24]

---

23 Joseph Smith Jr., MFP, 1:64.
24 Harold B. Lee, CR, April 1950, 96.

CHAPTER 4

THE HOLY PRIESTHOOD

THE RESTORATION OF THE PRIESTHOOD

"All the testimony," said Joseph Smith of the ancient prophecies contained in the Bible, "is that the Lord in the last days would commit the keys of the priesthood to a witness over all people."[1] And, in fact, among the very first items communicated to the young prophet by the Angel Moroni was a revised version of the prophecy of Malachi: "Behold I will reveal unto you the Priesthood, by the hand of Elijah the prophet, before the coming of the great and dreadful day of the Lord."[2]

Years later, Wilford Woodruff testified that those predictions had, in fact, been fulfilled:

> This is the privilege that we enjoy as Latter-day Saints. When the time had come, according to the decree of the Almighty, an angel visited the earth and committed the Priesthood to Joseph Smith and Oliver Cowdery, and gave them instructions and a promise that they should be inspired to lay it before the people. We have embraced this Gospel, and the Spirit of God enlightens our minds, so that we comprehend, by the inspiration of the Almighty, those principles that are necessary for our present and eternal salvation.[3]

From another perspective, of course, Latter-day Saint doctrine makes clear that the restoration of the priesthood was not a finite event that occurred and was exhausted with one or two angelic visitations, important and spectacular though they were. Rather, the restoration of the priesthood was a process, a process that is perhaps not fully complete even today. "The keys of this Priesthood," taught the Prophet Joseph Smith,

---

[1] Joseph Smith Jr., HC, 6:364.
[2] Joseph Smith Jr., HC, 1:12; Joseph Smith—History 1: 38–39.
[3] Wilford Woodruff, JD, 9:161.

consisted in obtaining the voice of Jehovah that He talked
with him—Noah—in a familiar and friendly manner, that He
continued to him the keys, the covenants, the power and the
glory, with which he blessed Adam at the beginning; and the
offering of sacrifice, which also shall be continued at the last
time; for all the ordinances and duties that ever have been
required by the Priesthood, under the directions and commandments of the Almighty in any of the dispensations, shall
all be had in the last dispensation, therefore all things had
under the authority of the Priesthood at any former period,
shall be had again, bringing to pass the restoration spoken of
by the mouth of all the Holy Prophets.[4]

THE PURPOSES OF THE PRIESTHOOD

What is the purpose of the priesthood and of its restoration?
Modern prophets and apostles have seen in it both earthly and heav-
enly purposes. "What is this priesthood given us for?" asked
President John Taylor.

That we may be enabled to build up the Zion of our God.
What for? To put down wrong and corruption, lasciviousness,
lying, thieving, dishonesty, and covetousness, with every kind
of evil, and also to encourage faith, meekness, charity, purity,
brotherly kindness, truthfulness, integrity, honesty, and everything that is calculated to exalt and ennoble mankind, that we
may be the true and proper representatives of God our Father
here upon the earth, that we may learn to know his will and
do it; that his will may be done on earth as in heaven. And
hence, Zion is spoken of as being the pure in heart.[5]

The claim that only those associated with the restored priesthood
are "the true and proper representatives of God our Father here upon
the earth" is a strong one, and will no doubt seem harsh to many. In
considering it, we must not forget that the latter-day prophets and
apostles of God have always repudiated any idea of coercing people to
accept the gospel, and we must keep in mind that their insistence that
the inhabitants of the earth hearken to the dictates of God's chosen

---

[4] Joseph Smith Jr., HC, 4:210–11.
[5] John Taylor, GK, 130–31.

servants stems not from personal vanity or greed for power, but from a zeal for the Lord. "Priests, bishops, and clergy, whether Catholic, Protestant, or Mahomedan," declared the Twelve Apostles in a statement issued not long after the assassination of Joseph Smith,

> will . . . have to yield their pretended claims to the priesthood, together with titles, honors, creeds and names; and reverence and obey the true and royal priesthood of the order of Melchisedech, and of Aaron; restored to the rightful heirs, the nobility of Israel; or, the dearth and famine will consume them, and the plague sweep them quickly down to the pit, as in the case of Korah, Dathan and Abiram, Who pretended to the priesthood, and rebelled against God's chosen priests and prophets, in the days of Moses.[6]

Of course, these people of other religions will not *merely* be asked to submit to the authority of the priesthood—though they must, of course, first do that. God's love for his children is great and it is even-handed. He is no respecter of persons, meaning that he loves all alike. "And he inviteth them all to come unto him and partake of his goodness; and he denieth none that come unto him, black and white, bond and free, male and female; and he remembereth the heathen; and all are alike unto God, both Jew and Gentile."[7] Church doctrine makes it clear that all peoples of the world will be invited to accept the priesthood and to receive its sacred ordinances, and it will be conferred upon them so that they can share the blessings they have been given with yet others, living and dead.

The words of the prophets make it clear that great and portentous issues are involved. "Satan," John Taylor observed,

> has held dominion, and rule, and power, over the human family, for generations and generations; and God is gathering

---

[6] The Twelve Apostles, MFP, 1:259. The language of the declaration seems somewhat unkind and judgmental by today's standards. Nineteenth century religious and political polemics were rougher than those to which we are generally accustomed; perhaps the recent murder of their leader and the on-going violence of sectarian mobs also affected their tone. In any case, I doubt if any Church leaders today would use the term "pretended" to describe the claims of most other religious believers. In fact, although a discussion of this would be beyond the scope of the present work, I seriously doubt that even Church leaders of the nineteenth century usually thought in those terms.
[7] 2 Nephi 26:33.

together a little nucleus here—a band of brethren clothed upon with the Holy Priesthood and the Spirit of God, by which they will be able to roll back the cloud of darkness that has overwhelmed the inhabitants of the earth, and plant the principles of truth, and establish the kingdom of God.[8]

A HEAVENLY AND EARTHLY PRIESTHOOD

This is, obviously, an unfathomably important mission. Prophets and sages and ordinary people have dreamed for centuries of a society that would be based on principles of justice, morality, peace, and kindness. The restoration of the priesthood is a step, say modern apostles and prophets, toward fulfilling that ancient vision. Joseph Smith spoke eloquently of the role that we, in The Church of Jesus Christ of Latter-day Saints, are called upon to play in the fulfillment of their dreams:

The heavenly Priesthood will unite with the earthly, to bring about those great purposes; and whilst we are thus united in one common cause, to roll forth the kingdom of God, the heavenly Priesthood are not idle spectators, the Spirit of God will be showered down from above, and it will dwell in our midst. The blessings of the Most High will rest upon our tabernacles, and our name will be handed down to future ages; our children will rise up and call us blessed; and generations yet unborn will dwell with peculiar delight upon the scenes that we have passed through, the privations that we have endured; the untiring zeal that we have manifested; the all but insurmountable difficulties that we have overcome in laying the foundation of a work that brought about the glory and blessing which they will realize; a work that God and angels have contemplated with delight for generations past; that fired the souls of the ancient patriarchs and prophets; a work that is destined to bring about the destruction of the powers of darkness, the renovation of the earth, the glory of God, and the salvation of the human family.[9]

Latter-day scripture likewise teaches that the purpose of the restored priesthood is not limited only to the temporal world. It is a

---

[8] John Taylor, JD, 5:157–58.
[9] Joseph Smith Jr., TPJS, 232.

link between this world and the next. By means of the ordinances of the priesthood, for example, human beings are prepared to behold the face of God.

> And this greater priesthood administereth the gospel and holdeth the key of the mysteries of the kingdom, even the key of the knowledge of God.
>
> Therefore, in the ordinances thereof, the power of godliness is manifest.
>
> And without the ordinances thereof, and the authority of the priesthood, the power of godliness is not manifest unto men in the flesh;
>
> For without this no man can see the face of God, even the Father, and live.[10]

Charles W. Penrose spoke of a future temple—where priesthood ordinances are performed—in which the visions of eternity will be opened to the view of all those who minister therein:

> The day is yet to dawn when the sons of Moses and Aaron, having become sanctified to the renewing of their bodies, will administer in that holy house, and the veil will be taken away, and they will gaze upon the glories of that world now unseen, and upon the faces of beings now to them invisible; but it will be when they have purified themselves from the evils of this world, and are really the servants of the living God, and temples of the Holy Ghost.[11]

Modern prophets have made it clear that priesthood authority also links this world and the next through the phenomenon of translation, by which select individuals have, on occasion, been transformed into a kind of mortal immortality, itself a bridge between this life and the life to come. The Prophet Joseph Smith taught that

> the doctrine of translation is a power which belongs to this Priesthood. There are many things which belong to the powers of the Priesthood and the keys thereof, that have been kept hid

---

10 Doctrine and Covenants 84:19–22.
11 Charles W. Penrose, JD, 21:49; compare Orson Pratt, JD, 14:275; 15:364–65.

from before the foundation of the world; they are hid from the wise and prudent to be revealed in the last times.[12]

SPIRITUAL AND TEMPORAL AUTHORITY

Indeed, although in the latter days the priesthood will come to exercise temporal authority under the guidance of its heavenly king, the priesthood's true uniqueness—what distinguishes it from other, merely human, instruments—consists precisely in its power to affect the eternal worlds beyond the grave.[13] As the Twelve Apostles said in 1845,

> This High Priesthood, or Apostleship, holds the keys of the kingdom of God, and power to bind on earth that which shall be bound in heaven; and to loose on earth that which shall be loosed in heaven. And, in fine, to do, and to administer in all things pertaining to the ordinances, organization, government and direction of the kingdom of God.
>
> Being established in these last days for the restoration of all things spoken by the prophets since the world began; and in order to prepare the way for the coming of the Son of Man.[14]

Brigham Young pointed to the almost inconceivable and endlessly ramifying power of the priesthood, saying that

> the Priesthood the Lord has again bestowed upon those who will receive it, is for the express purpose of preparing them to become proficient in the principles pertaining to the law of the celestial kingdom. If we obey this law, preserve it inviolate, live according to it, we shall be prepared to enjoy the blessings of a celestial kingdom. Will any others? Yes, thousands and millions of the inhabitants of the earth who would have received and obeyed the law that we preach, if they had had the privilege.[15]

---

12 Joseph Smith Jr., TPJS, 170.

13 Joseph Smith Jr., HC, 6:253, clearly distinguishes priesthood power from mere political power, and implies that the former is superior to the latter: "Although David was a king, he never did obtain the spirit and power of Elijah and the fullness of the Priesthood." The Prophet immediately adds, by the way, that "the Priesthood that he [David] received, and the throne and kingdom of David is to be taken from him and given to another by the name of David in the last days, raised up out of his lineage."

14 The Twelve Apostles, MFP, 1:253.

15 Brigham Young, JD, 8:35.

In fact, modern prophets have stated explicitly that priesthood authority—unlike political authority or corporate office or financial power—will itself be carried into the next life by those who received it here, and they will continue to exercise it. "When men leave this earth," said John Taylor,

> they leave it to occupy another sphere in another state of existence. And if . . . they hold the priesthood that administers in time and in eternity . . . they hold that priesthood in the eternal worlds, and operate in it there. It is an everlasting priesthood, that administers in time and in eternity. And the gospel that we have received unfolds to us principles of which we were heretofore entirely ignorant. It shows us the relationship that exists between God and man, and it shows us the relationship that exists between men who have dwelt upon the earth before and those who exist today. It shows that while God has revealed the priesthood to us upon the earth and conferred upon us those privileges, that in former generations he revealed the same priesthood to other men, and that those men holding that priesthood ministered to others here upon the earth; and that we are operating with them and they with us in our interests and in the interests of the church and kingdom of God, in assisting to build up the Zion of God, and in seeking to establish truth and righteousness upon the earth; and that there is a connecting link between the priesthood in the heavens and the priesthood upon the earth.[16]

On another occasion, President Taylor summarized both the temporal and eternal aspects of the priesthood's role:

> To bring about this desirable end—to restore creation to its pristine excellency and to fulfill the object of creation—to redeem, save, exalt, and glorify man—to save and redeem the dead and the living, and all that shall live according to its laws, is the design and object of the establishment of the priesthood on the earth in the last days. It is for the purpose of fulfilling what has not heretofore been done—that God's works may be perfected—that the times of the restitution of all things may

---

16 John Taylor, GK, 22–23.

be brought about, and that, in conjunction with the eternal priesthood in the heavens (who without us, nor we without them, could not be made perfect), we may bring to pass all things which have been in the mind of God, or spoken of by the Spirit of God, through the mouth of all the holy prophets since the world was.[17]

FULFILLING OUR PRIESTHOOD DUTY

Given the vastly important role that the priesthood is designed to play, both in redeeming the earth and reaching into the eternities, it is scarcely surprising that modern prophets and apostles have stressed the obligations of those who have received it and its ordinances. J. Reuben Clark treated this theme forcefully:

> Being in [the] last dispensation, representing our heavenly Father therein, we have great responsibilities. If the world is to be prepared for the Second Coming, we must do it. No one else has the knowledge. No one else has the authority. The responsibility is ours. The last dispensation has welded together all of the doctrines and principles of the gospel that were advanced in former dispensations. We have the priesthood bestowed by heavenly hands. We have the restoration of the keys, conferred in the Kirtland Temple when Moses and Elias and Elijah came. We have all of the authority, all of the principles that are necessary for the great work of preparation; and ours, I repeat, is the sole responsibility to go forward and see that our mission is carried out.[18]

President Brigham Young taught that the restoration of the priesthood would be accompanied, with the passage of time, by increases in human health, intelligence, and longevity. But this would not, he cautioned, come automatically. It would require our own effort and righteousness.

> The Prophet understood that what had been would be again; also that mankind would become blinder in the understandings, and make their days shorter and shorter, until they

---

[17] John Taylor, GK, 132.
[18] J. Reuben Clark Jr., CR, October 1953, 39–40.

would become almost extinct; and that then the Lord would begin to revive his Spirit and power and Priesthood among his children; and when he could get a people that would hearken to his voice, he would begin to add to their days, to their intellect, to their stature, and to every power and virtue of life, as at first bestowed upon the human family. How are we to magnify the Priesthood, unless we begin to perform our part towards bringing to pass this restoration? This is a work in which the female portion of the Latter-day Saints can be efficient co-labourers.[19]

President Young, too, sought to impress his listeners with the significance of the priesthood, as well as with the burdens, obligations, and blessings that come with acceptance of priesthood ordinances.

Remember it, brethren and sisters, and try to live worthy of the vocation of your high calling. You are called to be Saints—just think of and realize it, for the greatest honor and privilege that can be conferred upon a human being is to have the privilege of being a Saint. The honor of the kings and queens of the earth fades into insignificance when compared with the title of Saints. You may possess earthly power, and rule with an iron hand, but that power is nothing, it will soon be broken and pass away; but the power of those who live and honor the Priesthood will increase forever and ever.[20]

---

[19] Brigham Young, JD, 8:283.
[20] Brigham Young, JD, 17:119–20.

CHAPTER 5

REVELATION FROM GOD

THE CENTRALITY AND VALUE OF REVELATION

"Prayer," declared Marion G. Romney,

> is the means by which men communicate with God.
> Revelation is the means by which God communicates with
> men. Revelation is indispensable to an understanding of the
> gospel of Jesus Christ. The very nature of the gospel is such
> that without the active and constant operation of the principle
> of revelation, it could not be understood nor could it be had.[1]

Prayer, of course, has always been available to human beings, and, surely, there is scarcely in human history a man, woman, or child who has not, at least fleetingly, at some time of crisis sought help from a person or force more powerful than is to be found on earth. Revelation, on the other hand, God's communication to human beings, has been considerably more rare. Both the scriptures and secular history provide indisputable evidence that there have been many periods and many regions in which revelation has not been generally available to mankind.

This absence of revelation has not occurred because God did not wish to communicate his will or manifest himself to the inhabitants of earth. The Prophet Joseph Smith put the blame squarely on humanity itself:

> What is the reason that the Priests of the day do not get reve-
> lation? They ask only to consume it upon their lust. Their
> hearts are corrupt, and they cloak their iniquity by saying there
> are no more revelations. But if any revelations are given of God,
> they are universally opposed by the priests and Christendom at
> large; for they reveal their wickedness and abominations.[2]

---

[1] Marion G. Romney, CR, April 1964, 122.

[2] Joseph Smith Jr., MFP, 1:143. The scriptures clearly teach that God sometimes fails to manifest his power as he might otherwise do, because of human unbelief. See, for instance, Matthew 13:58.

In the latter days, however, God has chosen to reveal himself again to seers and prophets. "The day has already dawned," announced Wilford Woodruff,

> when the light of heaven is to fill the earth; the day in which the Lord has said that nothing should be kept hidden, whether it be things pertaining to one God, or many Gods, to thrones, principalities or powers; the day in which everything that has been kept from the knowledge of man ever since the foundation of the earth, must be revealed; and it is a day which the ancient prophets looked forward to with a great deal of interest and anxiety.[3]

It is in modern and continuing revelation, in the renewal of the ancient link between God and prophets, and, again, between prophets and a believing, obedient people, that the great power of this final dispensation largely consists. But it is the belief in ongoing revelation that has, at the same time, brought down upon the restored Church and its leaders the condemnation of the surrounding (religious) world. The Prophet Joseph Smith was forthright in his view of those who treasure up ancient revelations to dead prophets but refuse to grant the possibility of contemporary revelation to living ones:

> Compare this principle once with Christendom at the present day, and where are they, with all their boasted religion, piety and sacredness while at the same time they are crying out against prophets, apostles, angels, revelations, prophesying and visions, etc. Why, they are just ripening for the damnation of hell. They will be damned, for they reject the most glorious principle of the Gospel of Jesus Christ and treat with disdain and trample under foot the key that unlocks the heavens and puts in our possession the glories of the celestial world. Yes, I say, such will be damned, with all their professed godliness.[4]

Why do the prophets and apostles insist that the principle of revelation is so central to this dispensation? For the simple reason that we cannot be saved without it. "Growing into the principle of revelation," as Joseph Smith called it, is part of the very process of our salvation and

---

[3] Wilford Woodruff, DWW, 110.
[4] Joseph Smith Jr., MFP, 1:179.

exaltation. It is part of our becoming one with God, of our becoming like him in exaltation, of our having his "mind in us." John Taylor taught this doctrine:

> Cultivate the spirit of revelation that you have then, as the Scriptures said formerly, "As many as are led by the Spirit of God are the sons of God." Another passage, in speaking of certain individuals, tells them that they have received an unction from the Holy One, and they know all things, being instructed and taught by the Spirit of eternal truth. This is what the Bible speaks of in former times. "And ye need not," says he, "that any man should teach you, save the Anointing that is within you, which is true and no lie." Let men feel the anointing of the Spirit of the Lord and that Spirit will lead them into all truth, will bring things past to their remembrance and it will show them things to come, as it did in former times.[5]

Joseph Smith noted that when we are left to our own devices, we will necessarily fall prey to other powerful influences not divine:

> A man is saved no faster than he gets knowledge, for if he does not get knowledge, he will be brought into captivity by some evil power in the other world, as evil spirits will have more knowledge, and consequently more power than many men who are on the earth. Hence it needs revelation to assist us, and give us knowledge of the things of God.[6]

THE SURE WORD OF PROPHECY

Without revelation from God, we cannot have certainty. With it, we can know things that no book and no amount of study or speculation can teach us. Such was the understanding of the Prophet Joseph Smith, whose own quest for religious certainty and guidance was the occasion for the glorious appearance of the Father and the Son that opened this last dispensation.

> "We have a more sure word of prophecy, whereunto you do well to take heed, as unto a light that shineth in a dark place.

---

[5] John Taylor, JD, 14:366.
[6] Joseph Smith Jr., MFP, 1:143.

We were eye witnesses of his majesty and heard the voice of his excellent glory." And what could be more sure? When He was transfigured on the mount, what could be more sure to them? Divines have been quarreling for ages about the meaning of this.[7]

The Prophet knew whereof he spoke. "We can see," he once remarked, "that the doctrine of revelation far transcends the doctrine of no revelation; for one truth revealed from heaven is worth all the sectarian notions in existence.[8] Orson Pratt spoke on the same subject:

"He that believeth these words which I have spoken, him will I visit with the manifestations of my Spirit, and he shall know and bear record." It does not say, he shall merely have an opinion and bear record, but he shall know and bear record. . . . If you have believed these things with all of your hearts, and complied with the commands of the Most High, manifesting your faith by your works, then you have been put in possession of this knowledge, and you know, by the Spirit which he has poured out from heaven upon you, that they are true, and in force to all the world, and this Spirit gives you a knowledge concerning all truth. You are not like those who have no revelation of whom the ancient Apostle speaks, who were "Ever learning, and never able to come to the knowledge of the truth;" but you are of those, if you keep the commandments of God, who are not only learning from the word of God, but have a knowledge of all revealed truth by the power of the Spirit, the Comforter, which is a revelator, an unction to all those who receive it; and they are able to bear record of the things which they formerly believed to be true.[9]

It is the distinction and glory of the restored Church of Jesus Christ that it is once again led, as the true kingdom of God has always been led, by revelation from the Lord. The Church proclaims that the same principle that governed the people of God in biblical times governs them again. And what a blessing this is. We would be lost without it. As Marion G. Romney pointed out,

---

7 Joseph Smith Jr., MFP, 1:185.
8 Joseph Smith Jr., MFP, 1:206.
9 Orson Pratt, JD, 19:212.

The gospel deals with total truth—". . . knowledge of things as they are, as they were, and as they are to come." (D&C 3:4.) Such truth is not to be had through man's ordinary learning processes. His sensory powers are calculated and adapted to deal only with the things of this earth. Without revelation, man's intellect is wholly inadequate for the discovery of the ultimate truth with which the gospel deals. . . . It is my witness to you, however, that by the power of God, truth concerning the eternal verities with which the gospel deals has been in the past, is now being, and will in the future continue to be communicated to men from heaven by revelation. "Revelation" is the "governing law of conduct"—the age-old established rule of action or principle by which God communes with men.[10]

REVELATION YET TO COME

Members of The Church of Jesus Christ of Latter-day Saints believe in ongoing revelation, not merely in revelation that occurred in the opening scenes of this dispensation. It continues. And this principle, an exciting one for those who love to learn, suggests that we will, if we are faithful, know more in the future than we know now. "We believe," says the ninth Article of Faith, "that He will yet reveal many great and important things pertaining to the Kingdom of God." "There are great and glorious things yet to be revealed," declared Brigham Young. "We are but babes and sucklings in the knowledge of God and godliness. With all we know and understand by the Priesthood here in the midst of this people, we are mere infants before the angels in heaven."[11]

Although much has to do with the Lord's timetable itself, the words of modern Church leaders indicate that a significant limitation upon our ability to receive more is our own unrighteousness and lack of faith. "By and by," said Orson Pratt,

> when we will have faith in God, even as the brother of Jared had; and when we possess faith like unto his, we are promised in the Book of Mormon that all the great things which he saw shall be revealed unto us. But we shall have to obtain them as he obtained them—by faithfulness. By the quickening power

---

10 Marion G. Romney, CR, April 1964, 123.
11 Brigham Young, DBY, 94. Compare Harold B. Lee, SYHP, 72.

which was bestowed upon him, the brother of Jared beheld all the inhabitants of the earth that had been before his day, all who existed when he existed, and all who would exist even unto the end of the world. The power of God rested upon him and enlarged his vision, enabling him to see all these objects.[12]

Joseph Fielding Smith concurred, expressing his own patience and resignation to the will of the Lord in this matter, despite his own oft-demonstrated passion for scriptural and divine knowledge.

"Yea, verily I say unto you, in that day when the Lord shall come, he shall reveal all things—Things which have passed, and hidden things which no man knew, things of the earth, by which it was made, and the purpose and the end thereof— Things most precious, things that are above, and things that are beneath, things that are in the earth, and upon the earth, and in heaven." For my part, I am willing to wait until this time to learn the truth of these things. This information was given to the saints at one time in a former dispensation, but the Lord has said we may not have it in the days of wickedness. When the Gentiles "shall repent of their iniquity, and become clean before the Lord," then it shall be revealed again.[13]

When the day finally comes, it will be a glorious one. Orson Pratt echoed the rapturous visions of ancient Hebrew prophets in contemplating it:

Jeremiah has said that the time would come when the new covenant should take its full effect here upon the earth; that there would be no more need of ministers and priests to teach the people, although there would be need for ordinances to be administered, and for the priesthood to administer in other capacities; but so far as teaching the people to know the Lord was concerned it would be unnecessary. In that day no man would need to say to his neighbor, "Know ye the Lord." Why? Because all would know him, from the least unto the greatest, for Isaiah says they should all be taught of the Lord, all be righteous, all receive revelation and visions, all prophesy and

---

dream. That is, God would reveal by his Spirit in different ways, at different times and by different methods to his people those things that would comfort and build them up in their most holy faith.[14]

One thinks of the prophet Moses, when a young man ran to tell him that the Spirit was resting upon Eldad and Medad, who were prophesying in the midst of the camp of Israel. "My lord Moses," said Joshua, who seems to have feared that such goings-on would jeopardize the unique leadership role of his great mentor, "forbid them." But Moses was unconcerned. Indeed, he was delighted that someone else was experiencing the gift of prophecy, for it promised a reduction in the burden he had to carry. "Enviest thou for my sake?" he replied. "Would God that all the Lord's people were prophets, and that the Lord would put his spirit upon them!"[15] Likewise, today, a general Church membership upon which the Spirit rested even more than it does now would be far less of a burden upon bishops, stake presidents, and General Authorities. A Church in which each home and visiting teacher, each scoutmaster, each priesthood leader and Relief Society officer, each parent, were guided by the Spirit would be an unconquerable force for good. A society under the seal and guidance of the Spirit would be a paradise. Of such a day the prophet Isaiah spoke, when he prophesied of a future time in which

> they shall not hurt nor destroy in all my holy mountain: for the earth shall be full of the knowledge of the Lord, as the waters cover the sea.[16]

Brigham Young summed up his hope for the members of the Church in a way that, I think, both Moses and Isaiah would have approved:

> How will perfection be obtained? By all persons in the Kingdom of God living so as to be revelators from the heavens for themselves and for all they preside over, that everything they have to perform in this life—every worldly care and duty,

---

[14] Orson Pratt, JD, 15:238-39.
[15] Numbers 11:24-30.
[16] Isaiah 11:9.

and all their walk and conversation before each other and before the Lord, may be marked out by the spirit of revelation. Is this the way to perfection? It is. This is the Gospel of our Lord Jesus Christ; this is the Gospel of life and salvation.[17]

THE END KNOWN FROM THE BEGINNING

Latter-day prophets have spoken about the manner and content of the revelations that are to be expected in the last days. Joseph Fielding Smith, for instance, taught that we will someday understand the purpose of all things and realize that, contrary appearances notwithstanding, God was in control all along.

> When the end shall come, and the Lord makes known to us "all things," "things most precious, things that are above, and things that are beneath, things that are in the earth, and upon the earth and in heaven," then shall we discover that our Father knew the end from the beginning, and his plan is a perfect plan of salvation for every creature, both man and beast, and for the earth upon which we dwell.[18]

Bruce R. McConkie echoed an important Old Testament theme (one which had already been picked up and echoed by the apostle Peter in Acts 2:14-18) in teaching that revelatory visions would abound during the last days. "Visions," he explained,

> serve the Lord's purposes in preparing men for salvation. By them knowledge is revealed (2 Nephi 4:23), conversions are made (Alma 19:16), the gospel message is spread abroad, the church organization is perfected (D&C 107:93), and righteousness is increased in the hearts of men. And visions are to increase and abound in the last days, for the Lord has promised to pour out his "spirit upon all flesh," so that "old men shall dream dreams," and "young men shall see visions." (Joel 2:28-32)[19]

The Prophet Joseph Smith said that revelation will flow in such clearness and quantity in the last days that matters that have

---

[17] Brigham Young, DBY, 450.

[18] Joseph Fielding Smith, WP, 40–41.

[19] Bruce R. McConkie, DNTC, 2:445-46.

perplexed the greatest sages in human history will be made clear to even the most humble of God's children:

> Many things are insoluble to the children of men in the last days: for instance, that God should raise the dead, and forgetting that things have been hid from before the foundation of the world, which are to be revealed to babes in the last days.[20]

Even this revelation, the prophets and apostles indicate, will be but a foretaste of the full knowledge and understanding that will come to those who receive exaltation. "For now," wrote the apostle Paul, "we see through a glass, darkly; but then face to face: now I know in part; but then shall I know even as also I am known."[21] The Prophet Joseph Smith explained that, in the world to come,

> The white stone mentioned in Revelation 2:17, will become a Urim and Thummim to each individual who receives one, whereby things pertaining to a higher order of kingdoms, will be made known; and a white stone is given to each of those who come into the celestial kingdom, whereon is a new name written, which no man knoweth save he that receiveth it. The new name is the key word.[22]

TESTIMONY AND PERSONAL REVELATION

Personal revelation is, however, available even now to those who are willing to seek it and to accept it. Indeed, it is upon such revelation that secure conviction of the truthfulness of the gospel must rest, "for the testimony of Jesus is the spirit of prophecy."[23] "Do ye not suppose," asked the Book of Mormon prophet Alma the Younger,

> that I know of these things myself? Behold, I testify unto you that I do know that these things whereof I have spoken are true. And how do ye suppose that I know of their surety?

---

20 Joseph Smith Jr., HC, 5:424.
21 1 Corinthians 13:12.
22 Joseph Smith Jr., MFP, 1:168.
23 Revelation 19:10.

Behold, I say unto you they are made known unto me by the Holy Spirit of God. Behold, I have fasted and prayed many days that I might know these things of myself. And now I do know of myself that they are true; for the Lord God hath made them manifest unto me by his Holy Spirit; and this is the spirit of revelation which is in me.[24]

From the very beginning of The Church of Jesus Christ of Latter-day Saints in this dispensation, its leaders have encouraged all humankind to seek and obtain a personal witness of the truths they teach—a personal witness that is obtainable through (and only through) the Spirit of God. Said the Prophet Joseph Smith,

You remember the testimony which I bore in the name of the Lord Jesus, concerning the great work which He has brought forth in the last days. You know my manner of communication, how that in weakness and simplicity, I declared to you what the Lord had brought forth by the ministering of His holy angels to me for this generation. I pray that the Lord may enable you to treasure these things in your mind, for I know that His Spirit will bear testimony to all who seek diligently after knowledge from Him. I hope you will search the Scriptures to see whether these things are not also consistent with those things which the ancient Prophets and Apostles have written.[25]

It is this inner conviction, in fact, upon which the survival and the remarkable growth of the restored Church have rested. Wilford Woodruff, that great journal-keeper who was centrally involved in virtually all of the important events of the nineteenth-century Church, knew this well. "The pathway of the people of God," he said,

has been beset with difficulties. They have been environed with dangers. Dark clouds have almost enshrouded them. But amidst all these, the still, small voice of the Spirit of God has been heard. His Saints have had a testimony from Him that the course they have been led to take is the right one and that

---

[24] Alma 5:45-46.
[25] Joseph Smith Jr., TPJS, 29.

He will never fail to make known His mind and will to them so long as they live up to His requirements.[26]

Lorenzo Snow, who had considerable experience with personal revelation long before he became the fifth president of the Church, declared:

> We need assistance. We are liable to do that which will lead us into trouble and darkness, and those things which will not tend to our good, but with the assistance of that Comforter which the Lord has promised his Saints, if we are careful to listen to its whisperings, and understand the nature of its language, we may avoid much trouble and serious difficulty.[27]

THE NECESSITY OF PERSONAL REVELATION

Dependence upon the revelations of God is, however, hardly a characteristic of only the Saints in the past. Church authorities of this dispensation assure us that it remains essential. Heber C. Kimball is not alone in testifying that, in the difficult challenges that remain before us, "the time will come when no man or woman will be able to endure on borrowed light."[28] Most threatening of all, opposition will not always be obvious. It will take subtle and sometimes seductive forms, forms that will seem plausible, friendly, and good. Many times, inspired leaders warn us, we will require spiritual discernment to recognize challenges as challenges. "Satan," said David O. McKay,

> is still determined to have his way, and his emissaries have power given them today as they have not had throughout the centuries. Be prepared to meet conditions that may be severe, ideological conditions that may seem reasonable but are evil. In order to meet these forces, we must depend upon the whisperings of the Holy Spirit, to which you are entitled.[29]

Harold B. Lee gave similar advice, borrowing the words of his great predecessor in the presidency of the Church, Brigham Young:

---

[26] Wilford Woodruff, MFP, 3:160.
[27] Lorenzo Snow, JD, 19:341.
[28] Ezra Taft Benson, CR, October 1963, 18.
[29] David O. McKay, CR, April 1969, 97.

Were your faith concentrated upon the proper object, your confidence unshaken, your lives pure and holy, every one fulfilling the duty of his or her calling according to the priesthood and capacity bestowed upon you, you would be filled with the Holy Ghost, and it would be as impossible for any man to deceive and to lead you to destruction as for a feather to remain unconsumed in the midst of intense heat.[30]

In fact, leaders of the Church have long exhorted the Saints to seek spiritual confirmation and guidance even with regard to the instructions given by the General Authorities. We are not to be mere robots. (The plan accepted at the great Council in Heaven emphasized human agency. It was Lucifer's plan that sought to make of us automatons, and the Church of Jesus Christ has always placed a premium on freely chosen obedience, rather than coercion.) Ezra Taft Benson taught this clearly, again citing and affirming an important statement by Brigham Young:

> The . . . final test is the Holy Ghost—the test of the Spirit. By that Spirit we ". . . may know the truth of all things." (Moroni 10:5.) This test can only be fully effective if one's channels of communication with God are clean and virtuous and uncluttered with sin. Said Brigham Young: "You may know whether you are led right or wrong, as well as you know the way home; for every principle God has revealed carries its own convictions of its truth to the human mind . . . What a pity it would be if we were led by one man to utter destruction! Are you afraid of this? I am more afraid that this people have so much confidence in their leaders that they will not inquire of themselves of God whether they are led by Him. I am fearful they settle down in a state of blind self-security, trusting their eternal destiny in the hands of their leaders with a reckless confidence that in itself would thwart the purposes of God in their salvation, and weaken that influence they could give to their leaders did they know for themselves, by the revelations of Jesus, that they are led in the right way. Let every man and woman know, by the whispering of the Spirit of God to themselves, whether their leaders are walking

---

[30] Harold B. Lee, CR, October 1950, 130.

in the path that the Lord dictates, or not. This has been my exhortation continually."[31]

Continuing in the same conference address, Elder Benson explained how we are supposed to carry out our responsibility to evaluate the teachings of our Church leaders.

> How then can we know if a man is speaking by the spirit? The Bible, Book of Mormon, and Doctrine and Covenants give us the key. (See D&C 50:17-23; 100:5-8; 2 Nephi 33:1; 1 Corinthians 2:10-11.) President [J. Reuben] Clark summarized them well when he said: "We can tell when the speakers are moved upon by the Holy Ghost only when we, ourselves, are moved upon by the Holy Ghost. In a way, this completely shifts the responsibility from them to us to determine when they so speak . . . the Church will know by the testimony of the Holy Ghost in the body of the members, whether the brethren in voicing their views are moved upon by the Holy Ghost; and in due time that knowledge will be made manifest."[32]

CAUTIONS ON FUTURE REVELATION

It would be irresponsible, however, to end the matter here. Yes, the prophets and apostles of the restored Church have taught us the importance of seeking personal revelation and of taking the teachings of Church leaders before God for confirmation. But they have also warned us to distinguish divine revelation from personal whims, to test our perceptions against the inspired utterances of prophets ancient and modern. As quoted immediately above, the Prophet Joseph Smith not only taught us that "His Spirit will bear testimony to all who seek diligently after knowledge from Him," but also expressed his hope that we would "search the Scriptures to see whether these things are not also consistent with those things which the ancient Prophets and Apostles have written."[33] It is the same combination of study and faith, of careful thought and earnest prayer, that the Lord set forth to Oliver Cowdery even before the foundation

---

[31] Ezra Taft Benson, CR, October 1963, 17-18.
[32] Ezra Taft Benson, CR, October 1963, 18.
[33] Joseph Smith Jr., TPJS, 29.

of the Church.[34] Anything purporting to be revelation must be subjected to prayerful consideration and to faithful examination in the light of what the Lord has already revealed.

Marion G. Romney taught that not everything that claims to be a revelation from God really is such.

> Some . . . counterfeits are crude and easily detected, but others closely simulate true manifestations of the spirit. Consequently, people are confused and deceived by them. Without a key, one cannot distinguish between the genuine and the counterfeit. The Egyptians could not tell the difference between the power through which Moses and Aaron worked and that by which the magicians worked. On the day of Pentecost, the non-believers did not recognize that the apostles were speaking in tongues by the power of the spirit; on the contrary, they concluded that they were "drunken with new wine."[35]

Joseph Smith, too, cautioned us to be careful, and to be certain of what we have received and how we are to interpret it.

> We may look for angels and receive their ministrations, but we are to try the spirits and prove them, for it is often the case that men make a mistake in regard to these things. God has so ordained that when He has communicated, no vision is to be taken but what you see by the seeing of the eye, or what you hear by the hearing of the ear. When you see a vision, pray for the interpretation; if you get not this, shut it up; there must be certainty in this matter. An open vision will manifest that which is more important.[36]

A simple rule we have been admonised to follow, however, derives from the fact that the Church is a kingdom of order: Each of us has the right to receive revelation for himself or herself and for his or her stewardships. We have no right to receive or to proclaim revelation for the guidance of those who do not fall under our responsibility. (It is our natural human tendency, perhaps, to seek rather to

---

[34] Doctrine and Covenants 9:7–9. This is a consistent theme in the scriptures of the Latter-day Saints. Compare, for instance, Moroni 10:3–5 and Doctrine and Covenants 88:118; 109:7, 14.
[35] Marion G. Romney, CR, April 1956, 70.
[36] Joseph Smith Jr., MFP, 1:116.

advise others where it does not concern us, than to concentrate on our own duties. Certainly it is easier.) Brigham Young, for example, who was quoted above exhorting us to seek and receive personal revelation, nonetheless cautioned us about speaking of what we receive:

> If the Lord Almighty should reveal to a High Priest, or to any other than the head, things that are true, or that have been and will be, and show to him the destiny of this people twenty-five years from now, or a new doctrine that will in five, ten, or twenty years hence become the doctrine of this Church and Kingdom, but which has not yet been revealed to this people, and reveal it to him by the same Spirit, the same messenger, the same voice, the same power that gave revelations to Joseph when he was living, it would be a blessing to that High Priest, or individual; but he must rarely divulge it to a second person on the face of the earth, until God reveals it through the proper source to become the property of the people at large.[37]

John A. Widtsoe agreed, warning us not to be too free or casual in discussing the revelations, manifestations, or special gifts that we might obtain from the Lord:

> It is unwisdom, therefore, for those who have received such manifestations to send copies to others, to relate them by word of mouth in diverse places, and otherwise to scatter abroad a personal, sacred experience. There are times and places where testimony may be borne of our knowledge that the restored gospel is of the Lord, and of the goodness of the Lord to us, and when we may present evidence of our faith. It would be well to remember that the Lord Jesus Christ, while on earth, usually instructed those whom He had healed or otherwise blessed, that they should not tell others of the occurrence. Some things are done for the public good, others for private welfare.[38]

---

[37] Brigham Young, DBY, 338. This was, in fact, precisely the advise that Brigham Young gave to Lorenzo Snow when, in England, Elder Snow confided in him the personal revelation on eternal progression ("As man now is, God once was. As God now is, man may be.") that he (Elder Snow) had received in May 1840. The doctrine was not yet taught in the Church. Only later did Elder Snow mention it to the Prophet Joseph Smith, who confirmed that it was true and of God. He did not teach it openly until he was authorized to do so. See Heidi S. Swinton, "Lorenzo Snow," in Leonard J. Arrington, ed., *The Presidents of the Church* (Salt Lake City: Deseret Book, 1986), 153.
[38] John A. Widtsoe, ER, 1987 edition, 99.

Faithful Latter-day Saints know, and it has been the consistent testimony of latter-day prophets and apostles, that revelation for the Church will come through the proper channels. Not even counselors in the First Presidency have the prerogative to oppose their leader when he is acted upon by the revelations of God. Ezra Taft Benson taught this clearly:

> Will this Spirit be needed to check actions in other situations? Yes, and it could be used as a guide and a protector for the faithful in a situation described by Elder [Harold B.] Lee at the last general priesthood session of the Church when he said: "In the history of the Church there have been times or instances where Counselors in the First Presidency and others in high station have sought to overturn the decision or to persuade the President contrary to his inspired judgment, and always, if you will read carefully the history of the Church, such oppositions brought not only disastrous results to those who resisted the decision of the President, but almost always such temporary persuasions were called back for reconsideration, or a reversal of hasty action not in accordance with the feelings, the inspired feelings, of the President of the Church. And that, I submit, is one of the fundamental things that we must never lose sight of in the building up of the kingdom of God."[39]

How much less so, then, should the Church as a whole seek for guidance from those upon whom the mantle of the Prophet has not fallen. Again, Ezra Taft Benson spoke clearly, and in words that seem even more relevant today than when first he spoke them in 1967:

> Increasingly the Latter-day Saints must choose between the reasoning of men and the revelations of God. This is a crucial choice, for we have those within the Church today who, with their worldly wisdom, are leading some of our members astray. President J. Reuben Clark Jr., warned that "the ravening wolves are amongst us from our own membership and they, more than any others, are clothed in sheep's clothing, because they wear the habiliments of the Priesthood. . . . We should be careful of them."[40]

---

[39] Ezra Taft Benson, CR, October 1963, 18.
[40] Ezra Taft Benson, CR, October 1967, 34.

CHAPTER 6

ANCIENT AND MODERN PROPHECY

ANCIENT PROPHECY

Modern prophets and apostles teach that their ancient counterparts, the inspired writers and prophets of the Bible, foresaw and foretold our day. In this, of course, they are not entirely unique. "All people who have any confidence in the Old and New Testaments," said Orson Pratt,

> and who have read the pages of the Bible, are expecting certain great and important events to transpire upon the earth; they look for an entire change to come over the nations, and also for a universal kingdom to be established on the earth never to be overthrown. These things are so clearly predicted in the prophecies of the holy Prophets, that I believe all who profess any faith in the Bible are looking for something of this kind to take place.[1]

Leaders of The Church of Jesus Christ of Latter-day Saints are, however, unique in the way they interpret ancient prophecy as referring to specific events connected with the restoration of the gospel. Thus, says Bruce R. McConkie,

> Scripturalists are wont to refer to Isaiah as the Messianic prophet because of his many prophecies about the birth and ministry and death and resurrection of the Lord Jehovah. And truly he was; no Old Testament seer has left us a greater wealth of words about the Eternal Word than this son of Amoz, who prophesied in the days of Uzziah, Jotham, Ahaz, and Hezekiah, all kings of Judah, and who, according to tradition, was sawn asunder for the counsel he gave and the testimony of Jesus he bore. But what is of equal or even greater

---

[1] Orson Pratt, JD, 17:307.

import is that Isaiah's Messianic word shines forth far beyond time's meridian; he is the great prophet of the restoration. It is his voice that speaks of the restoration of the gospel in the last days, of the Coming forth of the Book of Mormon, of the raising of an ensign to the nations, of the gathering of Israel, of the building of the house of the Lord in the tops of the mountains, of the conversion of many Gentiles, of the building of Zion, of the Second Coming of the Son of Man, and of the millennial era of peace and righteousness. Truly, "great are the words of Isaiah."[2]

In fact, God's modern representatives, although they claim that revelation has been and continues to be received in recent years, have also insisted that the writings of the ancient prophets remain relevant to us today. Wilford Woodruff, for instance, taught that the prophecies of the New Testament, properly understood, could alert us to the fulfillment of God's promises.

The Savior, when speaking to his disciples of his second coming and the establishment of his kingdom on the earth, said the Jews should be scattered and trodden under foot until the times of the Gentiles were fulfilled. But, said he, when you see light breaking forth among the Gentiles, referring to the preaching of his Gospel amongst them; when you see salvation offered to the Gentiles, and the Jews—the seed of Israel—passed by, the last first and the first last; when you see this you may know that the time of my second coming is at hand as surely as you know that summer is nigh when the fig tree puts forth its leaves; and when these things commence that generation shall not pass away until all are fulfilled.[3]

President Joseph Fielding Smith explained, however, that even the recognition of the signs of the times requires discernment and spiritual sensitivity—which is, in a sense, revelation. These manifestations are not so obvious as to *force* faith upon those who do not wish to believe. Not yet, anyway. "The words of the prophets are rapidly being fulfilled," President Smith noted,

---

2 Bruce R. McConkie, MoM, 4:364–65.
3 Wilford Woodruff, JD, 14:5.

but it is done on such natural principles that most of us fail to see it. Joel promised that the Lord would pour out his spirit upon all flesh: the sons and daughters should prophesy, old men should dream dreams, and young men should see visions. Wonders in heaven and in the earth would be seen, and there would be fire, blood, and pillars of smoke. Eventually the sun is to be turned into darkness and the moon as blood and then shall come the great and dreadful day of the Lord. Some of these signs have been given; some are yet to come. The sun has not yet been darkened. We are informed that this will be one of the last acts just preceding the coming of the Lord.[4]

THE SPIRIT OF PROPHECY THEN AND NOW

Elder Orson Pratt had observed much the same tendency among people to ignore or fail to recognize the signs of God's activity in the world. "They do not understand the spirit of prophecy," he reflected.

They do not perceive that which is written by the ancient Prophets, much less will they understand that plainly written by the latter-day Prophets; consequently, all these things will overtake them unawares. Even the coming of Christ, so great an event as that is, will be to them as a thief in the night. After the kingdom of God has spread upon the face of the earth, and every jot and tittle of the prophecies have been fulfilled in relation to the spreading of the Gospel among the nations— after signs have been shown in the heavens above, and on the earth beneath, blood, fire, and vapour of smoke—after the sun is turned into darkness, and the moon shall have the appearance of blood, and the stars have apparently been hurled out of their places, and all things have been in com-motion, so great will be the darkness resting upon Christendom, and so great the bonds of priestcraft with which they will be bound, that they will not understand, and they will be given up to the hardness of their hearts.[5]

Wilford Woodruff, too, informed his listeners that the ancient predictions were indeed being fulfilled. "No man," he observed,

---

[4] Joseph Fielding Smith, CR, April 1966, 13.
[5] Orson Pratt, JD, 7:188-89.

can point to any of the revelations of God in the old prophets concerning events up to our day, but what have had their fulfillment. Everything that Jesus Christ spake concerning Judea and Jerusalem has had its fulfillment to the very letter. The Temple at Jerusalem was overthrown until not one stone was left upon another, and the Jews have been scattered and trodden under the feet of the Gentiles now for eighteen hundred years, and so they will remain until the times of the Gentiles are fulfilled, and that is pretty near. And, as the Lord has told us in these revelations, we are called upon to warn the world.[6]

But what good does it do us simply to know that the last days are at hand? Having that knowledge, based solely on ancient prophecies, we would still be at a loss as to what, precisely, we were to *do*. John Taylor recognized this problem, and gave counsel that is unique to the Latter-day Saints, for the leaders of The Church of Jesus Christ of Latter-day Saints are uniquely authorized to give it:

> The Gospel must again be preached as a warning unto all nations, and accompanied with it is to be a proclamation, "Fear God, and give glory to him, for the hour of his judgment is come." (Revelation 14:7.) But the people would very reasonably be heard to enquire, what can we do? What hope have we? If war comes, we cannot either prevent or avoid it. If plague stalks through the earth, what guarantee have we of deliverance? You say you have come as messengers of mercy to us, and as the messengers of the nations. What shall we do? Let Isaiah answer: he has told the tale of war, and defined the remedy. This shall be the answer of the messenger of the nations, that "the Lord hath founded Zion, and the poor of his people shall trust in it." (Isaiah 14:32.) Yes, says Joel, when this great and terrible day of the Lord comes, there shall be deliverance in Mount Zion, and in Jerusalem, as the Lord hath said, and in the remnant whom the Lord shall call. (Joel 2:32.) Yes, says Jeremiah, He will take them one of a city, and two of a family, and bring them to Zion, and give them pastors after his own heart, that shall feed them with knowledge and understanding. (Jeremiah 3:14-15.)[7]

---

6 Wilford Woodruff, JD, 18:112.

7 John Taylor, GG, 99.

MODERN PROPHECY REQUIRED

It is the testimony, not only of modern prophets and apostles but of millions of Latter-day Saints, that the "pastors after [God's] own heart" to whom the Lord's people are to give heed in the latter days are to be found in the restored Church of Jesus Christ. These shepherds are needed because it is only by modern day revelation that men and women will be able to recognize the signs of the last days, and because it is only through inspired guidance that they will know what to do about them. But, of course, the sheer fact that we need something does not mean that it will be *available* in our time of need. It is because of God's gracious love for his children that he has not left us alone in the trying times that will precede the return of the Savior. In supplying us with inspired prophets and apostles, furthermore, the Lord is behaving according to the same pattern that he established in his dealings with ancient Saints. "Surely the Lord God will do nothing," declared the ancient Hebrew prophet Amos, "but he revealeth his secret unto his servants the prophets."[8] "The Lord permits judgments to come upon the wicked," said Wilford Woodruff,

> but he never sends a great calamity upon the world without first sending Prophets and inspired men to warn the wicked of approaching chastisement, giving them, at the same time, space for repentance and means of escape, as witness the time of Noah, Lot, etc. And, "As it was in the days of Noah so shall it be in the days of the coming of the Son of Man." When the messengers of God have given a faithful warning to the wicked of their approaching overthrow, and the testimony is sealed, then will the Lord come out of his hiding-place and vex them with a sore vexation.[9]

Indeed, after the long interval we know as the Great Apostasy, our need for revelation is, if anything, even greater. Thus, John Taylor explained,

> As the world are ignorant of God and his laws, not having had any communication with him for eighteen hundred years; and

---

[8] Amos 3:7.
[9] Wilford Woodruff, JD, 10:218–19.

as all those great and important events must transpire, and as the Lord says he will "do nothing but what he reveals to his servants the Prophets," it follows that there must be revelations made from God; and if so, as a necessary consequence, there must be prophets to reveal them to. How did God ever reveal his will and purposes to Enoch, Noah, Abraham, Moses, the Prophets, Jesus, and his Disciples, and they to the people? God's messengers made known his will, and the people obeyed, or rejected it. If they were punished by floods, fire, plagues, pestilence, dispersions, death, etc., it was in consequence of their disobedience.[10]

Fortunately, as Orson Pratt assured his listeners, the prophets have given us a great deal of information about the last days, about what will occur during them and about how we are to equip and fortify ourselves to withstand the trials that they will present to us.

There are, in many revelations, not only in modern but in ancient prophecy, predictions touching the scenes of the last days, and the trials of the Saints; and we ought to be prepared for whatever is to come, troubles, distress, famine, war, or anything else.[11]

As Elder Pratt advised at another time,

The best thing for us to do is to depend upon what God reveals. If he gives us any knowledge regarding chronology, depend upon it; and he has given us a great deal of information with regard to the signs of the times. If he has not given us the age of the world, he has given us that whereby we may know that we live in the generation in which the times of the Gentiles will be fulfilled. And then we have other revelations, showing that when their times are fulfilled there is a speedy and short work to be accomplished in the gathering of the house of Israel from the four quarters of the earth. They are to be brought out of all nations, kindreds, tongues, and people with a mighty hand and outstretched arm. We are told that God will then perform wonders, miracles and signs, greater

---

10 John Taylor, GG, 95.
11 Orson Pratt, JD, 3:15.

than ever have been performed since the creation of the world; that he will bring back his covenant people. After the Jews have rebuilt Jerusalem, and after the Temple is erected, the Lord Jesus will come.[12]

Prophecy in Action

Ongoing modern revelation provides a map and a guide to the events and situations of the latter days. And just as a good map or guide lends feelings of security to those who carry it with them while they travel in unfamiliar territory, modern revelation gives those who accept it confidence even in difficult circumstances. Indeed, as God's servants explain, its chief value may be not so much the conveyance of detailed information about the future—since prophecies are frequently less than crystal clear and are often more easily understood after their fulfillment—as the assurance that, whatever happens, God knew about it and will enable his saints to triumph over it. Jedediah M. Grant recognized this, asking

> Why is it that the Latter-day Saints are perfectly calm and serene among all the convulsions of the earth—the turmoils, strife, war, pestilence, famine, and distress of nations? It is because the spirit of prophecy has made known to us that such things would actually transpire upon the earth. We understand it, and view it in its true light. We have learned it by the visions of the Almighty—by that spirit of intelligence that searches out all things, even the deep things of God.[13]

Indeed, as President Harold B. Lee explained,

> Prophecy may well be defined as history in reverse. Before our very eyes we are witnessing the fulfillment of prophecies made by inspired prophets in ages past. In the very beginning of this dispensation we were plainly told in a revelation from the Lord that the time was nigh at hand when peace would be taken from the earth and the devil would have power over his own dominion. (See D&C 1:35.) The prophets of our day also foretold that there should be wars and rumors of wars,

---

12 Orson Pratt, JD, 16:324–25.
13 Jedediah M. Grant, JD, 2:147.

and "the whole earth shall be in commotion, and men's hearts shall fail them, and they shall say that Christ delayeth his coming until the end of the earth. And the love of men shall wax cold, and iniquity shall abound." (D&C 45:26-27.)[14]

Because of the importance of this guide, continuing revelation, modern prophets have felt the same urgency in warning the peoples of the world that their ancient counterparts did. President Wilford Woodruff, for example, spoke movingly of the deep sense of responsibility that he felt:

> When I have the vision of the night opened continually before my eyes, and can see the mighty judgments that are about to be poured out upon this world, when I know these things are true, and are at the door of Jew and Gentile; while I know they are true and while I am holding this position before God and this world, can I withhold my voice from lifting up a warning to this people, and to the nations of the earth? I may never meet with this people again; I cannot tell how that may be. But while I live and see these things continually before my eyes I shall raise my warning voice.[15]

The prophet Ezekiel had sensed the same divinely imposed responsibility many centuries before. He recorded an inspired analogy that continues to be relevant today, and not merely to the prophets and apostles who lead The Church of Jesus Christ of Latter-day Saints. It expresses, powerfully, the obligation that rests upon all those who have received the message of the gospel, for "it becometh every man who hath been warned to warn his neighbor."[16] "Again the word of the Lord came unto me," recorded Ezekiel, "saying,"

> Son of man, speak to the children of thy people, and say unto them, When I bring the sword upon a land, if the people of the land take a man of their coasts, and set him for their watchman:
>
> If when he seeth the sword come upon the land, he blow the trumpet, and warn the people;
>
> Then whosoever heareth the sound of the trumpet, and

---

14 Harold B. Lee, IE, December 1970, 28.

15 Wilford Woodruff, DWW, 229–30.

16 Doctrine and Covenants 88:81.

taketh not warning; if the sword come, and take him away, his blood shall be upon his own head.

He heard the sound of the trumpet, and took not warning; his blood shall be upon him. But he that taketh warning shall deliver his soul.

But if the watchman see the sword come, and blow not the trumpet, and the people be not warned; if the sword come, and take any person from among them, he is taken away in his iniquity; but his blood will I require at the watchman's hand.

So thou, O son of man, I have set thee a watchman unto the house of Israel; therefore thou shalt hear the word at my mouth, and warn them from me.

When I say unto the wicked, O wicked man, thou shalt surely die; if thou dost not speak to warn the wicked from his way, that wicked man shall die in his iniquity; but his blood will I require at thine hand.

Nevertheless, if thou warn the wicked of his way to turn from it; if he do not turn from his way, he shall die in his iniquity; but thou hast delivered thy soul.[17]

It was this same sense of accountability that the apostle Paul was feeling toward the end of his ministry, when he called the elders of the church at Ephesus to meet with him in the nearby town of Miletus. When they arrived, he asked them to certify that he had, indeed, delivered the message of warning to them with which the Lord had entrusted him. "Wherefore," he said, "I take you to record this day, that I am pure from the blood of all men. For I have not shunned to declare unto you all the counsel of God."[18]

"We live in a momentous age," testified Wilford Woodruff, a modern successor to Ezekiel and Paul,

and our responsibilities are great before the Lord and to this generation. We have borne record of the calamities that should be poured out in the last days and they are coming to pass. For thus saith the Lord, "And after your testimony cometh wrath and indignation upon the people; for after your testimony cometh the testimony of earthquakes, that shall cause groanings in the midst of her, and men shall fall on the

---

17 Ezekiel 33:1–9.
18 Acts 20:26–27.

ground and not be able to stand; and also cometh the testimony of the voice of thunderings, and the voice of lightnings, and the voice of tempests, and the voice of the waves of the sea heaving themselves beyond their bounds. And all things shall be in commotion; and surely men's hearts shall fail them, for fear shall come upon all people; and angels shall fly through the midst of heaven, crying with a loud voice, sounding the trump of God, saying, Prepare ye, prepare ye, O inhabitant of the earth, for the judgment of our God is come: behold, and lo! the Bridegroom cometh, go ye out to meet him."[19]

HEEDING THE WARNING VOICE

We have faithful watchmen on the walls of Zion today, as the Saints of former times did anciently. The question is not whether we have prophets, but whether we will pay attention to their warning voices. One of them, President Ezra Taft Benson, framed the issue as clearly as it can be stated:

> Brethren and sisters, we don't need a prophet—we have one— we need a listening ear. And if we do not listen and heed, then, as the Doctrine and Covenants states, " . . . the day cometh that they who will not hear the voice of the Lord, neither the voice of his servants, neither give heed to the words of the prophets and apostles, shall be cut off from among the people." (D&C 1:14.)[20]

We must remember, though, that although ancient and modern prophets are divinely appointed to warn us, they are otherwise mortals like ourselves. As the apostle Paul acknowledged, even they "see through a glass, darkly."[21] There are clear indications that, in their eagerness to see the purposes of the Lord victorious, prophets have sometimes wished to hasten the process. But the Lord's timetable is more expansive than that of earthly mortals, whose lives are so pathetically brief. Wilford Woodruff, for example, may have expected the completion of the latter-day work to occur earlier than has, in fact, happened, yet even he expressed both caution about predicting the exact time and confidence about the ultimate outcome:

---

[19] Wilford Woodruff, JD, 10:216–17.

[20] Ezra Taft Benson, CR, October 1961, 71.

[21] 1 Corinthians 13:12.

I copied a revelation [from the Prophet Joseph Smith] more than twenty-five years ago, in which it is stated that war should be in the south and in the north, and that nation after nation would become embroiled in the tumult and excitement, until war should be poured out upon the whole earth, and that this war would commence at the rebellion of South Carolina, and that times should be such that every man who did not flee to Zion would have to take up the sword against his neighbor or against his brother. These things are beginning to be made manifest, but the end is not yet; but it will come, and that too much sooner than the world of mankind anticipate, and all those things spoken by the mouths of his Prophets will be fulfilled.[22]

However long the time they require, the prophecies will be fulfilled, and the lord's spokesmen assure us that those who think that things will go on forever as they seem to be now, will awake to find themselves greatly surprised. As Joseph Fielding Smith testified,

If the great and dreadful day of the Lord was near at hand when Elijah came, we are just one century nearer it today. "But no! Elijah, you are wrong! Surely one hundred years have passed, and are we not better off today than ever before? Look at our discoveries, our inventions, our knowledge and our wisdom! Surely you made a mistake!" So many seem to think, and say, and judging by their actions they are sure that the world is bound to go on in its present condition for millions of years before the end will come. Talk to them; hear what they have to say—these learned men of the world. "We have had worse times," they say. "You are wrong in thinking there are more calamities now than in earlier times. There are not more earthquakes, the earth has always been quaking but now we have facilities for gathering the news which our fathers did not have." "These are not signs of the times: things are not different from former times." And so the people refuse to heed the warnings the Lord so kindly gives to them, and thus they fulfill the scriptures.[23]

---

22 Wilford Woodruff, JD, 10:13.
23 Joseph Fielding Smith, WP, 283–84.

MODERN REVELATION CAN BE HAD BY ALL

As important and even essential as it is to have modern prophets to serve as watchmen against the trials of the latter days, there is yet a further promise. These same watchmen declare that we who are not among the apostolic leaders of The Church of Jesus Christ of Latter-day Saints can also obtain revelation for ourselves, in our own stewardships and responsibilities. Orson Pratt taught that a revealed knowledge of the events of the last days was available to all those who accept the gospel:

> When a man has this, though he may appeal to ancient Prophets to get understanding on some subjects he does not clearly understand, yet, as he has the spirit of prophecy in himself, he will not be in darkness; he will have a knowledge of the signs of the times; he will have a knowledge of the house of Israel, and of Zion, of the ten tribes and of many things and purposes and events that are to take place on the earth; and he will see coming events, and can say such an event will take place, and after that another, and then another; and after that the trumpet shall sound, and after that certain things will take place, and then another trump shall sound, etc.; and he will have his eye fixed on the signs of the times, and that day will not overtake him unawares.[24]

Charles W. Penrose testified that such revelation was, in fact, being received by those who had prepared themselves for it:

> The spirit which God has been pleased to pour out upon us in some degree opens our minds to a comprehension of these same things. When we take up the Bible or the Book of Mormon and read of the restitution to come, we can see it as the prophets saw it; for the same spirit that rested upon Isaiah and Jeremiah and upon Nephi and Moroni and others of the prophets that lived upon this continent, rests upon the people of God in these latter days. The same evidences are open to our vision, and we know as sure as we know that God lives that the day is close at hand when those events spoken of will transpire upon the earth.[25]

---

24 Orson Pratt, JD, 7:189.
25 Charles W. Penrose, JD, 20:294.

In a subsequent generation, Elder Bruce R. McConkie added his testimony of the same principle. "In seeking all these things," he said,

> not only is it our privilege to learn from holy writ, but if we are true and faithful in all things we can also see and feel the very things that came to those whose words we have canonized. Thus the Prophet Joseph Smith teaches and testifies: "Search the revelations of God; study the prophecies, and rejoice that God grants unto the world Seers and Prophets. They are they who saw the mysteries of godliness; they saw the flood before it came; they saw angels ascending and descending upon a ladder that reached from earth to heaven; they saw the stone cut out of the mountain, which filled the whole earth; they saw the Son of God come from the regions of bliss and dwell with men on earth; they saw the deliverer come out of Zion, and turn away ungodliness from Jacob; they saw the glory of the Lord when he showed the transfiguration of the earth on the mount; they saw every mountain laid low and every valley exalted when the Lord was taking vengeance upon the wicked; they saw truth spring out of the earth, and righteousness look down from heaven in the last days, before the Lord came the second time to gather his elect; they saw the end of wickedness on earth, and the Sabbath of creation crowned with peace; they saw the end of the glorious thousand years, when Satan was loosed for a little season; they saw the day of judgment when all men received according to their works, and they saw the heaven and the earth flee away to make room for the city of God, when the righteous receive an inheritance in eternity. And, fellow sojourners upon earth, it is your privilege to purify yourselves and come up to the same glory, and see for yourselves, and know for yourselves. Ask, and it shall be given you; seek and ye shall find; knock, and it shall be opened unto you."[26]

Indeed, the Prophet Joseph Smith taught that personal revelation was not only a privilege of the Saints in the latter days, but a necessity.

> Salvation cannot come without revelation; it is vain for anyone to minister without it. No man is a minister of Jesus Christ

---

[26] Bruce R. McConkie, MiM, 26.

without being a Prophet. No man can be a minister of Jesus
Christ except he has the testimony of Jesus; and this is the
spirit of prophecy. Whenever salvation has been administered,
it has been by testimony. Men of the present time testify of
heaven and hell, and have never seen either; and I will say that
no man knows these things without this.[27]

Many of us will no doubt feel inadequate reading such prophetic declarations as these. But Joseph Smith himself taught that revelation was a process that most of us would only gradually understand
and master, not something that we can expect to have perfected
overnight. And he expressly included inspired testimonies of Jesus,
which many hundreds of thousands if not millions of Latter-day
Saints have received, as instances of revelation. Thus, there are many
members of the Church who have experienced communication from
God and the Spirit and whose task is now to deepen and extend their
ability to do so. As he did on numerous other topics, the great
prophet of this dispensation offered inspired guidance on just how
we are to accomplish that:

A person may profit by noticing the first intimation of the
spirit of revelation; for instance, when you feel pure intelligence flowing into you, it may give you sudden strokes of
ideas, so that by noticing it, you may find it fulfilled the same
day or soon; (i.e.,) those things that were presented unto your
minds by the Spirit of God, will come to pass; and thus by
learning the Spirit of God and understanding it, you may
grow into the principle of revelation, until you become perfect
in Christ Jesus.[28]

And although it is not an easy principle to master, we are assured
that such mastery can and will be obtained. "For now we see through
a glass, darkly," wrote the apostle Paul, "but then face to face: now I
know in part; but then shall I know even as also I am known."[29] "The
time will come," prophesied Orson Pratt,

---

[27] Joseph Smith Jr., MFP, 1:115.
[28] Joseph Smith, TPJS, 151.
[29] 1 Corinthians 13:12.

when this people will become more fully revelators, and Prophets, and Seers themselves, and the earth will be filled with the knowledge of God, and even out of the mouth of babes and sucklings will the Spirit of God reveal things that have been kept secret from the foundation of the world; they will utter forth the things of God, helping to fill the earth with the knowledge of God, as the waters cover the great deep.[30]

PERSONAL REVELATION ESSENTIAL FOR EXALTATION

This "growing into the principle of revelation" is, however, not merely a useful tool for the here and now. It is the essence of what it means to be exalted. Hence its great—in fact inestimable—importance. Someday, indeed, the faithful Saints will be able to achieve the same oneness of mind with God the Father and the Son and the Holy Ghost that the three members of the Godhead now enjoy among themselves.[31]

Unfortunately, though, there is no one of us on the earth who has yet achieved such perfection, and in all our quest for true, God's true prophets warn that revealed knowledge, we must beware of those who, deliberately or by mistake, offer us counterfeits. "False prophets," reported Joseph Smith, "always arise to oppose the true prophets and they will prophesy so very near the truth that they will deceive almost the very chosen ones."[32] And they will become increasingly common as the advent of the Savior approaches, although they may not always, and perhaps will seldom, explicitly identify themselves as *prophets*. In order to counter their influence, the Saints will need an abundance of the spirit of discernment, which is itself a form of revelation. In this regard, a joint statement issued by Brigham Young, Heber C. Kimball, and Willard Richards offers both a warning and a promise of security to those who choose wisely:

Of the day and the hour of the coming of Christ no man knoweth. It is not yet, neither is it far off; there are prophecies

---

[30] Orson Pratt, JD, 19:219.

[31] John 17:20–23; compare 1 Corinthians 2:16; also Romans 8:27; 11:34; 12:2.

[32] Joseph Smith Jr., HC, 6:364.

yet to be fulfilled before that event takes place; therefore, let no man deceive the Saints with vain philosophy and false prophecy; for false prophets will arise, and deceive the wicked, and, if possible, the good; but while the wicked fear and tremble at surrounding judgments, the Saints will watch and pray; and, waiting the final event in patience, will look calmly on the passing scenery of a corrupted world, and view transpiring events as confirmation of their faith in the holy gospel which they profess, and rejoice more and more, as multiplied signs shall confirm the approach of the millennial day.[33]

---

[33] Brigham Young, Heber C. Kimball, Willard Richards, MFP, 2:64.

CHAPTER 7

A GREAT AND MARVELOUS WORK

THE RESTORATION OF THE CHURCH OF CHRIST

Modern prophets and apostles agree that the restoration of ancient Israel and its gathering were foretold by their ancient predecessors. It is this restoration and gathering, with the prophetic communications and the reestablished priesthood authority that make it possible, that constitutes the marvelous work and wonder that will mark off the last days. "There is," remarked Wilford Woodruff,

> no man upon the earth who believes in the literal fulfillment of prophecy as contained in the Old and New Testaments, but who must in his heart believe that the God of heaven will in the latter days set his hand to perform a great work and a wonder in the earth; and that he will call forth his Church out of the wilderness of darkness and establish it upon the foundation of apostles and prophets with Christ Jesus as the chief cornerstone. . . . There is no man that believes in the literal fulfillment of the revelations of God through the prophets who does not believe that the Lord will in the latter days gather a people together out of every nation under heaven, and that he will also gather the dispersed of Judah—the Jews—that have been trodden under the feet of the Gentiles for the last 1,800 years for shedding the blood of the Messiah.[1]

And, truly, it is a marvelous work and a wonder. Nowadays, as we enjoy the blessings of an international Church with wards and stakes and even temples on every inhabited continent, speaking scores of languages and reading the scriptures in many scripts, it is easy to forget how improbable this would have seemed to any ordinary observer when that Church was founded in 1830. Our observer would almost certainly have laughed at the pretentiousness of those half dozen obscure New York farmers who gathered under the leadership of a barely educated young man with the comically common name of Joseph Smith to establish a work that, they confidently asserted, would revolutionize the world. As President Woodruff went on to recall,

[1] Wilford Woodruff, DWW, 113–14.

This work, this marvelous work and a wonder, the work that will eventually fill the whole world—and neither man nor the devil can prevent it—commenced, as all the works of our God begin, in a small way. It was likened by the Savior to the mustard seed, the smallest of all seeds, put in the soil, which grew until the fowls of the air could lodge in the branches thereof. This certainly is characteristic of this Church and Kingdom, commencing as it did on the 6th day of April, 1830, with only six members. But the Lord told Joseph in one of the revelations that he was laying the foundation of a great work, how great he knew not.[2]

Yet, in spreading to every region and clime of the earth, the Church is doing only what the prophets have predicted it would do. For Joseph Smith and his associates were not making empty boasts. They were not hatching grandiose fantasies of self-glorification, nor were they arrogating to themselves a role to which they had no just claim. As Wilford Woodruff testified,

The Lord raised up Joseph Smith specially to do the work that he performed. He was ordained and appointed before he was born to come upon the stage of action in this age of God's mercy to man, through the loins of ancient Joseph who was a descendant of Abraham, Isaac and Jacob, to lay the foundation of this great and glorious dispensation—a dispensation that will be marked and distinguished in the annals of human history for its grand and mighty, and also its serious and awful events. The day has already dawned when the light of heaven is to fill the earth; the day in which the Lord has said that nothing should be kept hidden, whether it be things pertaining to one God, or many Gods, or to thrones, principalities or powers; the day in which everything that has been kept from the knowledge of man ever since the foundation of the earth, must be revealed; and it is a day to which the ancient prophets looked forward with a great deal of interest and anxiety. It is a day in which the Gospel is to be preached to every nation, tongue and people for a witness of what shall follow; a day in which the Israel of God who receive it in their dispersed and scattered condition are to gather together to the place appointed of God, the place where

---

2 Wilford Woodruff, JD, 24:52.

they will perform the "marvelous work and wonder" spoken of by the ancients who, in vision, saw our day; and where they will begin to inherit the promises made to the fathers respecting their children. The work that is to be so marvelous in the eyes of men has already commenced, and is assuming shape and proportions; but they cannot see it. It will consist in preaching the Gospel to all the world, gathering the Saints from the midst of all those nations who reject it; building up the Zion of God; establishing permanently in the earth His kingdom; preparing for the work of the gathering of the Jews and the events that will follow their settlement in their own lands, and in preparing for ourselves holy places in which to stand when the judgments of God shall overtake the nations.[3]

THE GATHERING OF THE HOUSE OF ISRAEL

The restoration of the gospel began with Joseph Smith's inquiry in the grove of trees near his home and with the glorious answer that came to him from the Father and the Son. But it can accurately be said that Joseph Smith's public, prophetic ministry commenced with the visitation of the angel Moroni and the revelation of the Book of Mormon. Elder Orson Pratt spoke of that visitation, during which the young prophet was informed of the existence of a portion of the house of Israel which had been previously unknown to the world:

This personage announced himself as a holy angel sent from God to communicate to him glad tidings of great joy. He was told that the day had arrived in which the Lord God was about to commence a great and marvelous work on the face of our globe, to bring about the fulfillment of the ancient prophecies in regard to the restoration to their own land of the scattered remnants of the House of Israel. He was also told that before this great work, of gathering the House of Israel, should take place the Church of God must be built up among the Gentile nations; that the Gospel must be preached to the Gentiles first, that the sound thereof must go to all people, nations and tongues, first to the Gentiles, that their times might be fulfilled; and then that the Gospel should go to the nations of the House of Israel, and they should be gathered in.[4]

---

3 Wilford Woodruff, JD, 24:51.
4 Orson Pratt, JD, 12:355.

Thus, the coming forth of the Book of Mormon marked the beginning of the great gathering of Israel. Indeed, Elder Pratt taught that this correlation, this link between the Book of Mormon and the gathering, was itself foretold in scripture:

> Here is a prediction in Isaiah, that before the Lord gathers Israel he would set up a sign, showing not only to us but to all people, nations and tongues in the four quarters of the earth that he is about to gather together all the people of the house of Israel. That sign is when these American Indians shall begin to know the Gospel taught and practiced by their ancient fathers. "When that day shall come it shall come to pass that kings shall shut their mouths, for that which had not been told them shall they see, that which they had not heard shall they consider; for in that day, for my sake, shall the Father work a work which shall be a great and marvelous work among them; and there shall be among them which will not believe it, although a man shall declare it unto them." (3 Nephi 21:8-9.)[5]

But the Book of Mormon is not only a symbol of the inception of the gathering of Israel. It is itself one of the greatest of all treatises on the subject of that gathering, proving that this great work of the latter days had been foreseen and explicitly discussed centuries before Christ and even before the Babylonian captivity had scattered the people of Judah. "Nephi saw that great promises were made to the Gentiles upon this land," remarked Joseph Fielding Smith,

> and that the Lord had a marvelous work for them to do in bringing forth the fulness of the Gospel and taking it to the seed of his brethren. The promise was made that after the Gentiles had scattered the Lamanites and had ill-treated them, the time would come when they would become nursing fathers unto them, and not only unto them but unto others of the scattered house of Israel. It was reserved for the Gentiles to gather the remnant of Israel, and to give them the blessings of the Gospel.[6]

And, in fact, the gathering has begun. "God," said Erastus Snow,

---

[5] Orson Pratt, JD, 18:18–19.
[6] Joseph Fielding Smith, WP, 144.

has set his hand to gather Israel, according to the Prophets; God has set his hand to establish his Zion; God has set his hand to build his kingdom in the earth, according to the prediction of the holy prophets. God is determined to work a work that shall be a marvelous work and a wonder, which he has commenced and will carry on to completion in his own peculiar way.[7]

Daniel H. Wells, too, testified to the fulfillment of the ancient prophecies in our own modern times:

We do know that the Lord has commenced his great and marvelous Work and he will continue it and break in pieces the wicked and ungodly nations until they shall become the kingdoms of our Lord and his Christ, and his kingdom which is now being set up will continue for ever and ever.[8]

THE RESTORATION OF JEW AND GENTILE

If the work of the Restoration was to commence in the obscurity of nineteenth-century frontier New York, it was certainly not to be confined there. But, while its effects were to be felt throughout the inhabited globe, and indeed have been, Church leaders remind us that these effects were to be particularly profound in the ancient land of the prophets, Palestine. Elder Milton R. Hunter observed:

Another phase of "a marvelous work and a wonder" would be the fulfilling of the covenants made by the Lord with the children of Israel. Nephi predicted that at the time that Jehovah would establish his gospel among the Gentiles in the land of promise he would remember the covenants he had made with the house of Israel—the covenant to return the Jews to Palestine, the covenant to establish Ephraim with the birthright in the promised land, the covenants with the Lamanites—and he would fulfill all of these covenants. . . . The Book of Mormon, as a portion of this "marvelous work and a wonder," would be given through the seed of Ephraim— who would have the birthright—or as Nephi stated, through the Gentiles, to the Jews, to the Lamanites, and to all of the

---

7 Erastus Snow, JD, 23:298.
8 Daniel H. Wells, JD, 10:199.

dispersed of the house of Israel, wherever they are throughout the world. This book would come forth to bear witness that Jesus is the Christ, the Savior of the world, to be a new witness to the Bible, and to help proclaim the gospel to the honest throughout the earth.[9]

Are the ancient prophecies in fact coming true? Manifestly, the answer is Yes. Ezra Taft Benson, a prophet of the latter days, is but one of many of God's servants who have recognized the Lord's hand in the events that have transpired over the past several decades in the Near East.

> The prophet Isaiah said that in the last days the Lord would proceed to do a marvelous work and a wonder; that the wisdom of their wise men should perish and the understanding of their prudent men should be hid (Isaiah 29:14; 2 Nephi 27:26). That prophecy, it seems to me, has been and is being fulfilled in what is transpiring over in Israel at the present time.[10]

And, once again, we must be careful not to lose sight of the wonder, the remarkable unlikelihood, of what we are seeing in and around the ancient land of Jerusalem. We are used to hearing about Israel on the nightly news and reading about it in newspapers and magazines. Yet there are few who would have imagined such a possibility at any time between, say, 200 and 1800 AD. The people of Judah, driven from their homeland for very nearly two thousand years, are back. Those who oppressed and scattered them, the Assyrians, the Babylonians, the Romans, are gone. Ancient Latin and ancient Egyptian are dead languages, known only imperfectly to an educated few. But Israel lives again, and once again, Hebrew, the tongue of the biblical prophets, is the everyday spoken language of shopkeepers, soldiers, mothers, and children.

The work of the gathering is not, of course, finished. The Twelve Apostles knew this in 1845:

---

9 Milton R. Hunter, CR, October 1958, 28. Joseph Fielding Smith, DS, 2:251, also taught that it is Ephraim that will take the lead in the labors of the last days, although he allowed a major role for others as well, including "the remnants of Joseph, found among the descendants of Lehi." Elder Orson Pratt taught that the Three Nephites, mentioned in the Book of Mormon, will also play a part in the "great and marvelous work" of the latter days. See JD, 18:21–22.
10 Ezra Taft Benson, TETB, 94.

A great, a glorious, and a mighty work is yet to be achieved, in spreading the truth and kingdom among the Gentiles—in restoring, organizing, instructing and establishing the Jews—in gathering, instructing, relieving, civilizing, educating and administering salvation to the remnant of Israel on this continent; in building Jerusalem in Palestine, and the cities, stakes, temples, and sanctuaries of Zion in America; and in gathering the Gentiles into the same covenant and organization—instructing them in all things for their sanctification and preparation—that the whole Church of the Saints, both Gentile, Jew and Israel, may be prepared as a bride, for the coming of the Lord.[11]

Much of the Work Lies in the Future

Decades later, Elder Franklin D. Richards continued to affirm that much remained to be done and that the most glorious elements of the task lie still in the future:

We have a great and marvelous work laid upon us, and its more marvelous features are still to be developed and made manifest. We yet see but a small part of it. The Lord has shown us all we can bear; all we can, in our present state of development, comprehend and apply.[12]

Wilford Woodruff agreed that we see only a portion of the full picture of the gathering. If we were to see it all at once, he seems to suggest, we might well be overwhelmed. Yet President Woodruff appears, at the same time, to exhort us to contemplate as much of the future work and glory as we possibly can, urging us not to let ourselves become depressed at the magnitude of the task before us but, rather, to allow ourselves to be inspired by the grandeur and the holiness of it.

If we could open the vision of our minds, and let it extend into the future and see this kingdom, and what it is bound to accomplish, and what we have to do, the warfare we have to pass through, we would certainly see that we have a great work on hand. We have not only to fight the powers of darkness, the invisible forces that surround us, but we have to war

11 The Twelve Apostles, MFP, 1:255.
12 Franklin D. Richards, JD, 26:300.

with a great many outward circumstances and to contend with a great many difficulties that we must of necessity meet, and the more of this we have to meet the more we should be stimulated to action, and to labour with all our power before the Lord for the establishment of righteousness and truth and the building up of the work of God, and to see that His name is honoured upon the earth.[13]

President Woodruff knew that much in this latter-day work—though not its ultimate outcome—depends upon us, upon ordinary men and women called upon to do quite extraordinary things. Though the Church has grown throughout the world and, in many cases, in the wealth and sophistication of its membership, our situation is really not so very different from that of the farmers and artisans who founded it on the sixth of April, 1830:

> These Elders of Israel were called from the various occupations of life to preach as they were moved upon by the Holy Ghost. They were not learned men; they were the weak things of this world, whom God chose to confound the wise, "and things which are not, to bring to nought things that are." We are here on that principle. Others will be gathered on that principle. Zion will be redeemed, Zion will arise, and the glory of God will rest upon her, and all that Isaiah and the other prophets have spoken concerning her will come to pass.[14]

Daniel H. Wells taught that the pace of the work, the speed with which the purposes of God will be fullfilled, rests in the hands of those who have been called to move it along:

> This great and marvelous work of the latter-days will be prolonged or hastened according to the faith and good works of the people engaged in it. If we pray, therefore, the Lord to hasten His work; to hasten the time when Zion shall be built up and redeemed; when the great and glorious Temple shall be erected to the name of the Most High God, and when His glory shall rest upon it in the form of a cloud by day and a pillar of fire by

---

13 Wilford Woodruff, JD, 4:230.
14 Wilford Woodruff, CD, 2:136.

night, let our righteousness conform with our holy desires; let us so live as to call down the blessings of heaven upon us.[15]

We will need all our prayerfulness, all our unity and righteousness, to carry out our part of the mission of this dispensation. For there will, unfortunately, be opposition to the latter-day work of the Lord. And some of that opposition will be powerful and deeply entrenched. The Twelve Apostles saw this clearly already in their declaration of 1845:

> There is also another consideration of vast importance to all the rulers and people of the world, in regard to this matter. It is this: As this work progresses in its onward course, and becomes more and more an object of political and religious interest and excitement, no king, ruler, or subject, no community or individual, will stand *neutral.* All will at length be influenced by one spirit or the other; and will take sides either for or against the kingdom of God, and the fulfillment of the prophets, in the great restoration and return of his long dispersed covenant people.
>
> Some will act the part of the venerable Jethro, the father-in-law of Moses; or the noble Cyrus; and will aid and bless the people of God; or like Ruth, the Moabitess, will forsake their people and their kindred and country, and will say to the Saints, or to Israel: *"This people shall be my people, and their God my God."* While others will walk in the footsteps of a Pharaoh, or a Balak, and will harden their hearts, and fight against God, and seek to destroy his people. These will commune with priests and prophets who love the wages of unrighteousness; and who, like Balaam, will seek to curse, or to find enchantments against Israel.[16]

ALL ARE CALLED TO THE WORK

But the words of the prophets leave no doubt about the ultimate outcome. President Wilford Woodruff, who was driven with his fellow Saints from state to state, whose prophet-leader was murdered by an anti-Mormon mob in Illinois, who suffered with the Church of God through virtually all of its trials in the nineteenth century,

---

15 Daniel H. Wells, JD, 23:307–8.
16 The Twelve Apostles, MFP, 1:257.

nonetheless had no reservations about prophesying the eventual triumph of the cause. His own experience, even amidst the pain, the injustice, and the bigotry, assured him of God's supporting hand:

> The Lord has said He would prove us whether we would abide in His covenant even unto death; indeed we have been tried from the commencement of this great work, but there has been an invisible hand at work for our defence all the time; the wicked have not seen the power that has sustained us, they cannot see the inside machinery that is at work in this kingdom, the nations of the earth cannot understand it, and they never can comprehend it, but the Latter-day Saints understand it, and they know that it is the power of God and the word of God, for the Lord has made proclamations and decrees, and covenants concerning Israel in the last days.[17]

Years later, Joseph Fielding Smith bore testimony of this same sustaining power. "When the Lord shall speak," he declared,

> the way will be opened for the accomplishment of his purposes, and all opposition will melt as the hoar-frost before the rising sun. "For thus saith the Lord, I will cut my work short in righteousness, for the days come that I will send forth judgment unto victory." (D&C 52:11.) "Behold I will hasten my work in its time." (D&C 88:73.)[18]

With this prophetic assurance supporting him, Elder Smith cautioned the Saints neither to lose hope nor to relax our efforts to build the Kingdom, merely because the promises of God seem, by our mortal timetable, to be slow of fulfillment:

> Nearly 100 years have passed since the site of Zion was dedicated and the spot for the temple was chosen, and some of the members of the Church seem to be fearful lest the word of the Lord shall fail. Others have tried to convince themselves that the original plan has been changed and that the Lord does not require at our hands this mighty work which has been predicted by the prophets of ancient times. We have not been

---

[17] Wilford Woodruff, JD, 4:230–31.
[18] Joseph Fielding Smith, WP, 271.

released from this responsibility, nor shall we be. The word of the Lord will not fail.[19]

The Lord's latter-day prophets and apostles have consistently sought to convey to us the importance of the effort in which we are involved, to urge us to consecrate our time and our talents and the material substance with which we have been blessed to the furtherance of this indescribably great cause. We may not be called upon to perform obvious heroics. We may not need to sacrifice our lives or to wear out our feet walking across a continent. Much of what we will be asked to do will be, as it is now, small. Seemingly unimportant acts of kindness and concern, time spent with young people, ordinances performed in holy places where fame and applause are unknown, all these are important steps to advance the building of Zion and to take the gospel of our Lord to the vast hosts of those, living and dead, who have not yet had the chance to hear it. "Wherefore," says the Lord, "be not weary in well-doing, for ye are laying the foundation of a great work. And out of small things proceedeth that which is great."[20]

Perhaps it is fitting, since we have heard so much in this chapter from the great latter-day apostle and prophet Wilford Woodruff, to give him the last word. From the books that preserve his teachings, his voice calls upon us, just as it did audibly for the Saints of his day, to dedicate ourselves anew to the service of God and our brothers and sisters:

> A great work is before us, a work worthy of intelligent beings—worthy of the most noble of spirits that ever existed around the throne of God in time or in eternity, in heaven or on the earth. Then, if we would feel right about this important subject, and look upon it as it is, we will go to work and labour with all our mights to build up the kingdom of our God, to carry out the purposes of the Lord, in the building up of Zion, the establishment of his kingdom, and restoration, and salvation of the house of Israel; we should listen strictly to those men who are the words of the Lord to us.[21]

---

[19] Joseph Fielding Smith, DS, 3:78.
[20] Doctrine and Covenants 64:33.
[21] Wilford Woodruff, JD, 4:233.

CHAPTER 8

THE RESTITUTION OF ALL THINGS

A RESTITUTION FORETOLD OF OLD

> Repent ye therefore, and be converted, that your sins may be blotted out, when the times of refreshing shall come from the presence of the Lord;
> And he shall send Jesus Christ, which before was preached unto you:
> Whom the heaven must receive until the times of restitution of all things, which God hath spoken by the mouth of all his holy prophets since the world began.[1]

One of the pervasive themes of the New Testament and of latter-day prophets and apostles is the notion of a "restitution of all things." Two things about that concept are immediately clear from the passage just cited from the Acts of the Apostles: First, the restitution or restoration of all things had been a part of the divine plan, and an element in the preaching of the prophets, from the very earliest era of scriptural history. "The Lord understood," John Taylor taught,

> that the time would come when the power of Satan, and the power of the wicked would be overthrown; when the Zion of God would be established; when a reign of righteousness would be introduced; when there would be a communion between the Priesthood on the earth and the Priesthood in the heavens, and when correct principles would be introduced, and the rule and government of God would be established in the earth, and continue until the kingdoms of this world would become the kingdoms of our God and His Christ, and He would reign with universal empire over the nations of the earth. This is a thing that has been spoken of by all the Prophets, and it is the time of the restitution of all things since the world was.[2]

---

[1] Acts 3:19-21.
[2] John Taylor, JD, 24:351.

Second, we learn from this passage in Acts that the great period of restitution was intended to occur near the very end of time, in connection with the second advent of the Lord Jesus Christ. Even as Peter was speaking the words quoted, Elder James E. Talmage remarked, that ancient apostle and prophet knew that he was speaking of "a time then far future, the time of restitution of which the prophets had spoken."[3] "It is apparent," wrote Joseph Fielding Smith, "that the restoration of all things was not the purpose to be accomplished during the meridian of time, when Christ was in his ministry. This great work was reserved for the last days."[4]

> The Lord indicated to the apostles, before his ascension, that the restoration of all things was not for their day or time, and that it was not for them "to know the times or the seasons, which the Father hath put in his own power." Peter and Paul made it very clear in their teachings that there should come another dispensation of the gospel to succeed that in which they lived, and this final dispensation should be given shortly before the second coming of the Son of God, to prepare mankind and the earth for the restoration of all things spoken of by all the holy prophets.[5]

It is the united testimony of God's modern prophets and apostles that the great process of restoration has begun. "I know by the . . . Spirit," declared Charles W. Penrose, "that God Almighty has sent his angels in these the last days to Joseph Smith and others, for the purpose of commencing this work of the restitution of all things. I know that work has begun to be ushered in."[6] Unshaken by the assassination of their leader, the Prophet Joseph Smith, the Quorum of the Twelve Apostles bore similar testimony in 1845 about the great work commenced by the Lord in their day: "He has given us the Holy Priesthood and Apostleship," they said, "and the keys of the kingdom of God, to bring about the restoration of all things as promised by the holy prophets of old.—And we know it."[7] Elder Bruce R. McConkie eloquently summarized the principal events of the Restoration:

---

[3] James E. Talmage, VM, 359–60.
[4] Joseph Fielding Smith, DS, 1:172.
[5] Joseph Fielding Smith, DS, 1:164.
[6] Charles W. Penrose, JD, 20:295.
[7] The Twelve Apostles, MFP, 1:263.

What glorious things have happened in this our day? The heavens have been opened, and the great God who upholds all things by his own power, accompanied by his Beloved Son has appeared to mortal man. An ancient American prophet, ministering in resurrected glory, has given the gold plates from which the Book of Mormon was translated. John, who baptized Jesus, came and conferred the Aaronic Priesthood upon Joseph Smith and Oliver Cowdery. Peter, James, and John—the holy three who were with Jesus in his ministry—have given their keys and powers to mortals, as have Moses, Elias, Elijah, Gabriel, Raphael, and divers angels. The true church has been organized; apostles and prophets once more speak the mind and will of the Lord; and scattered Israel is returning to the sheepfold of the Good Shepherd. Temples have risen in many nations, Israel is gathering, and the saints are in process of building up Zion and preparing for the return of the Lord. The gifts of the Spirit are being poured out upon the faithful oftentimes almost without measure. Truly, there are no words to describe, nor can any tongue tell, the glory and marvel of all that has come anew in our day as part of the promised restoration of all things.[8]

FUTURE ASPECTS OF RESTITUTION

Of course, Church leaders in this dispensation make clear that this restitution is not a one-time event. Rather, it is a process, and a process which is still underway. It was not completed by the coming forth of the Book of Mormon, nor by the restoration of the two priesthoods through the ministration of angels, nor by the mere organization of the Church, important though all these steps were.

They were part of the process, but not the sum total. This is why, for instance, Doctrine and Covenants 86:10, revealed on 6 December 1832, can still speak of "the restoration of all things spoken by the mouths of all the holy prophets since the world began" as something in the future. This also explains how the First Presidency of Brigham Young, Heber C. Kimball, and Jedediah M. Grant, urging the membership of the Church to greater efforts on behalf of the Lamanites, could say that "the time of restitution approaches; be up and doing, therefore, while the day lasts, while there is an

---

[8] Bruce R. McConkie, NWAF, 140–41.

opportunity of rendering them assistance and doing them service, that you may hear the approving words, 'Inasmuch as ye have done it unto one of the least of these my brethren, ye have done it unto me.'"[9] "We have gathered to these mountains," said Charles W. Penrose,

> that we may aid in this great work of restitution. We are build-ing these Temples that the Lord may come and restore further powers and keys and knowledge pertaining to the holy priest-hood, which has been held in reserve, for we have as yet only received the droppings of the shower to come; we have but received a few things compared with what remains to be revealed. There is not a principle nor a blessing referred to in these Scriptures, which has been enjoyed by the Saints of any former time, but what the Lord our God will restore and bestow upon his people of the latter times.[10]

Indeed, temples are an important component of the process of the restoration, as will become apparent throught the words of the prophets and apostles over the next few pages. And it can truly be said, in a sense, that, although the early events preceding the found-ing of The Church of Jesus Christ of Latter-day Saints were of cru-cial and glorious importance, the Restoration really came up to full speed with the great visions manifested to Joseph Smith and Oliver Cowdery in connection with the dedication of the Kirtland Temple in April of 1836. "God," explained Orson Pratt,

> has seen proper in the progress of this kingdom to restore to his servants holding the priesthood every key and power per-taining to the restitution of all things spoken of by the mouth of all the Holy Prophets since the world began. One of the first things that he condescended to restore was the fullness of the everlasting Gospel, just according to the prediction of the ancient Prophets—by the coming of an angel from heaven.[11]

Particularly important, in this regard, are the visitations of the ancient prophets Moses, Elijah, and Elias. Of the latter figure, Bruce R. McConkie taught that

---

[9] Brigham Young, Heber C. Kimball, Jedediah M. Grant, MFP, 2:178.
[10] Charles W. Penrose, JD, 20:296.
[11] Orson Pratt, JD, 15:45.

this mighty prophet holds "the keys of bringing to pass the restoration of all things spoken by the mouth of all the holy prophets since the world began, concerning the last days." (D&C 27:6; 77:9, 14–15; Matthew 17:11; Mark 9:12.) These keys have already been conferred upon man, and such things as have not already been revealed will be made known "in due time." (D&C 132:40, 45.)[12]

Joseph Smith informed his followers that the "restitution of all things spoken of by all the holy Prophets since the world was" will take place during "the dispensation of the fullness of times, when God shall gather together all things in one."[13] It is of the utmost importance to realize that this gathering together of "all things in one" is meant quite literally, as is the idea that "all things" that have ever pertained to previous dispensations of the fulness of the gospel will be restored. "We are living," said Joseph Fielding Smith,

> in the dispensation of the fulness of times into which all things are to be gathered, and all things are to be restored since the beginning. Even this earth is to be restored to the condition which prevailed before Adam's transgression. Now in the nature of things, the law of sacrifice will have to be restored, or all things which were decreed by the Lord would not be restored. It will be necessary, therefore, for the sons of Levi, who offered the blood sacrifices anciently in Israel, to offer such a sacrifice again to round out and complete this ordinance in this dispensation. Sacrifice by the shedding of blood was instituted in the days of Adam and of necessity will have to be restored.[14]

ANIMAL SACRIFICES ONLY TEMPORARY

The Prophet Joseph Smith explained, however, that the restoration of sacrifices did not mean the restitution of the full sacrificial system pertaining to the law of Moses. For it was the fulness of the gospel that was and is to be returned to earth, not the incomplete system that

---

[12] Bruce R. McConkie, MD, 636. Joseph Fielding Smith, DS, 1:172, explained that "The name Elias is more than a proper name; it is also a title. An Elias is one who goes before one greater than himself to prepare the way for the greater who is to follow. In this calling John [the Baptist] served."

[13] Joseph Smith Jr., TPJS, 252.

[14] Joseph Fielding Smith, DS, 3:94.

existed during the long partial apostasy of Israel when they were subject to the lesser law. "These sacrifices," said the Prophet,

> as well as every ordinance belonging to the Priesthood, will, when the Temple of the Lord shall be built, and the sons of Levi be purified, be fully restored and attended to in all their powers, ramifications, and blessings. This ever did and ever will exist when the powers of the Melchisedek Priesthood are sufficiently manifest; else how can the restitution of all things spoken of by the holy Prophets be brought to pass? It is not to be understood that the law of Moses will be established again with all its rites and variety of ceremonies; this has never been spoken of by the Prophets; but those things which existed prior to Moses' day, namely, sacrifice, will be continued.[15]

Joseph Fielding Smith, the Prophet's greatnephew who was himself an apostle and prophet of the Lord, further explained that sacrificial ordinances would only temporarily be reinstituted among the Saints, essentially to ensure the completeness of the Restoration:

> The sacrifice of animals will be done to complete the restoration when the temple spoken of is built; at the beginning of the millennium, or in the restoration, blood sacrifices will be performed long enough to complete the fulness of the restoration in this dispensation. Afterwards sacrifice will be of some other character.[16]

TWELVE TRIBES OF ISRAEL TO GATHER

For the work of this great last dispensation as explained by modern seers is, essentially, one of union and reunion, a welding together of nations, of generations, of earth and heaven in revelation, or of the living and the dead by means of the ordinances of the holy temple. This includes the gathering of Israel, which is an important part of this larger unifying process. "We believe in the literal gathering of Israel and in the restoration of the Ten Tribes: that Zion will be built

---

[15] Joseph Smith Jr., HC, 4:211–12.

[16] Joseph Fielding Smith, DS, 3:94. This principle, of at least temporary restitution in order to effect a complete restoration, may well be relevant to the nineteenth century Latter-day Saint practice of plural marriage. Orson Pratt, JD, 17:221, included that practice among the things that, since they had once been observed as part of the everlasting gospel, needed to be restored.

upon this [the American] continent; that Christ will reign personally upon the earth; and that the earth will be renewed and receive its paradisiacal glory."[17] Church leaders stress that this is, again, a *literal* gathering. "We are told," remarked Parley Pratt,

> by the Prophet of old, in the good old Bible, and by that peculiar Prophet that the Christian world (that portion of them that esteem the Bible) consider more clear, and more eloquent than any other, whose prophecies are on record—the Prophet Isaiah; we are told by him, that the Lord would, some time, "lift up a standard for the people," "an ensign for the nations," and that He would not only do this, but do it as a manifestation which should result in the great restoration of all things spoken of by the Prophets, in the restoration of the twelve tribes of Israel from the four quarters of the earth, to their own country, nationality, institutions, and religion; that they might again be nationalized, established, and reinstated in their covenant renewed unto them, as in days of old, and have their own Priesthood, rulers, governors, and consequently their own blessings.[18]

During the lifetime of Orson Pratt, of course, the gathering of the Jews to Palestine had scarcely begun. Indeed, it was hardly visible. "It is," he commented,

> very evident to every person who believes in the Scriptures of truth that, so far as the gathering of Israel and their becoming one nation in their own land are concerned, this prophecy has never yet been fulfilled, it is therefore among those great events which the Lord has decreed and determined to bring to pass in a period of time yet in the future; and he has pointed out, in this chapter [37] of Ezekiel, the manner and method in which he will commence the great work of the restitution of Israel.[19]

Today, however, the establishment of the Jews in their own state of Israel is an undeniable fact, which should be a sign to all observers of the faithfulness and power of God in keeping his promises. Elder Pratt also noted the commencement of the work of gathering and redeeming the scattered children of Israel in the western hemisphere,

---

17 Article of Faith 10.

18 Parley P. Pratt, JD, 1:173.

19 Orson Pratt, JD, 16:341.

a work whose eventual success is every bit as sure as the gathering of the Jews has proved itself to be. "Do you wonder then," he asked his hearers in the 1870s,

> that after forty-five years have passed away since the organization of this Church, and the voice of warning went forth to the Gentile nations, that God, in his mercy and power, should commence a work among this remnant of the house of Joseph, that wander as a multitude of nations upon the face of this continent? Recollect what Jacob said, concerning the seed of Joseph, in the 48th chapter of Genesis—they were to become a multitude of nations. They never were a multitude of nations in Palestine, neither in Asia, Europe, nor Africa, and if the prophecy is not fulfilled upon the great western continent, it will not be fulfilled at all. But it has been fulfilled on the continent of America; and we behold throughout the whole of this vast extent, from the frozen regions of the north, to Cape Horn in the south, a multitude of nations. Who are they? They are principally the remnants of one tribe, the remnants of the tribe of Joseph, and they are a multitude of nations in the midst of the earth. The Lord had commenced the gathering and restitution of the house of Israel among the very lowest specimens of humanity, and he will raise them up first, to carry on his great and marvelous work. The tens of thousands of Ephraim, and the thousands of Manasseh, will push the people together to the ends of the earth. Ephraim will not do the work alone, but he will be assisted by Manasseh. The Indians, and Lamanites, who will take hold in this great latter-day work, are the horns of Joseph, not to scatter the people, but to push them together.[20]

ALL THINGS TO BE GATHERED IN ONE

It is not enough, however, merely to gather the various peoples together. They must be unified in a common loyalty to the Lord and his ordinances, and the old enmities between them must be done away. Elder James E. Talmage indicated that

> the restoration is to be comprehensive; there shall be a united people, no longer two kingdoms each at enmity with the other; for: "The envy also of Ephraim shall depart, and the adversaries

---

[20] Orson Pratt, JD, 18:166–67.

of Judah shall be cut off: Ephraim shall not envy Judah, and Judah shall not vex Ephraim." (Isaiah 11:13.) With the words of a fond father the Lord thus speaks of His treatment of Israel and brightens their desolation with the promise: "For a small moment have I forsaken thee; but with great mercies will I gather thee. In a little wrath I hid my face from thee for a moment; but with everlasting kindness will I have mercy on thee, saith the Lord thy Redeemer." (Isaiah 54:7-8.)[21]

Indeed, the prophets teach that so complete will the unity and harmony be that, whether literally or symbolically, even the two physical lands of the gathering, the old Jerusalem of the east and the new Jerusalem, or Zion, of the west, will be brought together. As Joseph Fielding Smith said,

> The Lord revealed to the Prophet Joseph Smith that when he comes, as a part of the great restoration, this land surface will be brought back to its original form. When that time comes, the land of Zion (Western Hemisphere) and the land of Jerusalem "shall be turned back into their own place, and the earth shall be like as it was in the days before it was divided." John saw this day when "every island fled away, and the mountains were not found."[22]

The gathering and the unification that will attend it will not, however, be limited only to terrestrial space. It extends through time, as well. Erastus Snow saw an intimate link between the gathering of Israel and the welding together of Israel's various generations in the sealing ordinances of the house of the Lord:

> The Lord showed Ezekiel a valley full of dry human bones; and he asks him if those bones can live. Ezekiel answered, "O Lord God, thou knowest." The Lord then tells him to prophesy to the bones: O ye dry bones. Hear the word of the Lord; and as he did so there was a shaking, and behold the bones came together, bone to its bone; and according to the word of the Lord through him, flesh and skin and sinews came upon them, and the breath of life came into them, and lo, and

---

[21] James E. Talmage, AF, 330.
[22] Joseph Fielding Smith, DS, 3:75.

behold, they stood upon their feet an exceedingly great army. The Lord then tells the Prophet that these are the whole house of Israel; and that they complain of the non-fulfillment of the promises upon their head, saying, "Our bones are dried, and our hope is lost: all are cut off for our parts. "But he further tells him to prophecy unto them, saying, "Thus saith the Lord God; Behold, O my people, I will open your graves, and cause you to come up out of your graves, and bring you into the land of Israel," etc. And by whom shall this great and marvelous work be accomplished? I answer, by the thousands of Manasseh and the ten thousands of Ephraim; by this same people who shall search out and gather together the house of Israel, and who will come up as saviors upon Mount Zion.[23]

John Taylor, too, recognized the central role of the sealing ordinances in the work of the latter days. "The times of restitution spoken of by the prophets," he testified,

must take place; the restorer must come "before that great and terrible day of the Lord." The hearts of the fathers must be turned to the children, and the hearts of the children to the fathers, or the earth will be cursed. This great eternal marriage covenant lays at the foundation of the whole; when this was revealed, then followed the other. Then, and not till then, could the hearts of the fathers be turned to their children, and the hearts of the children to the fathers; then and not till then, could the restoration be effectually commenced, time and eternity be connected, the past, present, and future harmonize, and the eternal justice of God be vindicated; "Saviors come upon Mount Zion" to save the living, redeem the dead, unite man to woman and woman to man, in eternal, indissoluble ties; impart blessings to the dead, redeem the living, and pour eternal blessings upon posterity.[24]

THE EXPANSIVE NATURE OF RESTORATION

But President Taylor saw even this grand and expansive vision of the unification of Israel across all time and space as too small, too confined, too provincial. "We 'Mormons'," he observed,

---

[23] Erastus Snow, JD, 23:187.
[24] John Taylor, JD, 11:223.

think that we have made a wonderful stretch, for we say that all Israel is going to be saved, and we believe we are of Israel, and that we shall be gathered into the fold with them. And when we are gathered in with all the Israel of God, as we call them, that have lived in the various ages of the world up to the present time, we with them shall be redeemed and saved in the eternal kingdom of God. What else? Then His work will be accomplished, you may say. But I do not think it will, though it will certainly be a great work. This looks like the time of the restoration of all things, but in reality it is only a restoration of a few. Why, you may inquire, will you take in somebody besides the Israelites? Certainly. We are told they were beloved for the fathers' sakes, and in consequence of the promises made to the fathers. If they are brought in, it will be in consequence of these promises. I wonder if there were no other men of faith besides Abraham, Isaac, and Jacob, that existed previous to their days. And if there were, I want to know if they knew anything about God, and obtained promises for their offspring.[25]

Given the vastness of the work in which we are engaged, one which ranges across all time and all earthly space, which concerns both those who have passed on before us and those who will come after us in all the nations of the globe, it is hardly surprising that our brothers and sisters on the other side of the veil are deeply interested in the labors of this dispensation. "We have never said that we would do it alone," said Parley P. Pratt,

but rather that the powers of the heavens that have gone before us and been perfected in the same Gospel, were engaged in it, and wish to help to do it. Nothing short of this fond union of the Saints who have gone before us with the living Latter-day Saints, will ever bring about and complete that great restoration that we have all been looking for, and believing in, that all the Prophets have prophesied of since the world began; nothing short of these united powers can possibly attain to that which is designed, hence they in the other world will attend to their part of it; they are doing it now. But by and bye they will have to be ministers on the earth, and to

---

25 John Taylor, JD, 1:156–57.

the Latter-day Saints, and we have to be prepared to have the vail rent, and to be united more perfectly in our co-operations with them, and they with us.[26]

Indeed, Church authorities remind us that there are powers and authorities that needed to come from behind the veil, where they had been taken by those earlier prophets who had possessed them. It is for this reason that angelic ministrations have been so prominent a part of the establishment of this Church and kingdom in the latter days. "Remember, remember," Parley Pratt, Willard Richards, John Taylor, and W. W. Phelps exhorted members of the Church in a joint declaration,

> that the priesthood and the keys of power are held in eternity as well as in time, and, therefore, the servants of God who pass the veil of death are prepared to enter upon a greater and more effectual work, in the speedy accomplishment of the restoration of all things spoken of by his holy prophets.[27]

Charles W. Penrose further explained that

> God has commenced the great work of restitution of all things by restoring the Gospel in its primitive simplicity, and every principle and ordinance belonging thereto, with the authority and power to administer therein. Every man that has lived upon the earth in past ages, who has held the keys in any dispensation of God's mercy to man, has come down from the place whence he has gone, and restored those keys; they have all brought their priesthood, their authority, and the spirit and power belonging thereunto, and ordained living men to the authority which they themselves held.[28]

A COMMINGLIING OF RESURRECTED AND MORTAL SAINTS

And when the work is sufficiently far along, these now-angelic beings will openly mingle with the Saints in a grand and glorious

---

[26] Parley P. Pratt, JD, 4:13–14.
[27] Parley P. Pratt, Willard Richards, John Taylor, W. W. Phelps, HC, 7:189.
[28] Charles W. Penrose, JD, 20:295.

reunion of the faithful living and the righteous dead. President John Taylor declared that

> Adam, Seth, Enoch, and the faithful who lived before the flood, will possess their proper inheritance. Noah and Melchizedek will stand in their proper places. Abraham, with Isaac and Jacob, heirs with him of the same promise, will come forward at the head of innumerable multitudes, and possess that land which God gave unto them for an everlasting inheritance. The faithful on the continent of America will also stand in their proper place; but, as this will be the time of the restitution of all things, and all things will not be fully restored at once, there will be a distinction between the resurrected bodies and those that have not been resurrected; and, as the scriptures say that flesh and blood cannot inherit the kingdom of God, neither doth corruption inherit incorruption; and although the world will enjoy just laws—an equitable administration, and universal peace and happiness prevail as the result of this righteousness; yet, there will be a peculiar habitation for the resurrected bodies. This habitation may be compared to paradise, whence man, in the beginning, was driven.[29]

"Surely," Joseph Fielding Smith remarked, pursuing the same theme,

> the earth will be in commotion as it readjusts itself to assume its paradisiacal glory. All this must come to pass, because it is a part of the great restoration, and all things are to be restored, both in heaven and in earth in this dispensation. Among these changes the City of Enoch with its inhabitants is to return and join in the grand celebration at the coming of Christ to reign, and all the prophets of old and the righteous saints shall be gathered in the grand assembly of rejoicing.[30]

Indeed, inspired teachings indicate that the resurrection itself can be viewed as a component part of this great reunifying restoration, as it brings together the severed spirits and bodies of those who have died. "Not only will the earth be restored," wrote President John Taylor,

---

[29] John Taylor, GK, 217-18.
[30] Joseph Fielding Smith, WP, 310.

but also man; and those promises which, long ago, were the hope of the Saints, will be realized. . . . The tombs will deliver up their captives, and, reunited with the spirits which once animated, vivified, cheered, and sustained them while in this vale of tears, these bodies will be like unto Christ's glorious body. They will then rejoice in that resurrection for which they lived, while they sojourned below.[31]

THE EARTH TO BECOME PARADISE

It is difficult, if not impossible, for fallen human beings to imagine the grandeur of all this. John Taylor attempted, nonetheless, to sketch the scene for us. "What," he asked,

will be the effects of the establishment of Christ's kingdom, or the reign of God on the earth? It is the doing away with war, bloodshed, misery, disease, and sin, and the ushering in of a kingdom of peace, righteousness, justice, happiness, and prosperity. It is the restoration of the earth and man to their primeval glory and pristine excellence; in fact, the "restitution of all things spoken of by all the prophets since the world began."[32]

All the fondest dreams of political reformers and utopian theorists will be realized. But the linking of all the generations of humankind, living and dead, the compensation for all past losses long thought beyond recompense, the joyous reunion between peoples and the even more joyous reunion of lost, fallen, alienated humanity with its heavenly parents far transcends the most exalted fantasies of mortal idealists. Again, President Taylor:

The time of the restitution of all things will be ushered in; the earth resume its paradisiacal glory, and the dead and the living Saints possess the full fruition of those things for which they lived, and suffered, and died. These are the hopes that the ancient Saints enjoyed; they possessed hopes that bloomed with immortality and eternal life; hopes planted there by the Spirit of God, and conferred by the ministering of Angels, the

---

[31] John Taylor, GK, 217.
[32] John Taylor, GK, 216.

visions of the Almighty, the opening of the Heavens, and the promises of God. They lived and died in hopes of a better resurrection. How different to the narrow, conceited, groveling views of would-be-philosophers, of sickly religionists, and dreaming philanthropists![33]

With such good cause, believing Latter-day Saints join with the Twelve Apostles under Brigham Young, and call for others to join them in the all-important task of building up the kingdom of our God.

We once more invite all the kings, presidents, governors, rulers, judges, and people of the earth, to aid us, the Latter-day Saints; and also, the Jews, and all the remnants of Israel, by your influence and protection, and by your silver and gold, that we may build the cities of Zion and Jerusalem, and the temples and sanctuaries of our God; and may accomplish the great restoration of all things, and bring in the latter-day glory.[34]

But whether others join us or not, and, indeed, whether we ourselves prove individually faithful or not, the work will be done. It will triumph. It cannot fail, for God has so decreed. "As God has dealt in former times," prophesied John Taylor,

so will he in the latter, with this difference, that he will accomplish his purposes in the last days; he will set up his kingdom; he will protect the righteous, destroy Satan and his works, purge the earth from wickedness, and bring in the restitution of all things.[35]

---

[33] John Taylor, GG, 81–82.
[34] The Twelve Apostles, MFP, 1:264.
[35] John Taylor, GG, 95.

CHAPTER 9

ADAM-ONDI-AHMAN

Not far from the town of Gallatin, in Daviess County, Missouri, there is a place known to the people as "Spring Hill." Here a settlement of the Saints was started in 1838. This hill is on the north of the valley, through which runs Grand River, described by the Prophet Joseph as a "large, beautiful, deep and rapid stream, during the high waters of spring." In the spring and summer the surrounding valley is most beautiful, with its scattered farms discernible as far as the eye can reach. The citizens here go about their daily tasks all unaware of the wondrous occurrences which have taken place in this beautiful valley and on this hill. They are equally oblivious to the momentous events soon to be staged there.[1]

THE PLACE WHERE ADAM DWELT

The place to which Joseph Fielding Smith referred is known in Latter-day Saint scripture and theology as Adam-ondi-Ahman. It played a fundamental role in the earliest scriptural history of the earth, and it will emerge from neglect and obscurity to play a role every bit as central in the events of the latter days. It is, of course, the future of the place that concerns us here, but that future cannot be understood without at least a passing reference to its past. Orson Pratt explained that

> Adam-ondi-ahman, the Valley of God, where Adam dwelt, was located about fifty miles north of Jackson County, in the State of Missouri. The Lord has revealed to us that Adam dwelt there towards the latter period of his probation. Whether he had lived in that region of country from the earliest period of his existence on the earth, we know not. He might have lived thousands of miles distant, in his early days. It might have been upon what we now term the great eastern hemisphere, for in those days the eastern and western hemispheres were one, and were not divided asunder till the days of Peleg.[2]

[1] Joseph Fielding Smith, WP, 287.
[2] Orson Pratt, JD, 16:48.

But the importance of the site does not derive from the mere fact that Adam slept there. Rather, it is what happened there only shortly before Adam's death that gives it its significance and that foreshadows what the scriptures and prophets promise is yet to occur there in days to come. "Three years before the death of Adam," wrote Joseph Fielding Smith,

> he called together his children, including all the faithful down to the generation of Methuselah, all who were high priests, "with the residue of his posterity who were righteous, into the valley of Adam-ondi-Ahman, and there bestowed upon them his last blessing." (D&C 107:53.) At this grand gathering the Lord appeared and administered comfort unto Adam, and said unto him: "I have set thee to be at the head; a multitude of nations shall come of thee, and thou art a prince over them forever." The assembly arose and blessed Adam and called him Michael, the prince, the arch-angel. Then Adam stood up in the midst of the congregation—and no such a gathering on any other occasion has this world ever seen—"and notwithstanding he was bowed down with age, being full of the Holy Ghost (he) predicted whatsoever should befall his posterity unto the last generation." And all this is written in the book of Enoch, which shall be revealed in due time. (D&C 107:54 57.)[3]

Orson Pratt described the event in similar terms, saying that

> in that valley Adam called together Seth, Enos, Cainan, Mahalaleel, Jared, Enoch, Methusaleh and all the high Priests and righteous of his descendants for some seven or eight generations. Three years before his death he there stood up, being bowed with age, and preached to that vast assembly of people, and pronounced upon them his great and last patriarchal blessing, and they rose up by the authority and power and revelation of the holy Priesthood which they held, and pronounced their blessing upon their great common progenitor Adam, and he was called the Prince of Peace, and the Father of many nations, and it was said that he should stand at the head of and rule over his people of all generations, notwithstanding he was so aged. That was the blessing pronounced,

---

[3] Joseph Fielding Smith, WP, 288–89.

three years before his death, upon the great head, Patriarch and Prophet of this creation, the man whom God chose to begin the works of this creation, in other words to begin the peopling of this earth.[4]

We do not depend solely upon ancient writings about this great event for what we know of it. At least one prophet in modern times has actually seen the great council. "I saw Adam in the valley of Adam-ondi-Ahman," testified Joseph Smith.

> He called together his children and blessed them with a patriarchal blessing. The Lord appeared in their midst, and he (Adam) blessed them all, and foretold what should befall them to the latest generation. . . . This is why Adam blessed his posterity; he wanted to bring them into the presence of God. They looked for a city, etc., "whose builder and maker is God." (Hebrews 11:10.) Moses sought to bring the children of Israel into the presence of God, through the power of the Priesthood, but he could not. In the first ages of the world they tried to establish the same thing; and there were Eliases raised up who tried to restore these very glories, but did not obtain them; but they prophesied of a day when this glory would be revealed. Paul spoke of the dispensation of the fullness of times, when God would gather together all things in one, etc.; and those men to whom these keys have been given, will have to be there; and they without us cannot be made perfect.[5]

ADAM IS THE ANCIENT OF DAYS

Why is it important for us to know about this grand event from the ancient scriptural past? Prophets have testified that it is important for us today to understand something of the ancient conference because yet another such council will be held in the latter days at the same place—a council that will actually see to the accomplishment of that which the patriarch Adam was seeking to do at the beginning of human history. We will have to pass through much tribulation before that time, as the Prophet Joseph Smith, using the apocalyptic language of Daniel and of the Revelation of John, made apparent:

---

[4] Orson Pratt, JD, 17:186–87.
[5] Joseph Smith Jr., TPJS, 158–59.

The "Horn" made war with the Saints and overcame them,
until the Ancient of Days came; judgment was given to the
Saints of the Most High from the Ancient of Days; the time
came that the Saints possessed the Kingdom. This not only
makes us ministers here, but in eternity.[6]

It is the arrival of this rather mysterious figure, the Ancient of
Days, that will put an end to the troubles of the Saints. Who is he?
Joseph Fielding Smith provides a clear answer:

The world at large is in ignorance regarding this wonderful
character, the Ancient of Days. Much has been written of him,
but mostly without knowledge. He is, so the Lord informs us,
no other than Adam, our ancient father. As Michael, the arch-
angel, he fought the battles against Lucifer in the beginning,
and he shall also sound the trumpet when all the dead shall
awake (D&C 29:26), and he shall lead the fight in the final
battle with Lucifer. (D&C 88:111-14.) As Adam he was
known as the first man on the earth, as by virtue of that
honor, he becomes "the father of all, the prince of all, the
ancient of days," (D&C 27:11.) He holds the keys of salvation
for this earth, under the direction of the Holy One, "who is
without beginning of days, or end of life," even Jesus Christ.
(D&C 78: 16.)[7]

As the Ancient of Days, Adam will summon a council much like
the one over which he presided as a mortal many thousands of years
before. The time for this, modern apostles and prophets have assured
us, is not far off. Again, we turn to Joseph Fielding Smith for information on the subject:

Not many years hence there shall be another gathering of high
priests and righteous souls in this same valley of Adam-ondi-
Ahman. At this gathering Adam, the Ancient of Days, will
again be present. At this time the vision which Daniel saw will
be enacted. The Ancient of Days will sit. There will stand
before him those who have held the keys of all dispensations,
who shall render up their stewardships to the first Patriarch of

---

the race, who holds the keys of salvation. This shall be a day of judgment and preparation.[8]

CHRIST WILL RECEIVE THE KINGDOM

The Prophet Joseph Smith also offers interesting insight into the coming council:

> Daniel in his seventh chapter speaks of the Ancient of Days; he means the oldest man, our Father, Adam—Michael. He will call his children together and hold a council with them to prepare them for the coming of the Son of Man. He (Adam) is the father of the human family, and presides over the spirits of all men, and all that have had the keys must stand before him in this grand council. This may take place before some of us leave this stage of action. The Son of Man stands before him, and there is given him glory and dominion. Adam delivers up his stewardship to Christ, that which was delivered to him as holding the keys of the universe, but retains his standing as head of the human family.[9]

When Adam presents the keys of his priesthood responsibility to Christ, the Savior's second advent will be very near at hand indeed, for he will come to claim what is, and what the leaders of his chosen priesthood will have formally certified to be, rightly his. Joseph Fielding Smith taught of this, noting that

> Daniel speaks of Adam as the Ancient of Days. In this dispensation the Ancient of Days will sit in the valley of Adam-ondi-Ahman; and the judgment will be set; Christ will come; and the kingdom will be turned over to Christ; and he will be sustained in his calling as King of Kings and Lord of Lords.[10]

Elder Bruce R. McConkie, too, discussed the anticipated council, saying:

> Before the great and dreadful day when the Lord is to return— "In flaming fire taking vengeance on them that know not God,

---

[8] Joseph Fielding Smith, WP, 289.
[9] Joseph Smith Jr., HC, 3:386–87.
[10] Joseph Fielding Smith, DS, 1:106.

and that obey not the gospel of our Lord Jesus Christ" (2 Thessalonians 1:8)—there is to be an appearance at a place called Adam-ondi-Ahman. There Adam, the Ancient of Days, will sit in council with his children; there Christ will come, and to him shall be given "dominion, and glory, and a kingdom, that all people, nations, and languages, should serve him: his dominion is an everlasting dominion, which shall not pass away, and his kingdom that which shall not be destroyed." (Daniel 7.) The place where this gathering will take place has been specified by revelation (D&C 116), and so imminent is its occurrence that the Prophet Joseph Smith was led to remark, "This may take place before some of us leave this stage of action."[11]

Our own Church leader have indicated that the proceedings of this long-prophesied council will have profound implications for the governments that will be exercising power over the inhabitants of the earth at that time. As Joseph Fielding Smith put it,

Daniel speaks of the coming of Christ, and that day is near at hand. There will be a great gathering in the Valley of Adam-ondi-Ahman; there will be a great council held. The Ancient of Days, who is Adam, will sit. The judgment—not the final judgment—will be held, where the righteous who have held keys will make their reports and deliver up their keys and ministry. Christ will come, and Adam will make his report. At this council Christ will be received and acknowledged as the rightful ruler of the earth. Satan will be replaced. Following this event every government in the world, including the United States, will have to become part of the government of God. Then righteous rule will be established. The earth will be cleansed; the wicked will be destroyed; and the reign of peace will be ushered in.[12]

But the Savior will not rule directly in every detail around the world. As he has always done, he will rely upon the priesthood leaders that he has selected and who are accountable to him for the manner in which they carry out their stewardships. "Until this grand council is held," President Smith wrote elsewhere,

---

[11] Bruce R. McConkie, MD, 732.
[12] Joseph Fielding Smith, DS, 3:13–14.

Satan shall hold rule in the nations of the earth; but at that time thrones are to be cast down and man's rule shall come to an end—for it is decreed that the Lord shall make an end of all nations. (D&C 87:6.) Preparation for this work is now going on. Kingdoms are already tottering, some have fallen; but eventually they shall all go the way of the earth, and he shall come whose right it is to rule. Then shall he give the government to the saints of the Most High.[13]

THE ORGANIZATION OF THE KINGDOM TO BE MANIFEST

Church teachings reveal that it will be imperative, therefore, that the priesthood itself be properly organized at this time. And, in fact, the thorough organization of the priesthood will be one of the chief tasks begun in the council at Adam-ondi-Ahman. "This," explained Orson Pratt,

> explains the reason why our father Adam comes as the Ancient of days with all these numerous hosts, and organizes them according to the records of the book, every man in his place, preparatory to the coming of the Son of Man to receive the kingdom. Then every family that is in the order of the Priesthood, and every man and every woman, and every son or daughter whatever their kindred, descent or Priesthood, will know their place.[14]

"It will be found then," said Elder Pratt,

> who it is who have received ordinances by divine authority, and who have received ordinances by the precepts and authority of men. It will then be known who have been joined together in celestial marriage by divine authority, and who by wicked counsels, and by justices of the peace who did not believe in God at the time that they did it, or those who have been married merely until death shall part them. It will then be known that those who have received the ordinances of marriage according to the divine appointment are married for all

---

13 Joseph Fielding Smith, WP, 290.
14 Orson Pratt, JD, 17:186.

eternity; it will then be known that their children are the legal heirs to the inheritances, and glories, and powers, and keys and Priesthood of their fathers, throughout the eternal generations that are to come; and every man will have his family gathered around him which have been given unto him by the sealing of the everlasting Priesthood, and the order and law which God has ordained, and none other.[15]

Elder Pratt saw the proper organization of families as part and parcel of the effort to properly lay out the order the priesthood, in preparation for assuming the great responsibility of regulating all governmental and public matters throughout the world under the direction of the Savior himself. Until then, Elder Pratt maintained, neither the priesthood nor, indeed, the Restoration will be complete. "This man," he said, referring to Father Adam,

will sit upon his throne, and ten thousand times ten thousand immortal beings—his children—will stand before him, with all their different grades of Priesthood, according to the order which God has appointed and ordained. Then every quorum of the Priesthood in this Latter-day Saints Church will find its place, and never until then. If we go behind the vail we will not see this perfect organization of the Saints of all generations until that period shall arrive. That will be before Jesus comes in his glory.[16]

Elder Pratt taught that the current organization of The Church of Jesus Christ of Latter-day Saints will be merged into an even larger institution, composed of the priesthood and its leaders from all the times that have gone before:

Then we will find that there is a place for the First Presidency of this Church; for the Twelve Apostles called in this dispensation; for the twelve disciples that were called among the remnants of Joseph on this land in ancient times; for the twelve that were called among the ten tribes of Israel in the north country; for the Twelve that were called in Palestine, who administered in the presence of our Savior; all

---

[15] Orson Pratt, JD, 17:188.
[16] Orson Pratt, JD, 17:187.

the various quorums and councils of the Priesthood in every dispensation that has transpired since the days of Adam until the present time will find their places, according to the callings, gifts, blessings, ordinations and keys of Priesthood which the Lord Almighty has conferred upon them in their several generations. This, then, will be one of the grandest meetings that have ever transpired upon the face of our globe.[17]

AN ACCOUNTING OF PRIESTHOOD STEWARDSHIP

Thus, the process of perfecting the priesthood will include even those who have preceded this dispensation, the righteous dead, as well as the living of the dispensation of the fulness of times. John Taylor explained this as follows:

> Then they will assemble to regulate all these affairs, and all that held keys of authority to administer will then represent their earthly course. And as this authority has been handed down from one to another in different ages, and in different dispensations, a full reckoning will have to be made by all. All who have held the keys of priesthood will then have to give an account to those from whom they received them. Those that were in the heavens have been assisting those that were upon the earth; but then, they will unite together in a general council to give an account of their stewardships, and as in the various ages men have received their power to administer from those who had previously held the keys thereof, there will be a general account.[18]

President Taylor set forth the process as one that will be familiar to those who know the priesthood order of the contemporary Church, which is an earthly reflection of the heavenly pattern that will be brought to earth with the coming of the Ancient of Days and, ultimately, of the Savior. "Those under the authorities of the Church of Jesus Christ of Latter-day Saints," he said,

> have to give an account of their transactions to those who direct them in the priesthood; hence the elders give an account

---

[17] Orson Pratt, JD, 17:187.
[18] John Taylor, GK, 216–17.

to presidents of conferences; and presidents of conferences to presidents of nations. Those presidents and the seventies give an account to the twelve apostles; the twelve to the First Presidency; and they to Joseph, from whom they, and the twelve, received their priesthood. This will include the arrangements of the last dispensation. Joseph delivers his authority to Peter, who held the keys before him, and delivered them to him; and Peter to Moses and Elias, who endowed him with this authority on the Mount; and they to those from whom they received them. And thus the world's affairs will be regulated and put right, the restitution of all things be accomplished, and the kingdom of God be ushered in. The earth will be delivered from under the curse, resume its paradisiacal glory, and all things pertaining to its restoration be fulfilled.[19]

But none of this will be done for the glory of mortal human beings, or merely for the sake of their acquiring power over other mortals. Rather, the perfecting of the priesthood and its assumption of political authority will prepare a people and a world to receive the Savior at his return, to serve him and to worship him. "Why all this organization?" asked Orson Pratt.

Why all this judgment and the opening of the books? It is to prepare the way for another august personage whom Daniel saw coming with the clouds of heaven, namely the Son of Man, and these clouds of heaven brought the Son of Man near before the Ancient of days. And when the Son of Man came to the Ancient of days, behold a kingdom was given to the Son of Man, and greatness and glory, that all people, nations and languages should serve him, and his kingdom should be an everlasting kingdom, a kingdom that should never be done away.[20]

Perhaps one of the fullest descriptions of the tasks of the great meeting has been given to us by Joseph Fielding Smith:

This council in the valley of Adam-ondi-Ahman is to be of the greatest importance to this world. At that time there will be a

---

[19] John Taylor, GK, 217.
[20] Orson Pratt, JD, 17:186.

transfer of authority from the usurper and impostor, Lucifer, to the rightful King, Jesus Christ. Judgment will be set and all who have held keys will make their reports and deliver their stewardships, as they shall be required. Adam will direct this judgment, and then he will make his report, as the one holding the keys for this earth, to his Superior Officer, Jesus Christ. Our Lord will then assume the reins of government; directions will be given to the Priesthood; and He, whose right it is to rule, will be installed officially by the voice of the Priesthood there assembled. This grand council of Priesthood will be composed, not only of those who are faithful who now dwell on this earth, but also of the prophets and apostles of old, who have had directing authority. Others may also be there, but if so they will be there by appointment, for this is to be an official council called to attend to the most momentous matters concerning the destiny of this earth.[21]

In fact, President Smith said, only a very small number of people will know about the great council at Adam-ondi-Ahman when it occurs, though all people will learn about it eventually as they experience the great blessings of peace and order and truth that will flow from it.

When this gathering is held, the world will not know of it; the members of the Church at large will not know of it, yet it shall be preparatory to the coming in the clouds of glory of our Savior Jesus Christ as the Prophet Joseph Smith has said. The world cannot know of it. The Saints cannot know of it— except those who officially shall be called into this council— for it shall precede the coming of Jesus Christ as a thief in the night, unbeknown to all the world.[22]

---

[21] Joseph Fielding Smith, WP, 291.
[22] Joseph Fielding Smith, WP, 291.

CHAPTER 10

A DAY OF POWER

Accompanying and, indeed, making possible the restoration of the Lord's Church in the latter days was a restoration of priesthood authority through the ministration of angels. When Joseph Smith and Oliver Cowdery knelt in the presence, first, of the resurrected John the Baptist and then, later, before the ancient apostles Peter, James, and John, they received power. Prophets and apostles of this dispensation emphasize that it was power that had not been had among ordinary mortals since the collapse of the early Christian church, and it is entirely and utterly unique to The Church of Jesus Christ of Latter-day Saints. This power and authority has been exercised by members of the Church ever since, not least in the great program of preaching the gospel and gathering God's children into his restored Kingdom.

Citing instructions given by the Prophet Joseph Smith, Elder Bruce R. McConkie referred to this power and alluded to the goal toward which bearers of the priesthood should be working:

> "What is meant by the command which saith: Put on thy strength, O Zion—and what people had Isaiah reference to?" Answer: "He had reference to those whom God should call in the last days, who should hold the power of priesthood to bring again Zion, and the redemption of Israel; and to put on her strength is to put on the authority of the priesthood, which she, Zion, has a right to by lineage; also to return to that power which she had lost." (D&C 113:7–8.) When the work here proclaimed is fully accomplished, the Millennium will be upon us, and no unclean person will be left to go into Jerusalem or Zion or any of the cities of the earth, for the wicked will be burned at His coming.[1]

THE DAY OF POWER STILL FUTURE

But even though the marvelous power of the priesthood that now exists in the Church is a power that can "bind on earth" and

---

[1] Bruce R. McConkie, NWAF, 572.

have it then "bound in heaven," an authority whose reach extends beyond death so that "the gates of the spirit world shall not prevail against it," is not yet at the full,[2] the "day of power" has not yet come. W. W. Phelps, David Whitmer, and Parley P. Pratt made this clear in a proclamation that dates back to the earliest years of the Church. "All the prophets," they said,

> from Moses to John the Revelator, have spoken concerning these things. And in all good faith, by direct revelation from the Lord, as in days of old, we commenced the glorious work, that a holy city, a new Jerusalem, even Zion, might be built up, and a temple reared in this generation, whereunto, as saith the Lord, all nations shall be invited. First, the rich and the learned, the wise and the noble, were to be invited; and after that cometh the day of His power.[3]

"The Elders of this Church have gone forth among many nations," Orson Pratt explained decades later, when the efforts of the missionaries had taken the gospel throughout North America, to Europe, and the isles of the sea.

> They rejoice in the power that is made manifest, in some measure. God has said that they should go and preach the Gospel to all nations of the earth; and that signs should follow them that believe. "In my name they shall do many wonderful works. In my name they shall cast out devils, speak in other tongues; and the eyes of the blind shall be opened." The Elders have found this to be true. As far as the people have had faith, they have seen this power, in some measure, displayed. But this can not be said, comparatively, to be the day of his power. When the day of the power of the Lord shall come, then will be a time when not only the sick, the lame and the blind, but also the very elements will be wrought upon by the power of God, as the Lord has spoken, and be subservient to the commands of his servants.[4]

---

[2] The quoted passages are from Matthew 16:18–19. The translation is my own; the Greek word *hades*, which the King James Version misleadingly renders as "hell," represents the destination of *all* the dead, both good and evil, and need have no negative moral connotation. It is equivalent to the Hebrew *sheol*, and precisely equivalent to what Latter-day Saints typically call "the spirit world."

[3] W. W. Phelps, David Whitmer, Parley P. Pratt, et al., HC, 2:129.

[4] Orson Pratt, JD, 16:151.

After the Times of the Gentiles Are Fulfilled

When will the day of the Lord's power come? Elder Pratt and others have connected its arrival with the timetable of the Church's missionary efforts:

> Another revelation upon this subject says, that after the times of the Gentiles are fulfilled, the servants of God should be sent forth to Israel. What shall then take place? Behold, "then cometh the day of my power." "Then," when the servants of God turn from the Gentile nations, and shall go forth by commandment of the Almighty, being sent by His Church, the voice of His people, and the Holy Spirit, unto the nations of Israel, "then cometh the day of my power," saith the Lord. What kind of power? He goes on to tell us, that it should come to pass, that the tribes and nations of Joseph should hear the Gospel in their own tongue, and in their own language, through those who are sent forth and ordained unto this power through the gift of the Holy Ghost shed forth upon them, for the revelations of Jesus Christ.[5]

Like so much else in the dispensation of the fulness of times, the day of God's power is connected with the gathering of Israel. Orson Pratt used a passage from the prophet Ezekiel to illustrate this to his nineteenth-century hearers:

> Let us quote prophecy to show what the day of the Lord's power means, when the people of Israel will be willing. The first to which I will call your attention will be found recorded in the 20th chapter of Ezekiel, commencing at the 33rd verse—"As I live, saith the Lord God, surely with a mighty hand, and with a stretched out arm, and with fury poured out, will I rule over you. And I will bring you out from the people, and will gather you out of the countries wherein ye are scattered, with a mighty hand, and with a stretched out arm, and with fury poured out. And I will bring you into the wilderness of the people, and there will I plead with you face to face. Like as I pleaded with your fathers in the wilderness of the land of Egypt, so will I plead with you, saith the Lord God."[6]

---

5 Orson Pratt, JD, 2:262.
6 Orson Pratt, JD, 14:65.

Elder Pratt taught that we could know that all of this was beginning to be fulfilled when the sign was given of the coming forth of
the Book of Mormon—or, as he expressed it, the appearance of "the
writings of Joseph"—and its joining with "the Jewish record," the
Bible.

> Then we may look out for the restitution of Israel; as soon as
> the times of the Gentiles are fulfilled, we may look out for the
> day of the Lord's power, when he will cause the very powers of
> heaven to shake for the benefit of his people. The powers of
> eternity will be moved to bring about the great work of the
> restitution of the house of Israel. Then the mountains shall
> tremble, and the little hills shall skip like lambs, as is prophe-
> sied by the Psalmist David. Then all things shall feel the
> power of God, and his arm will be made bare in the eyes of all
> the nations, until the ends of the earth shall see the salvation
> of God, manifested in behalf of his covenant people Israel. It
> will be emphatically the day of the Lord's power.[7]

Knowing that the sign of the Book of Mormon had already been
given, Elder Pratt naturally assumed that the final fulfillment of the
prophecies would come very soon.

> Individuals are now sitting in this Tabernacle who will carry
> this message. The young among us will go forth to the ends
> of the earth and declare to the scattered remnants of Israel,
> wherever found, the comforting words that, "The times of the
> Gentiles are fulfilled, that the day is come for the covenant
> which God made with the ancient fathers of Israel to be ful-
> filled;" and you will have the pleasure of gathering them up by
> thousands, tens of thousands, and hundreds of thousands,
> from the islands of the sea and from all quarters of the earth;
> for that will be a day of power far more than it is while the
> Gospel continues among the Gentiles.[8]

---

[7] Orson Pratt, JD, 18:168.

[8] Orson Pratt, JD, 14:64–65.

[9] The leaders of the ancient church had to learn this fact as well, and to teach it to the early
Saints, when the Savior did not return immediately as some had expected. See the warning at 2
Peter 3:3–4, 8–10.

The Natural Branches of Israel Converted

Of course, the word *soon* clearly means one thing to us and, often, quite another to the Lord.[9] Nonetheless, since the Book of Mormon has now been available to the world for well over a century and a half, we can confidently expect that the great day of God's power is now significantly closer than it was in 1830. And, in fact, the evidence is mounting with each passing year that the great day is approaching. For the prophets have indicated that the restoration of the lost children of Israel in the Americas would be an important part of the day of God's power—and descendants of Lehi are joining the Church by the tens and hundreds of thousands throughout North, Central, and South America. This was not yet the case in the time of Wilford Woodruff, although that great prophet maintained his faith that the time would come. "We cannot do a great deal for that people," he said,

> only pray for them, and treat them kindly, until the power of God begins to rest upon them, and they are waked up by the visions of heaven, and the angels begin to converse with them. They will be inspired by the spirit of the power of God, like other branches of Israel, and the day will come when the poor Utahs, and Piedes, and other degraded tribes in these mountains will again feel they possess souls among men as their fathers did before them. The ten tribes will also come in remembrance before the Lord, and they will again return with outstretched arms to their lands, and be led by leaders inspired by the Spirit and power of God, and they will come with visions, revelations, and prophets, and they will be baptized and ordained under the hands of the children of Ephraim, who bear the Holy Priesthood on the earth at that time, and they will be crowned with glory, power, immortality, and eternal lives before God.[10]

> They, by and by, will receive the gospel. It will be a day of God's power among them, and a nation will be born in a day. Their chiefs will be filled with the power of God and receive the gospel, and they will go forth and build the new Jerusalem, and we shall help them. They are branches of the

---

[10] Wilford Woodruff, DWW, 120.

house of Israel, and when the fulness of the Gentiles has come in and the work ceases among them, then it will go in power to the seed of Abraham.[11]

The Prophet Joseph Smith said that that day would also see the conversion of the Jews. Their reception of the gospel, and, indeed, the preaching of the gospel to them, has been delayed until after the time of the Gentiles as a result, in large part, of their rejection of the prophets and of the Son of God himself.[12]

> Christ, in the days of His flesh, proposed to make a covenant with them, but they rejected Him and His proposals, and in consequence thereof, they were broken off, and no covenant was made with them at that time. But their unbelief has not rendered the promise of God of none effect; no, for there was another day limited in David, which was the day of His power; and then His people, Israel, should be a willing people;—and He would write His law in their hearts, and print it in their thoughts; their sins and their iniquities He would remember no more.[13]

Orson Pratt attempted to impress upon his audience the great manifestation of divine power that would be involved in restoring God's ancient covenant people to their place of honor with the Lord. It would not, he said, be one of the usual routine events of human history. For, as he rightly pointed out,

> Israel have never been willing to receive Jesus from the day that they were cut off as bitter branches that brought forth no good fruit, until the present period. Generation after generation has passed away, and they still remain in unbelief, and they still remain in their scattered condition among all the nations and countries of the earth. But when the day of the Lord's power shall come, when he shall send forth his servants with the power of the priesthood and apostleship to the nations and to the scattered remnants of the house of Israel that dwell in the islands of the sea afar off, he will show forth his power in that

---

11 Wilford Woodruff, DWW, 121.
12 See, for example, Acts 13:46; Romans 11:25.
13 Joseph Smith Jr., HC, 1:313.

day in such a conspicuous manner that all Israel, as it were, will be saved. As it is written by the Apostle Paul, "Blindness in part hath happened to Israel until the fulness of the Gentiles be come in, and so all Israel shall be saved." All Israel in that day will hear the voice of the Lord and the voice of his servants; all Israel, in that day, will see the arm of the Lord made bare in signs and mighty wonders in effecting the restoration of his chosen people to their own land.[14]

The Saints Will Go Forth in Power

Even here, Elder Pratt pointed out, the Lord will work through his mortal servants, the Saints and the bearers of the holy priesthood, and it is through them that his power will, in large part, be displayed:

This will be when the times of the Gentiles are fulfilled, and you Elders of Zion are sent to the house of Israel. You will go in the Lord's power, and so great will be that power that you will have influence over them. You will tell them that their warfare is accomplished, that their iniquity is pardoned, and that they have received at the Lord's hand double for all their sin; and the Lord will bear witness of this by his mighty power, with a mighty hand and an outstretched arm will the Lord do this, and with fury poured out. Poured out upon whom? Upon all the nations and kingdoms of the Gentiles who will not receive the truth, their times being fulfilled. It will be expressly the day of the Lord's judgment, or, in other words, the hour of the Lord's judgment, that is spoken of in the 14th chapter of Revelations, when the angel brings the Gospel.[15]

"But," inquires one, "have you any testimony from the Scriptures to prove that that day will be a day of power?" Hear what the Lord says by the mouth of the Psalmist David, "Thy people shall be willing in the day of thy power." They are not willing now and have not been willing for eighteen centuries past. But when the day of his power comes they will be willing to hearken, they will gather up to their promised land, for it will be the day of the Lord's power. In what respect will there

---

14 Orson Pratt, JD, 14:332.
15 Orson Pratt, JD, 14:65.

be power manifested then? As power was manifested when the Lord brought Israel from the Egyptian nation into the wilderness of Sinai and spoke to them by his own voice, so will the power of Almighty God be made manifest among all the nations of the earth when he brings about the redemption and restoration of his people Israel; or, in other words, the former display of power will be eclipsed, for that which was done in one land, among the Israelites and Egyptians in the wilderness, will be performed among all nations.[16]

"If we had the voice of a trumpet," said Elder Pratt on another occasion,

and could make our speech heard unto the ends of the earth, we would say to all the nations of our globe—to all peoples, kindreds, and tongues, "Hear ye, when the Lord sends forth a proclamation to Israel that are in your midst; for then shall be fulfilled that which is written, that all nations shall see the salvation of God, for His arm shall be made bare in the eyes of all people; it shall be made bare in power, in signs, in wonders, and in mighty miracles, to bring about His purposes unto the house of Israel."[17]

Sounding a similar theme, Elder Bruce R. McConkie taught:

The elders of Israel by preaching the message of the restoration are inviting men to come to that supper [of the Lamb]. "For this cause I have sent you," the Lord says to his missionaries, "that a feast of fat things might be prepared for the poor; yea, a feast of fat things, of wine on the lees well refined, that the earth may know that the mouths of the prophets shall not fail; Yea, a supper of the house of the Lord, well prepared, unto which all nations shall be invited. First, the rich and the learned, the wise and the noble; And after that cometh the day of my power; then shall the poor, the lame, and the blind, and the deaf, come in unto the marriage of the Lamb, and partake of the supper of the Lord, prepared for the great day to come."[18]

---

16 Orson Pratt, JD, 14:65. Elder Pratt's comments echo the prophecies of Jeremiah 16:14–15; 23:7–8.

17 Orson Pratt, JD, 2:262.

18 Bruce R. McConkie, MD, 469, citing Doctrine and Covenants 58:6-11; 65:3.

A Day of Worldwide Judgment

"There is a day of power coming," Orson Pratt declared,

> a day of wonders and a day of mighty deeds, when the power of the Lord, in great judgment, will be upon the nations of the wicked; and also when his glory shall be upon his covenant people who shall be restored to their own lands. The message with which we are now entrusted is a part of the great and last warning message to the nations of the earth, first to the Gentiles, and last to the house of Israel. And when we get through warning the Gentiles, the proclamation which the Lord has given us, shall be delivered to Israel in the islands of the sea and among the various nations; and they shall gather home to the land of their inheritance. Then Jerusalem shall be redeemed and a temple established upon its former foundation in the holy land. Then the nations of the earth will see a fulfillment of our words.[19]

When that day comes, say the modern apostles and prophets of God, men and women will no longer be left to doubt whether or not the Lord lives and whether or not it would be wise to obey him. "For I, the Lord, rule in the heavens above, and among the armies of the earth; and in the day when I shall make up my jewels, all men shall know what it is that bespeaketh the power of God."[20] But, by that point, it will apparently be too late for the truly wicked to escape the fate they have courted for so long. "The day is nigh at hand," announced Wilford Woodruff,

> when He will make bare His arm of power, and show the world that there is a God in Israel, who will no longer bear the blasphemies of the wicked without bringing them to judgment, but He will send forth those angels, those messengers who dwell in the presence of God, who are waiting with their sharp sickles in their hands to reap down the earth; but this will not be until the Gospel has been fully offered to the Gentiles; then the bitter branches will be broken off.[21]

---

[19] Orson Pratt, JD, 20:148.
[20] D&C 60:4; compare Malachi 3:16–4:3.
[21] Wilford Woodruff, JD, 4:231.

This time will not, however, come without conflict and opposition. Indeed, the words of the Lord's spokesmen raise the possibility that it may well be the devil's opposition to the work of the Lord, some of which we can see even now, that will call forth his power from behind the veil. For the "arm of the Lord," as it is depicted in scripture, is his sword arm, and its appearance is not a good sign for the wicked or for those who fight against him. Orson Pratt foresaw the day when the world would be divided into two warring camps:

> **After the kingdom of God has spread upon the face of the earth, and every jot and tittle of the prophecies have been fulfilled in relation to the spreading of the Gospel among the nations—after signs have been shown in the heavens above, and on the earth beneath, blood, fire, and vapour of smoke—after the sun is turned into darkness, and the moon shall have the appearance of blood, and the stars have apparently been hurled out of their places, and all things have been in commotion, so great will be the darkness resting upon Christendom, and so great the bonds of priestcraft with which they will be bound, that they will not understand, and they will be given up to the hardness of their hearts. Then will be fulfilled that saying, That the day shall come when the Lord shall have power over his Saints, and the Devil shall have power over his own dominion.**[22]

THE POWER OF GOD TO BE A PROTECTION

That this struggle will be a real one, with real risks and real casualties, is clearly indicated by the warnings that the prophets and apostles of God have given to us. Indeed, we know already that the exhortation to "endure to the end" is a serious one and not mere empty words, for all around us we see the effects of temptation, of immorality in the media, of drugs, of greed and materialism, of opposition, of crime and violence, and there are few members of the Church indeed who cannot name at least some of their brothers and sisters who have fallen victim to these forces, deployed against us by our adversary the devil. Yet our leaders assure us that things are very likely to get still worse before the return of our Savior. "The servants of God," said Orson Pratt,

---

[22] Orson Pratt, JD, 7:188–89.

will need to be armed with the power of God, they will need to have that sealing blessing pronounced upon their foreheads that they can stand forth in the midst of these desolations and plagues and not be overcome by them. When John the Revelator describes this scene he says he saw four angels sent forth, ready to hold the four winds that should blow from the four quarters of heaven. Another angel ascended from the east and cried to the four angels, and said, "Smite not the earth now, but wait a little while." "How long?" "Until the servants of our God are sealed in their foreheads." What for? To prepare them to stand forth in the midst of these desolations and plagues, and not be overcome.[23]

The great day of God's power will be a time of purification, both within and beyond the Church. Mere nominal membership in the restored Kingdom will not be enough to save those who have set at naught the counsels of the Lord's servants and have trampled him under their feet.[24] "The time of the division will come soon enough," predicted Orson Pratt.

It will be in the great day of the Lord's power, when his face shall be unveiled in yonder heavens, and when he shall come in his glory and in his might. Then the heavens will be shaken and the earth will reel to and fro like a drunken man. "Then," saith the Lord, "I will send forth mine angels to gather out of my kingdom all things that offend and that do iniquity."[25]

Bruce R. McConkie was explicit in saying that, in the time of God's power, there will be members of the Church who will be found unworthy to participate fully in the work and the blessings of the great latter-day cause.

"There has been a day of calling," a day in which all the elders of the kingdom were invited to come forward and build the New Jerusalem, "but the time has come for a day of choosing." The response of his early Latter-day Saints having been inadequate, the Lord will now choose when he will, those who

---

23 Orson Pratt, JD, 15:366.
24 See 1 Nephi 19:7; Alma 5:53; Helaman 12:2; 3 Nephi 28:35.
25 Orson Pratt, JD, 17:113.

are to accomplish the great work. "And let those be chosen that are worthy." When the day comes, none but those who qualify by obedience and righteousness will participate in the work. "And it shall be manifest unto my servant" the President of the Church who then governs the kingdom "by the voice of the Spirit, those that are chosen; and they shall be sanctified; and inasmuch as they follow the counsel which they receive, they shall have power after many days to accomplish all things pertaining to Zion." (D&C 105:14–37.)[26]

Just as they always have, the blessings of God will attend those who, through faithfulness, overcome opposition.[27] "We are to be operated upon by the Holy Ghost," said Orson Hyde,

and undergo such a material change by its power that we can abide the day of burning in which the Son of God will be revealed with the same comfort that Shadrach, Meshach, and Abednego did in the fiery furnace. They were cast into that devouring element and moved as pleasantly and as agreeably as the fish moves in the sea, its native element. When that day comes, it will be made to appear who is pure; for it will bear upon every individual; and those who are not right and pure will be devoured and destroyed. If we are faithful, we can abide that day and feel that we are wrapped in nothing more than in a blaze of glory, because we shall be prepared for it. But if we do not live our religion, we shall be consumed in that day; and it will be a day that no creature can dodge. Hypocrisy and deceit will then be no shield. Pure and unadulterated goodness alone will enable us to stand in that day. We shall then know who possesses the qualifications of Saints, and who does not; and we shall have to be tested, and that strongly, compared with that to which we are now subjected. The two will be so different, so widely apart from each other, that we cannot now imagine the difference.[28]

GREAT TASKS TO BE ACCOMPLISHED

President Heber C. Kimball, though somewhat overly optimistic about the time involved, nevertheless echoed the teaching of other

---

[26] Bruce R. McConkie, NWAF, 619.
[27] See 2 Nephi 2.
[28] Orson Hyde, JD, 5:355.

prophets and apostles in saying that future bearers of the priesthood would enjoy an even greater portion of divine power in carrying out their tasks than did the faithful leaders and members of the Church in the nineteenth century. "I am talking," he said,

> to the men that hold the Priesthood. And I cannot but think that the little boys before me will have that Priesthood which we hold, and many of them will see the day when they will have power to raise the dead. They will have power to do many things we do not have power to do.[29]

Indeed, given the immense and trying difficulties that loom before the Saints before the coming of the Lord, additional power is a necessity. And it is perhaps largely for this reason that the time before the Savior's second advent has been as long as it has been. We have, still, much to learn before we will be prepared to carry out our assigned mission.[30] Joseph Fielding Smith explained that, in the early days of the Church,

> it was made plain that the elders would have to be endowed with power from on high and go forth to declare the gospel to the nations and "push the people together from the ends of the earth," before Zion could be built. So the Lord in the very beginning instructed the saints that the building of the New Jerusalem and its sacred temple would be deferred until many other things were accomplished, and they had passed through much tribulation.[31]

Lorenzo Snow promised that

> if we succeed in passing through the approaching fiery ordeals with our fidelity and integrity unimpeached, we may expect at the close of our trials, a great and mighty outpouring of the Spirit and power of God—a great endowment upon all who shall have remained true to their covenants.[32]

---

[29] Heber C. Kimball, JD, 6:123.
[30] Again, in this context too, see 2 Peter 3:3–4, 8–10.
[31] Joseph Fielding Smith, DS, 3:78.
[32] Lorenzo Snow, TLS, 120.

ENEMIES TO BE VANQUISHED

For the teachings of the prophets offer assurance that the cause of righteousness will triumph, however dismal and dark the situation may appear. We are not to sit nervously on the sidelines, reckoning the odds and trying to cast our lot with the winner. We are to commit ourselves, now and wholeheartedly, to the cause of God. Obviously, the battle of good and evil will not be one between equals. The Lord does not lose. He will remain relatively silent for a while, aiding his Saints from his heavenly throne, communicating with them and their leaders by revelation and inspiration, and supporting them with his spirit, but when he openly enters the conflict, it will be over. Orson Hyde touched on this theme, citing the words of Nephi from the Book of Mormon:

> "And it came to pass that I beheld that the great mother of abominations did gather together multitudes upon the face of all the earth, among all the nations of the Gentiles, to fight against the Lamb of God. And it came to pass that I, Nephi, beheld the power of the Lamb of God, that it descended upon the Saints of the Church of the Lamb, and upon the covenant people of the Lord, who were scattered upon all the face of the earth; and they were armed with righteousness and with the power of God in great glory." (1 Nephi 3:47–50.) In view of the sentiment contained in the foregoing quotation, I am led to believe that whatever branch of the great and abominable church shall lead the way to fight against the Lamb of God, will have a greater task to perform than they are aware of. It is not merely a little handful of Latter-day Saints that they have to contend with; but, it is with all the celestial powers. This, however, they do not believe; and, consequently, like the unthinking horse, they rush to the onset.[33]

"However much our enemies may howl," said Orson Pratt,

> whatever may be our future tribulations, the Lord God has decreed that Zion shall become a strong nation, that the armies of Israel shall become very great, and not only very great, but they will be sanctified before him, and there will be such a power made manifest in their midst, that their banners

---

[33] Orson Hyde, JD, 5:140.

will be terrible to all the nations of the earth. They will not be terrible because we outnumber the nations, but this terror of Zion which will be among the nations, will be because of the power of the great Jehovah that will be manifested in their midst, something that the nations will discern and understand; and when telegraphic dispatches are sent forth to the most distant parts of the earth, it will be said—"Who can stand before the armies of Zion? Behold, the Lord God is with them as a cloud by day, and as a pillar of fire by night."[34]

Speaking of the same yet-future time of crisis and victory, Heber C. Kimball testified that

the day is to come when one shall chase a thousand, and two put ten thousand to flight. When that day comes, the Lord will make the enemies of His people flee as if there were thousands after them, when there is only one; and that is the way that God will deal with our enemies. The day of God Almighty is at hand, when He will show forth His power, and when He will deliver His people from all their enemies.[35]

ONE LIKE UNTO MOSES TO COME

Modern revelation indicates that when the great struggle reaches its peak of intensity, the Lord will raise up a figure specially suited to lead his people to success in the conflict. The Prophet Joseph Smith wrote about this personage in an 1832 letter to W. W. Phelps that now forms a part of the Doctrine and Covenants:

Thus saith the still small voice, which whispereth through and pierceth all things, and oftentimes it maketh my bones to quake while it maketh manifest, saying: and it shall come to pass, that I, the Lord God, will send one mighty and strong, holding the sceptre of power in his hand, clothed with light for a covering, whose mouth shall utter words, eternal words; while his bowels shall be a fountain of truth, to set in order the house of God, and to arrange by lot the inheritances of the Saints, whose names are found, and the names of their fathers, and of their

---

[34] Orson Pratt, JD, 17:306.
[35] Heber C. Kimball, JD, 4:375.

children enrolled in the book of the law of God: while that man, who was called of God, and appointed, that putteth forth his hand to steady the ark of God, shall fall by the shaft of death, like as a tree that is smitten by the vivid shaft of lightning; and all they who are not found written in the book of remembrance shall find none inheritance in that day but they shall be cut asunder, and their portion shall be appointed them among unbelievers, where are wailing and gnashing of teeth.[36]

Orson Pratt also preached about this coming leader, referring his listeners to another discussion of the subject that is to be found in Doctrine and Covenants 103:15–20. "God will shield us by his power," Elder Pratt promised,

if we are to be led forth out of bondage as our fathers were led, at the first. This indicates that there may be bondage ahead, and that the Latter-day Saints may see severe times, and that unless we keep the commandments of God, we may be brought into circumstances that will cause our hearts to tremble within us, that is, those who are not upright before God. But if this people should be brought into bondage, as the Israelites were in ancient days, Zion must be led forth out of bondage, as Israel was at the first. In order to do this God has prophesied that he will raise up a man like unto Moses, who shall lead his people therefrom.[37]

Elder Pratt returned to the subject several years later, offering even more detail about the role to be played by the great leader of the Saints in the crisis of the latter days. And, although it is evident that Elder Pratt's deep yearning for the return of the Savior led him to underestimate the time remaining before the prophecies would be fulfilled—for, truly, "of that day and that hour knoweth no man, no, not the angels which are in heaven, neither the Son, but the Father"[38]—his portrayal of the "man raised up like unto Moses" is surely true to what the prophets have consistently taught:

The days are coming—I know they are close at hand—when the young and rising generation that are now sitting in this

---

[36] D&C 85:6–9.
[37] Orson Pratt, JD, 15:362.
[38] Mark 13:32; compare Matthew 24:36.

congregation, and who are spread forth upon the face of the land, throughout these mountains and valleys, will see the turning point for Zion. What will they see? They will see a man raised up like unto Moses in days of old—a man to whom the Lord will reveal himself, as he did to his servant Moses, by angels, by visions, by revelation from the heavens, and will give unto him commandments, and make him an instrument in his hands, to redeem the people and to establish them in their everlasting inheritance upon the face of this American continent. Will he show forth his power in that day as he did unto his servant Moses and to Israel? Yes, only more abundantly, more extensively than in the days of Moses, for there is a larger continent than the land of Egypt, in which the Lord will make manifest his power—a greater people than the Egyptians, among whom he will work. Consequently he will show forth his power unto all the inhabitants of this land. He will fulfill the plain predictions of the Prophet Isaiah that the Lord shall make bare his arm in the eyes of all the nations, until all the ends of the earth shall see the salvation of God.[39]

THE PRIESTHOOD OF GOD WILL PREVAIL

With the eventual victorious result of the great conflict in mind, Elder Orson Hyde offered some very pragmatic advice to those who attempt to fight the work of God and to oppose those whom the Lord has chosen as his servants in the last days. "Be not . . . too anxious or forward," he counseled,

> to persecute and destroy the men in whose hands Heaven has placed your destiny, lest, when the day of their power cometh they may remember all your acts, and reward you according to your deeds. These men are bound to overcome; and he that overcometh shall have power over the nations, and shall rule them with a rod of iron. "Be wise, therefore, O ye kings; be instructed, ye judges of the earth. Kiss the Son, lest he be angry, and ye perish from the way, when his wrath is kindled but a little. Blessed are all they that put their trust in him." (Psalms 2:10, 12.)[40]

---

[39] Orson Pratt, JD, 21:177–78.
[40] Orson Hyde, JD, 7:53.

Thus, the outcome is certain. As Charles W. Penrose declared,

The day will not be far distant when the Priesthood of God will have the balance of power, and their rule and dominion now in the hands of the wicked upon the face of all the earth will be taken away from the corrupt and the wicked, and given into the hands of the Saints of the Most High God, and he will reign for ever and ever. Amen.[41]

Under the Savior and his Father, the redeemed and righteous Saints of God will rule the earth, and unrighteousness and corruption will cease to trouble them. Purchased by the Redeemer's blood, sanctified by the Spirit, acting in meekness and holiness before the Lord, they will share in the divine glory and, as the scriptures have promised, "inherit the earth."[42] "We talk about kings and nobles," said George Q. Cannon,

and we have admired their glory; but the day is not far distant when there will be thousands of men in Zion holding more power, and having more glory, honor, and wealth than the greatest and the richest of the nobles of the earth. The earth and its fulness are promised unto us by the Lord our God, as soon as we have the wisdom and experience necessary to wield this power and wealth. Shall we not be patient, then, and diligent when we have so much assistance given unto us? Shall we not plod unwearyingly and unmurmuringly forward in the path God has marked out for us, when we have the help, the comfort, and the consolation which he gives us day by day?[43]

---

[41] Charles W. Penrose, JD, 20:129.
[42] See Psalms 37:11; Matthew 5:5; 3 Nephi 12:5.
[43] George Q. Cannon, JD, 11:175.

CHAPTER 11

THE COMING FORTH OF RECORDS

And righteousness will I send down out of heaven; and truth will I send forth out of the earth, to bear testimony of mine Only Begotten; his resurrection from the dead; yea, and also the resurrection of all men; and righteousness and truth will I cause to sweep the earth as with a flood, to gather out mine own elect from the four quarters of the earth, unto a place which I shall prepare, an Holy City, that my people may gird up their loins, and be looking forth for the time of my coming; for there shall be my tabernacle, and it shall be called Zion, a New Jerusalem.[1]

One of the most prominent features of the dispensation of the fulness of times is the vast avalanche of knowledge and understanding that it has brought and continues to bring with it. This is true in secular regards as well as in matters of the spirit. Computers, telecommunications, aerospace technology, spectacular advances in medicine and pharmacology and genetics, revolutionary discoveries in archaeology—all of these have come toward us at an ever-increasing pace in recent decades. Joseph Smith, for instance, lived in a manner that was, technologically, not very different from the way in which his medieval ancestors or the people of ancient Rome or Jerusalem had lived. He watched no television, listened to no radio, never spoke on a telephone. He never heard a record or a cassette tape or a compact disc. For transportation, although steam locomotives were beginning to enter the picture during his lifetime, he relied mostly on his feet, or on those of a horse, or on a horse-drawn carriage. Yet in the century and a half or so that has elapsed since the Prophet's martyrdom, we have largely replaced the modes of transportation known to scores of generations of our ancestors, turning instead to automobiles and jet aircraft. Even the smallest town or the most isolated cabin can be linked to any other place in the world. We can dial a friend in Tokyo

---

[1] Moses 7:62.

or watch a press conference in Jerusalem or enjoy a recording of the Vienna Philharmonic Orchestra any time we want.

Such discoveries are of immense value. We rarely die from simple diseases or from minor wounds. Women can face childbirth with little of the fear that once accompanied bringing babies into the world. The Church, too, benefits. The words of modern prophets and apostles can be sent around the globe virtually instantaneously. Indeed, they themselves can be physically present anywhere in the world within hours, making it practically possible, for perhaps the first time in history, for apostolic authority to hold a church organization together over large geographical distances and to guard against apostasy. But these and hundreds of other innovations, important as they are, pale in signficance when compared to the quantities of new knowledge about God and his commandments that have come to the world since the beginning of the restoration of the gospel in the early nineteenth century.

THE COMING FORTH OF THE BOOK OF MORMON

This explosion of new and restored insights began with the revelation of an ancient record, buried in a hill in rural New York state. "Let us take the Book of Mormon," said the Prophet Joseph Smith,

> which a man took and hid in his field, securing it by his faith, to spring up in the last days, or in due time; let us behold it coming forth out of the ground, which is indeed accounted the least of all seeds, but behold it branching forth, yea, even towering, with lofty branches, and God-like majesty, until it, like the mustard seed, becomes the greatest of all herbs. And it is truth, and it has sprouted and come forth out of the earth, and righteousness begins to look down from heaven, and God is sending down His powers, gifts and angels, to lodge in the branches thereof.[2]

Speaking of the three standard works that had been canonized by his day (the Bible, the Book of Mormon, and the Doctrine and Covenants), the Prophet saw the influence of the ancient scriptures spreading throughout the whole world, coupled with ongoing revelation to the people of modern times:

---

[2] Joseph Smith Jr., TPJS, 98.

"Then said He unto them, therefore every scribe which is instructed in the kingdom of heaven, is like unto a man that is an householder, which bringeth forth out of his treasure things that are new and old." For the works of this example, see the Book of Mormon coming forth out of the treasure of the heart. Also the covenants given to the Latter-day Saints, also the translation of the Bible—thus bringing forth out of the heart things new and old, thus answering to three measures of meal undergoing the purifying touch by a revelation of Jesus Christ, and the ministering of angels, who have already commenced this work in the last days, which will answer to the leaven which leavened the whole lump.[3]

Indeed, the prophets and apostles of the modern Church have always taught that people living in the last days were and are a major audience for the Book of Mormon, and this not just by chance. The book, as we have it, was *intended* to address us today. "The Lord made a promise to Moroni," said Orson Pratt,

also to Mormon, and to many other Prophets who dwelt on this land in previous generations, that these plates should never be destroyed, but that they should be preserved by his hand, and that they should be brought forth out of the earth in the latter days, for the purpose of bringing about the gathering of his people from the ends of the earth, and the bringing in of the fullness of the Gentiles and fulfilling their times, after which the translation of these records should go to all the remnants of the house of Israel, scattered abroad on the face of the whole earth; and that these records should be instrumental in the hands of God in gathering Israel from the four quarters of the earth.[4]

Joseph Fielding Smith agreed, pointing out that

each of the major writers of the Book of Mormon testified that they wrote for future generations. Nephi said: "The Lord God promised unto me that these things which I write shall be kept and preserved, and handed down unto my seed, from

---

[3] Joseph Smith Jr., MFP, 1:69.
[4] Orson Pratt, JD, 15:183.

generation to generation" (2 Nephi 25:21). His brother Jacob, who succeeded him, wrote similar words: "For [Nephi] said that the history of his people should be engraven upon his other plates, and that I should preserve these plates and hand them down unto my seed, from generation to generation" (Jacob 1:30). Enos and Jarom both indicated that they too were writing not for their own peoples but for future generations (see Enos 1:15-16; Jarom 1:2).[5]

RECORDS STILL TO BE REVEALED

But the Lord's revelations to us of the dispensation of the fulness of times were certainly not completed with the coming forth of the Book of Mormon. Though Latter-day Saints have far more knowledge concerning divine things than any other people on earth, we have not yet received all that the Lord would like to give to us. And modern prophets have said that the responsibility for this fact lies more with us than with our Father in Heaven. "There is so much knowledge that is withheld from us," lamented Joseph Fielding Smith.

> To many questions we have to postpone the answers. If we had the faith we could answer them. The Lord is withholding knowledge from us because of our unworthiness. Read what is written in the 27th chapter of 2nd Nephi, the 26th chapter of 3rd Nephi, the 3rd and 4th chapters of Ether. In these chapters the Lord tells us that he is withholding from the world and from the Church the greatest revelation that was ever written. It is the history of this world from the beginning thereof to the ending. The Lord says, in the 27th chapter of 2nd Nephi, that it shall not come forth in the days of wickedness.[6]

But we are not without hope for greater light and knowledge. "We believe . . . that God . . . will yet reveal many great and important things pertaining to the Kingdom of God."[7] That is why the Church has been blessed with the continued presence of prophets and apostles. And they have hinted, and more than hinted, over the years, about what we have to look forward to if we are righteous and faithful. Even

---

5 Ezra Taft Benson, TETB, 58.
6 Joseph Fielding Smith, DS, 2:304–5.
7 Article of Faith 9.

the Book of Mormon itself has not yet been completely revealed to us. "Joseph did not translate all of the plates," said Brigham Young. "There was a portion of them sealed, which you can learn from the Book of Doctrine and Covenants."[8] "Why are these plates of Mormon sealed?" asked Elder Bruce R. McConkie.

> The answer is obvious. They contain spiritual truths beyond our present ability to receive. Milk must precede meat, and whenever men are offered more of the mysteries of the kingdom than they are prepared to receive, it affects them adversely. In instructing his Jewish disciples, for instance, Jesus said: "Go ye into the world, saying unto all, Repent, for the kingdom of heaven has come nigh unto you. And the mysteries of the kingdom ye shall keep within yourselves; for it is not meet to give that which is holy unto the dogs; neither cast ye your pearls unto swine, lest they trample them under their feet. For the world cannot receive that which ye, yourselves, are not able to bear; wherefore ye shall not give your pearls unto them, lest they turn again and rend you." (JST, Matthew 7:9–11.) Thus also Alma said: "It is given unto many to know the mysteries of God; nevertheless they are laid under a strict commandment that they shall not impart only according to the portion of his word which he doth grant unto the children of men, according to the heed and diligence which they give unto him." (Alma 12:9.)[9]

The fact that these records were not permitted to be translated, and the fact that we still today do not have them, seems to indicate that there is a great deal more yet to be revealed to us. Certainly President Wilford Woodruff thought so. "Perhaps," he said,

> when the remainder of the plates, which were delivered to the Prophet Joseph, and which he was commanded not to translate come forth, we may learn many more things pertaining to our labor on the earth which we do not know now. But be this as it may, all this internal work is left for the Holy Ghost to reveal to the living oracles, as they guide, lead, dictate, and direct the people day by day.[10]

---

8 Brigham Young, JD, 19:38.
9 Bruce R. McConkie, NWAF, 443–44.
10 Wilford Woodruff, DWW, 234.

MORE ANCIENT AMERICAN RECORDS

But even the plates delivered to the Prophet, including the sealed portion, represent but a small part of the records kept by the Jaredites and the Nephites, records which will, according to modern seers, be revealed and published for the benefit of the Saints of God in the last days. Speaking of the plates of Ether, for instance, Elder Orson Pratt noted that

> they are not yet found. We have the Book of Ether, that is not one-hundredth part of the contents of those twenty-four plates. But a very short account. Whoso findeth these twenty-four plates will have power to get the full account; for they give a history from the days of Adam through the various generations to the days of the flood, from the days of the flood down to the days of Peleg, and from the days of Peleg to the Tower, which was very nearly contemporary with Peleg. And from that time for some sixteen or eighteen centuries after they landed on this continent. The prophecies of their Prophets in different generations, who published glad tidings of joy upon the face of all the northern portion of this continent. Their records and doings are all to come to light, and these will help to fulfill the words of our text that the knowledge of God will cover the earth as the waters cover the great deep.[11]

Furthermore, Elder Pratt pointed out,

> The records of the ancient Nephites . . . existed in great numbers and are of great importance, records kept by their Kings, records of the history of the Nephites for over a thousand years, records of their proceedings and of the things that God had revealed to them, records that were secret, and not permitted to come forth in the days of weakness, records that revealed all things from the foundation of the world to the end thereof, records that were kept when Jesus administered to the Nephites, the ninety-ninth part of which was not written by Mormon, all of which are to come forth. What for? To teach the Latter-day Saints how to organize, how to be prepared for the things that are coming. Then we will know something

---

[11] Orson Pratt, JD, 16:53.

about what is termed the United Order, when we get hold of these records of the experience of the Nephites for 165 years in the Order; the experience of the people of this great western hemisphere, from the northern to the southern extremity; they will have left some records of their acts and doings that cannot fail to be of great worth to the people of these latter times.[12]

Indeed, Joseph Smith and Oliver Cowdery are said to have seen large numbers of ancient American records, far beyond the relatively small number of plates given to the Prophet for translation. Consider the following account given by Brigham Young, which surely must rank as one of the most tantalizing stories from early Latter-day Saint history:

When Joseph got the plates, the angel instructed him to carry them back to the hill Cumorah, which he did. Oliver says that when Joseph and Oliver went there, the hill opened, and they walked into a cave, in which there was a large and spacious room. He says he did not think, at the time, whether they had the light of the sun or artificial light; but that it was just as light as day. They laid the plates on a table; it was a large table that stood in the room. Under this table there was a pile of plates as much as two feet high, and there were altogether in this room more plates than probably many wagon loads; they were piled up in the corners and along the walls. The first time they went there the sword of Laban hung upon the wall; but when they went again it had been taken down and laid upon the table across the gold plates; it was unsheathed, and on it was written these words: "This sword will never be sheathed again until the kingdoms of this world become the kingdom of our God and his Christ."[13]

President Heber C. Kimball, too, knew the story, for he speaks of

the vision that Joseph and others had, when they went into a cave in the hill Cumorah, and saw more records than ten men could carry[.] There were books piled up on tables, book upon book. Those records this people will yet have, if they accept of

---

12 Orson Pratt, JD, 19:14.

13 Brigham Young, JD, 19:38. Whether this cave actually exists in the hill in New York, or whether what Oliver and Joseph saw was a vision of something that exists elsewhere, is not clear.

the Book of Mormon and observe its precepts, and keep the commandments.[14]

THE EARTH TO BE FILLED WITH KNOWLEDGE

But the Latter-day Saints are not to expect only records from the ancient peoples of the Book of Mormon. Rather, the last days will see a flood of ancient documents from many places. (Perhaps, though they are certainly not to be considered scripture, the discoveries from Nag Hammadi in Egypt, and the recovery of the Dead Sea Scrolls, as well as many other document finds in the past century or so, should be seen as a small part of this influx of knowledge from the past.) Orson Pratt spoke forcefully on this subject. "Certain records," he said,

> which God has promised to bring to light in his own due time, will far exceed anything that has been revealed through the Book of Mormon or the Bible, or that which has come to us through the Abrahamic record taken from Egyptian papyrus, or that which is contained in the vision of Moses, revealing to him the history of the creation of the world. All these will be as a drop in the bucket in comparison with the eternal knowledge that will yet flow down from heaven upon the heads of the Latter-day Saints before this generation shall pass away. The earth will be filled with the knowledge of God, as the waters cover the great deep, and the things of all nations will be revealed.[15]

It is obvious that this was a subject that fired the thoughts of Elder Pratt. That great nineteenth-century apostle, isolated though he was on the American frontier and occupied as he always was with extensive missionary journeys, yearned "to be one who possessed great knowledge, and to be a greater follower of righteousness, and to possess a greater knowledge."[16] His hunger for truth led him to remarkable efforts in mathematics and astronomy, as well as in the

---

14 Heber C. Kimball, JD, 4:105. These may have been, at least partially, the texts from which Mormon abridged his account. In that case, what we have in the Book of Mormon would be the cream of the broader records' spiritual content, at least as we are privileged to know it now, while the content of the large collection of plates would be heavily political and relatively secular (see 1 Nephi 9:2–4). Frankly, many ancient archives have turned out to be largely made up of inventory lists. But there is no doubt that we would love to learn much, much more about the Book of Mormon peoples and their rich and miraculous history.

15 Orson Pratt, JD, 20:76.

16 See Abraham 1:2.

study of Hebrew and other subjects. Yet what he desired most was a knowledge of the things of God. "We might now stop and say no more about the bibles that are yet to come," he commented, scarcely able, himself, to have done any such thing.

> From what little I have said the strangers present may begin to believe the truth of that Scripture which says, "And there are also many other things which Jesus did, the which, if they should be written every one, I suppose that even the world itself could not contain the books that should be written." (John 21:25.) The Lord has not, because of unbelief and wickedness of the people, permitted these things to come forth to be trampled under the feet, as swine would trample jewels under their feet. But as soon as the righteousness of the people shall warrant, he will reveal these hidden treasures of knowledge, and they will understand and comprehend the great things of God; and not only will records be brought forth, but the minds of men, and minds of women, and minds of children, and the minds of all the people who believe, will be like a fountain of light and intelligence, and they will be able to comprehend all records and books inspired from on high.[17]

Though it led him again to overestimate the speed of the Lord's timetable, Elder Pratt's enthusiasm for the knowledge that will be revealed is surely something we can and should share. His desire should be our desire. "We have every reason," he said,

> to believe that the time is not far distant, and that there are some living among the young now upon the earth, that will live to behold great numbers of revelations given, and will behold other books come forth and other records translated by the Urim and Thummim, that same instrument that Joseph Smith used in the translation of the Book of Mormon, which will again come forth and be revealed to the seer and revelator that God will raise up by which these ancient records will be brought to light. Then these great things will be known, then we shall rejoice in the greater fulness of knowledge and understanding, according to the promise; and when we rend that veil of unbelief, spoken of in the Book of

---

17 Orson Pratt, JD, 19:219.

Mormon, and when it is taken away from our midst, and we exercise faith in God, even as the ancient man of God, the brother of Jared, did, then will the Lord reveal to this people what was shown to this man.[18]

RECORDS OF THE ANCIENT PATRIARCHS

Among these restored ancient texts will be many that will cast new light on the history and peoples of what we generally call the Old Testament, or the Hebrew Bible. For, although we do not now, by and large, possess materials that go back so far, Latter-day Saint theologians know that writing and the keeping of records go back to the very origins of the race.[19] That the patriarch Abraham actually possessed some of these documents is apparent from the book of Abraham that we have in our modern Pearl of Great Price. But it is also evident that he passed on to us only a portion of what he had from them, and it seems likely that the other materials he had were lost still in ancient times:

> But the records of the fathers, even the patriarchs, concerning the right of Priesthood, the Lord my God preserved in mine own hands; therefore a knowledge of the beginning of the creation, and also of the planets, and of the stars, as they were made known unto the fathers, have I kept even unto this day, and I shall endeavor to write some of these things upon this record, for the benefit of my posterity that shall come after me.[20]

But God has the power to bring back what is lost. Indeed, this is one of the greatest of divine miracles, repeated throughout all his works. He restores the gospel, the Church, and the priesthood. Through the miracle of the Atonement, he restores innocence after transgression. Through the gift of resurrection, he restores life after death. And he will restore knowledge that has been lost through carelessness, neglect, and transgression. Orson Pratt, for example, expected the return of the words of Adam, the patriarch of all patriarchs:

> He must have spoken concerning all the following dispensations, that were to be revealed from time to time to the children

---

[18] Orson Pratt, JD, 19:216.
[19] Moses 6:5–6, 46.
[20] Abraham 1:31.

of men. He must have spoken concerning the spreading of his posterity after the days of Noah, and of the great work of God being established on the earth in the latter days, and concerning the second advent of the Son of God, concerning the great day of rest, the period when Satan should be bound. All these things were written in the Book of Enoch, who was present on that occasion. And this book is to be testified of, in due time, to the Saints of the last days.[21]

Elder Pratt also taught the Saints of his day to anticipate the recovery of yet more writing from the early prophet Enoch, of whom the Bible (as we now have it) knows little more than that he "walked with God: and he was not; for God took him."[22] We are privileged to possess considerably more information about that great ancient figure in the book of Moses. But Elder Pratt maintained that there was even more to come:

Enoch prophesied of all things, as well as his great ancestor, Adam. A few of his words are translated, and brought to light by the Prophet Joseph Smith, and published in the various publications of this Church—in the Evening and Morning Star, the Pearl of Great Price, etc. This prophecy, though very short, as far as it has been revealed, unfolds marvelous principles, showing that his eyes were opened to see things that were past, and things in the future, all of which were recorded in the Book of Enoch, which is to be brought to light and revealed in the latter times.[23]

RECORDS OF THE HOUSE OF ISRAEL

Church leaders in this dispensation have indicated that we will learn more, too, of figures from the story of Israel itself, who come later in biblical history than the founding patriarchs of humankind. "The prophecies of Joseph in Egypt were very great," Orson Pratt pointed out,

and we are told in the Book of Mormon that there were a great many given to him. When we have all those, also the

---

[21] Orson Pratt, JD, 16:48–49.
[22] Genesis 5:24.
[23] Orson Pratt, JD, 16:49.

prophecies of Neum, a great Prophet who prophesied concerning Christ; also those of Zenos and Zenock, and others of which only bare reference is given; and then again when the ten tribes of Israel come from the north country, they will bring with them their records which they have kept since seven hundred and twenty years before Christ, which will contain an account of the hand of God dealing among that lost people, which doubtless will be exceedingly interesting as well as instructive.[24]

Indeed, Elder Pratt reminded his hearers,

The Lord has told us that he would bring forth those brass plates that Lehi and the families that came with him from Jerusalem, some six hundred years before Christ, brought with them, which contain the history of the creation, and the writings of inspired men down to the days of Jeremiah; they came out in Jeremiah's day. We are informed in the Book of Mormon that they contained many prophecies very great and extensive in their nature. And when these plates, now hidden in the hill Cumorah, are brought to light we shall have the history of the Old Testament much more fully, with the addition of a great many prophecies that are not now contained in that record.[25]

Even the records of the ten lost tribes, who vanished from the history of the Bible when the northern kingdom of Israel was destroyed in the eighth century B.C., will be revealed to the Latter-day Saints in days to come. As Elder Pratt taught, "when the ten tribes of Israel come from the north country, they will bring with them their records which they have kept since seven hundred and twenty years before Christ, which will contain an account of the hand of God dealing among that lost people, which doubtless will be exceedingly interesting as well as instructive."[26] There will then come a merging of the records of the various peoples, as the witnesses of these different groups combine to reinforce one another, and as each people rejoices in the workings of God among brothers and sisters from whom they had for so long been separated. The political unity of the children of God in the last days will be based upon the foundation of their

---

24 Orson Pratt, JD, 19:218–19.
25 Orson Pratt, JD, 19:218.
26 Orson Pratt, JD, 19:218–19.

controlling stories, which will be seen to be themselves unified, since they come from the same God. "It was predicted," said Elder Pratt,

> by one of the ancient American prophets, who lived in those days, that when God should bring these ten tribes from the north country, they would bring their records with them. And it should come to pass that they should have the records of the Nephites, and the Nephites should have the records of the Jews, and the Jews and the Nephites should have the records of the lost tribes of the house of Israel, and the lost tribes of Israel should have the records of the Nephites and the Jews. "It shall come to pass that I will gather my people together, and I will also gather my word in one." Not only the people are to be gathered from the distant portions of our globe, but their records, or bibles, will also be united in one.[27]

At least one apostle has explained that the flood of new information and insight, which began in the early nineteenth century but is destined to increase in speed and volume as the Millennium draws nearer, will also include material pertaining to personalities in the New Testament. Elder Pratt declared that

> there is still another record to come forth. John the Baptist is said by the highest authority to be one of the greatest Prophets ever born of a woman; but we have very little written in the Jewish record concerning him. We have a revelation in the Doctrine and Covenants concerning the record of John, that great Prophet. And we are promised that if we were faithful as a people, the fullness of the record of John shall hereafter be revealed to us. When we get this, I think we shall have still more knowledge in regard to doctrine and principle, and things that are great and marvelous, of which we know very little, if anything about.[28]

Openness to More Revelation to Come

Of course, Church leaders have always taught that one of the glorious aspects of the dispensation of the fulness of times consists in

---

[27] Orson Pratt, JD, 19:172.
[28] Orson Pratt, JD, 19:218.

the fact that the Latter-day Saints will not be dependent merely upon the spiritual experiences of dead and departed people. They will receive their own revelations, as well as being permitted to feast upon a greater library of ancient scriptures than probably any other group of God's mortal children has known. Indeed, said Charles W. Penrose, our membership in The Church of Jesus Christ of Latter-day Saints and our sustaining of our leaders, modern-day prophets, commits us to expect and to accept future revelation. While we treasure the truths given in the past, we seek the disclosure of yet more and greater truths.

> By lifting up our hands to heaven in this way, we show to God and to angels, that we are ready at any time, if the Lord has a word of revelation to communicate to us, to receive it, no matter how it may come; whether by the inspiration of the Holy Ghost, or otherwise; by means of the Urim and Thummim, if he sees fit to restore it to the Church, which he will do as sure as we are gathered here to-day, and a man will stand up like unto Moses, who will communicate the word of the Lord unto us, line upon line and precept upon precept, until God brings forth everything needed for the building up of his work; and the things kept hidden from the foundation of the world will be brought forth, and all the ancient records that have been lost will be brought to light, by men through whom God shall operate by means of the Urim and Thummim as well as by the inspiration of the Holy Ghost.[29]

It is this openness to all the truths of God and the cosmos, this refusal to be limited to past creeds and the writings of dead Saints, however great, that constitutes one of the chief glories of the gospel and of the Church and Kingdom of God in the latter days. It is a major portion of the sheer excitement of being a Latter-day Saint. "There is nothing too great to be withheld from the Saints of God in the last dispensation of the fulness of times," exclaimed Orson Pratt.

> Hear what the Prophet Joseph Smith said, when confined in Liberty Jail. As well may the puny arm of man attempt to stop the waters of the Missouri River as to try to prevent the

---

[29] Charles W. Penrose, JD, 21:47.

Almighty from pouring down knowledge upon the Latter-day Saints. It will come; it will come like a mighty flood, it will come like a mighty ocean, and there will be no mental darkness upon the whole face of the earth. The laws by which the earth is governed, by which the materials were governed, by which intelligence produces intelligence, by which one material cleaves to another, and by which all the various mechanisms are performed, will be revealed in their times and in their seasons. And then the Lord will not stop there; but he will unfold other systems and heavens that shall come into connection with ours.[30]

---

[30] Orson Pratt, JD, 20:76-77.

CHAPTER 12

SAVIORS ON MOUNT ZION

But upon mount Zion shall be deliverance, and there shall be holiness . . .

And saviours shall come up on mount Zion to judge the mount of Esau; and the kingdom shall be the Lord's.[1]

Throughout Latter-day Saint scripture, tradition, and prophecy runs the concept of Zion. The word has many senses, but, biblically, its primary reference is to the hill upon which King Solomon built his temple.[2] In the broader canon of scripture known to members of The Church of Jesus Christ of Latter-day Saints, Zion is defined as "the pure in heart,"[3] a usage that is certainly related to the city of Zion established by the prophet Enoch.[4] For these reasons, the concept of Zion is closely connected to the idea of the temple, as well as with a society of the righteous who have gathered to a place centered on the temple. And we are told by modern prophets and apostles that one of the most significant events of the last days will be the building of a great temple in the city of New Jerusalem, also known as the city of Zion,[5] which will be located in Jackson County, Missouri, or the land of Zion.[6]

WHAT IT MEANS TO BE A SAVIOR

It is hardly surprising, therefore, that God's chosen servants in the latter days have seen in the phrase "saviors on Mount Zion" a reference to the work of the holy temples. Elder Orson Hyde explained in memorable terms what the term *savior* implies:

It is said, that "Saviors shall come up on Mount Zion to judge the Mount of Esau; and the kingdom shall be the Lord's."

---

[1] Obadiah 1:17, 21.
[2] 1 Kings 8:1; 2 Samuel 5:6–7.
[3] Doctrine and Covenants 97:21.
[4] Moses 7:18-19.
[5] See Doctrine and Covenants 45:66–67.
[6] See Doctrine and Covenants 58:49–50; 62:4; 63:48; 72:13; 84:76; 104:47.

Some men think the way they are going to be saviors is to get as many wives as they can, and save them; now, they may slip up on that, if that is their view, and their feelings extend no further. I will tell you what a savior is; if I see a family who are starving for want of bread, and are thirsting and fainting for water, and an individual should give them bread and water, he has saved them; that is the kind of savior I would give the most for, under some circumstances that I have been placed in, and I would prize that savior more precious than gold. If I were in danger of falling from a precipice, or from a building, as I have said before, and had no means of saving myself, if some kind friend would come along, and put forth his hand and help to save me, he is my savior; so if a man rescues me from a galling yoke of oppression, under which I must faint and die, he is my savior. Saviors shall come upon Mount Zion, and they shall judge the Mount of Esau. This is the kind of savior that will judge the ungodly, and give them their due.[7]

Still, as we might be able to deduce from Elder Hyde's remarks, the notion of a "savior" is broader, more inclusive, than service in the temples alone. It involves all of the ways in which we can serve, and help to save, our fellow human beings. It can certainly also include the very tangible acts, alluded to by Elder Hyde, of giving food and drink to those who need it. It will require, for its full realization, a greater sense of love than we have perhaps yet experienced.

Lorenzo Snow publicly wondered if the Saints of his day had yet learned the kind of love that they needed to be "saviors on Mount Zion." "When one brother is not willing to suffer for his brother," Elder Snow reflected,

how is it in his power to manifest that he has love for his brother? I tell you it is in our folly and weakness that we will not bear with our brethren; but if they trespass upon our rights we immediately retaliate, and if they tread upon our toes we immediately jump upon theirs, the same as the people do in the Gentile world, where it is thought necessary to act in a state of independence, and to defend oneself against aggressors.[8]

---

[7] Orson Hyde, JD, 2:67–68.
[8] Lorenzo Snow, TLS, 119.

These things, he said, ought not so to be. And there would come a time, Elder Snow prophesied, when, like it or not, such attitudes would have to be done away.

> There is a day coming that we will have to suffer for each other, and even be willing to lay down our lives for each other, as Jesus did for the Twelve Apostles in His day, and as they did for the cause which He established. When I see a brother that has been trespassed against, and then he turns round and jumps upon the offender, then I say, how far is that brother from the path of duty, and I say to him you must learn to govern yourself, or you never will be saved in the kingdom of God.[9]

TAKING RESPONSIBILITY FOR OTHERS

It is in loving unity under the direction of the Lord's chosen prophets that we will be enabled to carry out our responsibility to be "saviors" of his children. "We expect to be saviors on Mount Zion in the last days," declared George A. Smith.

> We all exercise faith that God may give to our President wisdom and understanding to foresee the evils with which we may be threatened, and to take measures to avert them. Suppose that he comes forward and tells us how to prepare, and we neglect his counsel, then the watchman is clear, and we are liable to the dangers and difficulties resulting from disobedience. If the King of Egypt had not observed the counsels of Joseph almost the whole people would have been destroyed. As it was, those who did not obey Joseph's counsel were under the necessity of selling all their property, and ultimately themselves, for slaves to the king, in order to obtain that bread which they could have laid up during the seven years of plenty, if they had obeyed Joseph's counsel.[10]

Perhaps, accordingly, a useful way of organizing the statements of modern prophets on the subject of being "saviors on Mount Zion" is to break them down along the lines of what the First Presidency in recent years has defined as the threefold mission of the Church,

---

[9] Lorenzo Snow, TLS, 119.
[10] George Albert Smith, JD, 12:142.

which is (1) to perfect the Saints, (2) to proclaim the gospel, and (3) to redeem the dead. (Each one of these tasks requires and reflects a practical love for our brothers and sisters of the kind that Elder Snow wanted the Saints to develop.) "We will not finish our work," declared President Joseph F. Smith, "until we have saved ourselves, and then not until we shall have saved all depending upon us; for we are to become saviors upon Mount Zion, as well as Christ."[11]

Church leaders remind us that such a task, of course, will demand every bit of devotion, every ounce of energy and dedication that we can summon to its execution. And even then we will just manage to achieve it. The Prophet Joseph Smith begged us to understand the magnitude of our obligation and to waste no time in getting to work to fullfill our responsibility. "I would advise all the Saints," he said,

> to go with their might and gather together all their living relatives to this place, that they may be sealed and saved, that they may be prepared against the day that the destroying angel goes forth; and if the whole Church should go to with all their might to save their dead, seal their posterity, and gather their living friends, and spend none of their time in behalf of the world, they would hardly get through before night would come, when no man can work; and my only trouble at the present time is concerning ourselves, that the Saints will be divided, broken up, and scattered, before we get our salvation secure; for there are so many fools in the world for the devil to operate upon, it gives him the advantage oftentimes.[12]

CHRIST, OUR SAVIOR, IS OUR MODEL

For all the urgency of the assignment, though, Latter-day Saints are never to lose sight of the fact that they can be saviors only because a greater Savior than they paid the price for their sins and the sins of those for whom they labor. The teachings of God's spokesmen leave no room for misunderstanding on this point. No single one of us is necessary to the process; some of us will fail, but the work will go on and will triumph. The one necessary and indispensable act of salvation was that carried out by our Redeemer. Without him, no amount

---

[11] Joseph F. Smith, JD, 19:264.
[12] Joseph Smith Jr., TPJS, 330–31.

of missionary labor and no amount of temple service would avail us. No youth programs or sacrament meeting speeches, however fine, would save anybody. We will be "saviors on Mount Zion," if at all, under and through our Redeemer, Jesus Christ. If we labor in him, our success is assured. "We shall be the saviors of men sooner or later if we are faithful," said Heber C. Kimball, "and shall have power to redeem and save mankind through the atonement made by Jesus Christ."[13] Lorenzo Snow made much the same point some years later. "In order for us to effect the purposes of God," he said,

> we shall have to do as Jesus did—conform our individual will to the will of God, not only in one thing, but in all things, and to live so that the will of God shall be in us. We have the same Priesthood that Jesus had, and we have got to do as He did, to make sacrifice of our own desires and feelings as He did, perhaps not to die martyrs as He did, but we have got to make sacrifices in order to carry out the purposes of God, or we shall not be worthy of this holy Priesthood, and be saviors of the world. God intends to make us saviors not only of many that now dwell on the earth, but of many in the spirit world: He will not only place us in a position to save ourselves, but He will make us competent to assist in the redemption of many of the offspring of the Almighty.[14]

We will be most effective to the extent that we are most like Christ. But this Christlikeness, suggested Elder Snow, may not always come in ways that we would have chosen:

> Our suffering is for the same reason as Christ's. It has not been with the Latter-day Saints the most delightful thing that could be imagined to suffer as they have suffered—and what for? For the same as Jesus suffered, to a certain extent—for the salvation of the world. And although in this life very many of them may not receive that which we offer to them, the day will come, through the progress of things in eternity, when they will receive it, and they will be thankful that we came into the world and suffered in their interests as we have.[15]

---

[13] Heber C. Kimball, JD, 10:101.
[14] Lorenzo Snow, JD, 23:341–42.
[15] Lorenzo Snow, TLS, 118.

MAGNIFYING OUR CALLINGS AS SAINTS

The first of our obligations is to perfect the Saints, to teach, preach, and exemplify the gospel in our own families and congregations. (Some may think that our first obligation is to perfect *ourselves*. But it seems clear that such perfection will come only as we serve the Saints, as we labor in the mission field to bring the gospel to others, and as we worship and renew our covenants in the temples of the Most High. It must come concurrently with such labors, for, if we waited until we ourselves were perfect before commencing them, they would never be begun.) To the extent that the assemblies of the Saints are well-instructed in both doctrine and conduct, to the degree that they are prayerful and obedient, they will be empowered to carry out the remainder of their mission to the world at large. President John Taylor explained that one of the reasons for the very physical gathering of the Saints together, for their perilous journey over oceans, mountains, and deserts, was so that they could instruct and strengthen one another in preparation for, once again, crossing those natural barriers to take the words of truth to those who had not yet heard them. "Why," he asked,

> should we be thus gathered together? That there may be a body of people found to whom God can communicate his will, that there might be a people who should be prepared to listen to the word and will and voice of God: that there might be a people gathered together from the different nations who, under the influence of that spirit should become saviors upon Mount Zion; that they might, under the inspiration of the Almighty, and through the power of the Holy Priesthood which they should receive, go forth to those nations and proclaim to the people the principles of life, that they might indeed become the saviors of men.[16]

Today, with our great ease of international communication and transportation, the physical gathering together of the Saints in one place is no longer essential. They can be in contact with the apostles and prophets who lead them as easily nowadays as if they were all located in the same town. But the fundamental obligation of teaching one another remains. As Lorenzo Snow explained,

---

[16] John Taylor, JD, 19:302.

It becomes the duties of fathers in Israel to wake up and become saviors of men, that they may walk before the Lord in that strength of faith, and that determined energy, that will insure them the inspiration of the Almighty to teach the words of life to their families, as well as to teach them when they are called into this stand. Then all our words will savor of life and salvation wherever we go, and wherever we are.[17]

OUR RESPONSIBILITY TO DO MISSIONARY WORK

Our next great obligation, thus, is that of missionary service. "Those," said Joseph F. Smith, "who have embraced the Gospel—and especially those who are endowed with the authority of the Holy Priesthood, and are called to be saviors upon Mount Zion—ought to be the first and foremost in this good work of being saviors of their neighbors, and of their fellow creatures on the earth."[18] "Love is one of the chief characteristics of Deity," the Prophet Joseph Smith taught,

> and ought to be manifested by those who aspire to be the sons of God. A man filled with the love of God, is not content with blessing his family alone, but ranges through the whole world, anxious to bless the whole human race. This has been your feeling, and caused you to forego the pleasures of home, that you might be a blessing to others, who are candidates for immortality, but strangers to truth; and for so doing, I pray that heaven's choicest blessings may rest upon you.[19]

Modern apostles and prophets have consistently taught that members of the Church have a special obligation to seek the welfare of the descendants of Lehi. Yet they have often rebuked the Latter-day Saints, also, for not having taken this responsibility seriously enough. "We have forgotten," said Orson Pratt,

> who we are; we have forgotten in a measure what God has been doing with us as a people; we have forgotten his purposes that he has determined to accomplish in our day and generation;

---

[17] Lorenzo Snow, JD, 4:158.
[18] Joseph F. Smith, JD, 25:250.
[19] Joseph Smith Jr., MFP, 1:120.

we have forgotten the degraded, forlorn condition of the sons of Joseph; we have forgotten the predictions of the holy Prophets among their fathers, who so earnestly prayed to the most High for themselves and their children to the latest generation, whose prayers have been recorded in the records of eternity and preserved in the archives of heaven, to be answered upon the heads of their posterity in the last days. We have forgotten these things to a great extent, and are dwelling at ease in Zion, and neglecting the great redemption of Israel.[20]

There is great danger in such neglect, not only for the Lamanites and the other remnants of Book of Mormon peoples, but for those of Ephraim who have been assigned by God to take the gospel to them. Said Elder Pratt,

Without this people become the saviours of Israel, we shall be accounted as salt that has lost its savor, and therefore no longer good for anything but to be trodden under the feet of Israel, or of our enemies. Whosoever will not extend the hand of mercy to redeem this people [the Lamanites] will go down, and lose their influence with God and all good men. We are placed here as saviours upon the mountains, and God has placed us here because we understand principles that they are ignorant of. We know about God; we have learned something of Jesus Christ and of the redemption wrought out by him; we have also learned some little of the future state of man. We are in possession of knowledge which is hid from all the rest of the world.[21]

Brigham Young, too, urged his listeners to remember their divinely given mandate and our obligation to God and to those who are our fellow descendants from the great biblical patriarchs. "We are the descendants of Abraham," he stated.

Here are the Lamanites—descendants of Joseph, and the seed of Israel is scattered through the nations; and as Joseph was a savior to his father's house, let us live in obedience to the counsel given us, that we can become saviors to his whole father's house in the latter days.[22]

---

[20] Orson Pratt, JD, 9:175–76.
[21] Orson Pratt, JD, 9:176.
[22] Brigham Young, JD, 10:338.

"One thing is certain," President Young declared to his listeners, and that is that

> if we magnify our calling as Elders in Israel, we are the saviors of the children of men, instead of being their destroyers. We were ordained to save the people, and to save them in the manner the Lord has pointed out. The Savior came not to call the righteous, but sinners to repentance; and we preach to the people, and call upon them to be saved—not the righteous, but we call upon sinners; for those that are well, need no physician, but they that are sick.[23]

It is not our position to judge who is to hear the gospel and who is not. All of our Heavenly Father's children who live upon the earth, or who have ever lived upon the earth, are to have the opportunity to hear and understand it so that they can choose either to accept it or to reject it. John Taylor made our obligation utterly clear in this respect:

> And in regard to the world, what ought our feelings to be towards them? A feeling of generosity, a feeling of kindness, a feeling of sympathy, with our hearts full of charity, long-suffering and benevolence, as God our Father has, for he makes his sun to rise on the evil as well as the good; he sends his rain on the unjust as well as the just. And while we abjure the evils, the corruptions, the fraud and iniquity, the lasciviousness and the lyings and abominations that exist in the world, whenever we see an honorable principle, a desire to do right, whenever we see an opening to promote the happiness of any of these people, or to reclaim the wanderer, it is out duty to do it, as saviors on Mount Zion.[24]

Elder Orson Hyde similarly urged us to perform our duty, promising us that, if we did, we would receive one of the greatest of all earthly rewards, the love and respect of our brothers and sisters. "Are we willing," he asked,

> to put forth our hand and aid in rolling forth this work, by collecting the people together from wretchedness and want?

---

[23] Brigham Young, JD, 1:359.
[24] John Taylor, JD, 19:305.

What shall we gain by doing this? We shall gain numbers that will look up to us as their friends and benefactors, and hail us as their saviors.[25]

REDEEMING THE DEAD THROUGH TEMPLE WORK

It is doubtful that service in the temple will bring so tangible a reward of gratitude from those for whom the service is performed. For the vast majority of them have gone beyond the veil, and only rarely are they permitted to communicate with those still in mortality. There is, likewise, little or no public recognition of those who have labored long and hard for the redemption of the dead. This is not, of course, to say that temple work is thankless, only to say that it is surely among the most selfless (and, therefore, Christlike) forms of service available to us in this life. Its rewards come in the sense of satisfaction and peace that attend temple worship and will come later in the gratitude of many, many of those who have passed away.

But the work before us is vast. Hundreds of millions of people have lived and died without hearing the message of the gospel and, therefore, without having had even the choice of accepting or rejecting it with its saving ordinances. And the great prophet of this dispensation warned that the time we have to accomplish our mission in this regard is severely limited. "The Saints have not too much time," said Joseph Smith, "to save and redeem their dead and gather together their living relatives, that they may be saved also, before the earth will be smitten, and the consumption decreed falls upon the world."[26] Elsewhere, the Prophet taught that

> in the days of Noah, God destroyed the world by a flood, and He has promised to destroy it by fire in the last days: but before it should take place, Elijah should first come and turn the hearts of the fathers to the children, etc. Now comes the point. What is this office and work of Elijah? It is one of the greatest and most important subjects that God has revealed. He should send Elijah to seal the children to the fathers, and the fathers to the children.[27]

---

25 Orson Hyde, JD, 2:67.
26 Joseph Smith Jr., TPJS, 330.
27 Joseph Smith Jr., TPJS, 337.

It is this sense of urgency that drives our modern apostles and prophets to build temples throughout the world, wherever the Saints may dwell. It was this sense of urgency that led the Prophet Joseph Smith, during the last months of his life, even while he sensed his impending martyrdom, to work down in the Nauvoo stone quarries, pushing the construction of the temple along with almost a sense of desperation. He knew how important the powers of the temple were to the salvation of all mankind:

> Let us suppose a case. Suppose the great God who dwells in heaven should reveal Himself to Father Cutler here, by opening the heavens, and tell him, "I offer up a decree that whatsoever you seal on earth with your decree, I will seal it in heaven; you have the power then; can it be taken off? No. Then what you seal on earth, by the keys of Elijah, is sealed in heaven; and this is the power of Elijah, and this is the difference between the spirit and power of Elias and Elijah; for while the spirit of Elias is a forerunner, the power of Elijah is sufficient to make our calling and election sure.[28]

With a similar understanding in mind, Lorenzo Snow lamented the unwillingness of the Saints of his day to commit themselves to the work of redeeming the dead with the devotion that it deserves:

> It is the case with many in this community that instead of preparing themselves for positions in the eternal world, they have been satisfied with the cares of this life, and attending to those things which have been for the comfort of themselves and their wives and children; they have been satisfied in exercising themselves in this small way of ambition. They have forgotten the salvation of their forefathers, and that on them lay the responsibility of laying a holy and pure foundation upon which their posterity may build and obtain life and salvation, and upon which the generations to come might return back to their pristine purity. Instead of being sanctified this day as the people might have been had they sought it diligently, they are weak in their intellects, weak in their faith, weak in their power in reference to the things of God, and many of them this day, setting aside their being saviors of

---

[28] Joseph Smith Jr., MFP, 1:206.

men, are incapable of administering salvation to their individual wives and children. This, brethren, whatever you may
think about it, is a solemn consideration, and you must know
it, for at the present you do not see this as you want to see it,
and as you should see it.[29]

Brigham Young registered similar disappointment with the
Saints. Although he is famous as a colonizer and a genius in matters
of administration and practical affairs, Brigham Young was first and
foremost a prophet and apostle of God. His great talents for worldly
accomplishment were dedicated to a purpose that transcended mere
mortality. Among other things, he was passionate about the work for
the dead. Not long before the completion of the St. George Temple,
the first temple built by the Latter-day Saints in the West, and only
a short time before his death, President Young spoke to the people of
St. George. He pled with them to recognize the importance of service
in the temple and to give it their utmost in dedication and effort.
"Now," he said,

> those that can see the Spiritual Atmosphere, can see that many
> of the Saints are still glued to this earth, and lusting and long-
> ing after the things of this world, in which there is no profit.
> It is true we should look after the things of this world and
> devote all to the building up of the Kingdom of God . . . [but]
> suppose we were awake to this thing, namely the salvation of
> the human family, this house would be crowded . . . from
> Monday Morning until Saturday Night . . . . All of the angels
> of heaven are looking at this little handful of people, and stim-
> ulating them to the salvation of the human family . . . . When
> I think upon this subject I want the tongues of Seven
> Thunders to wake up the people.[30]

SAVIORS OR SALT THAT HAS LOST ITS SAVOR

Church leaders have taught that one of the reasons why we have
been called to be Saints is to do the work for those others of God's
children who have not had our privileges. We are certainly not to sit

---

[29] Lorenzo Snow, JD, 4:155.

[30] Brigham Young sermon, 1 January 1877, St. George Temple Book, Church Archives, as cited
in Eugene England, *Brother Brigham* (Salt Lake City: Bookcraft, 1980), 228.

back and bask in our blessings, taking no thought for others. If we do, it is as if we are soldiers who have deserted our posts and gone away without leave. "For," the Lord said of the Latter-day Saints, "they were set to be a light unto the world, and to be the saviors of men; And inasmuch as they are not the saviors of men, they are as salt that has lost its savor, and is thenceforth good for nothing but to be cast out and trodden under foot of men."[31] "God is looking upon us," testified President John Taylor,

> and has called us to be saviors upon Mount Zion. And what does a savior mean? It means a person who saves somebody. Jesus went and preached to the spirits in prison; and he was a savior to that people. When he came to atone for the sins of the world, he was a savior, was he not? Yes, And we are told in the revelations that saviors should stand upon Mount Zion; and the kingdom shall be the Lord's. Would we be saviors if we did not save somebody? I think not. Could we save anyone if we did not build temples? No, we could not; for God would not accept our offerings and sacrifices. Then we came here to be saviors on Mount Zion, and the kingdom is to be the Lord's.[32]

It is a huge work that lies before us, but it is largely for this purpose that we have been called and that earlier Saints were led to gather together from the distant quarters of the earth. As Brigham Young explained,

> The ordinance of sealing must be performed here man to man, and woman to man, and children to parents, etc., until the chain of generations is made perfect in the sealing ordinances back to Father Adam; hence, we have been commanded to gather ourselves together to come out of Babylon, and sanctify ourselves, and build up the Zion of our God, by building cities and temples, redeeming countries from the solitude of nature, until the earth is sanctified and prepared for the residence of God and angels.[33]

---

[31] D&C 103:9–10.
[32] John Taylor, GK, 287.
[33] Brigham Young, DBY, 407.

Much has already been done. But as the kingdom grows in this, the dispensation of the fulness of times, the pace of the work for the dead will increase. Of necessity, prophetic discourse makes clear, it must. "To accomplish this work," said Brigham Young,

> there will have to be not only one temple but thousands of them, and thousands and tens of thousands of men and women will go into those temples and officiate for people who have lived as far back as the Lord shall reveal.[34]

But, although all our persistence and dedication will be required, we will not be without divine help. "When his Kingdom is established upon the earth, and Zion built up," explained President Young, speaking of these events as if they were all yet in the future, as, in a sense, their final realization actually is,

> the Lord will send his servants as saviors upon Mount Zion. The servants of God who have lived on the earth in ages past will reveal where different persons have lived who have died without the Gospel, give their names, and say, "Now go forth, ye servants of God, and exercise your rights and privileges; go and perform the ordinances of the house of God for those who have passed their probation without the Gospel, and for all who will receive any kind of salvation; bring them up to inherit the celestial, terrestrial, and telestial kingdoms," and probably many other kingdoms not mentioned in the Scriptures; for every person will receive according to his capacity and according to the deeds done in the body, whether good or bad, much or little.[35]

THE MISSION OF THE 144,000

The testimony of both ancient and modern revelation is that, indeed, there will be found those who will do the saving work for their brothers and sisters, and the redemption of the dead will be accomplished. President John Taylor sets the stage for an examination of this issue:

---

[34] Brigham Young, DBY, 394.
[35] Brigham Young, DBY, 407.

Without going into the full investigation of the history and excellency of God, the Father of our Lord Jesus Christ . . . let us reflect that Jesus Christ, as Lord of lords, and King of kings, must have a noble race in the heavens, or upon the earth, or else he can never be as great in power, dominion, might, and authority as the scriptures declare. But here, the mystery is solved. John says: "And I looked, and, lo, a Lamb stood on the mount Sion, and with him an hundred forty and four thousand, having his Father's name written in their foreheads." (Revelation 14:1.)[36]

John the Revelator's number of 144,000 may not be taken literally, or as expressing a precise number by some. As the product of twelve times twelve thousand, it connotes completeness and perfection and echoes both the twelve tribes of Israel and the twelve apostles of the Lamb. The Prophet Joseph Smith clarified the meaning of this language, speaking of service in the temple of God.

I am going on in my progress for eternal life. It is not only necessary that you should be baptized for your dead, but you will have to go through all the ordinances for them, the same as you have gone through to save yourselves. There will be 144,000 saviors on Mount Zion, and with them an innumerable host that no man can number. Oh! I beseech you to go forward, go forward and make your calling and your election sure; and if any man preach any other Gospel than that which I have preached, he shall be cursed; and some of you who now hear me shall see it, and know that I testify the truth concerning them.[37]

So the work will be done, whether we as individuals participate in it or not. But surely each one of us would wish to enjoy the blessings that come from obedience and service to God. "If we obey this law, preserve it inviolate, live according to it," promised Brigham Young,

we shall be prepared to enjoy the blessings of a celestial kingdom. Will any others? Yes, thousands and millions of the

---

[36] John Taylor, GK, 29.
[37] Joseph Smith Jr., HC, 6:365.

inhabitants of the earth who would have received and obeyed the law that we preach, if they had had the privilege. When the Lord shall bring again Zion, and the watchmen shall see eye to eye, and Zion shall be established, saviors will come upon Mount Zion and save all the sons and daughters of Adam that are capable of being saved, by administering for them.[38]

THE CHALLENGE OF BEING SAVIORS

In a very real sense, the division between vicarious temple work and missionary service is an artificial one. Both aim to take the ordinances of the priesthood to those who have not yet received them. The only real difference is the location of those to whom the ordinances are offered. "In these latter days," remarked Wilford Woodruff,

> Saviors have come up on Mount Zion, and they are laboring to save the world—the living and the dead. The Lord required this at our hands, and if we do not labor to promote this cause and to build it up, we shall be under condemnation before him.[39]

It is all the same work. The dead are not really dead; they are every bit as alive as those in mortality, except that they live in a different place.

Indeed, even dividing temple work from the concept of perfecting the Saints is a difficult thing to do, in practice. For the goal of all our efforts, in our youth programs, in our sacrament meetings, in our welfare service, is to help people get their lives in order so that they may receive and keep the ordinances and covenants of the priesthood and raise up a posterity that will do the same. "The first thing you do," advised the Prophet Joseph Smith,

> go and seal on earth your sons and daughters unto yourself, and yourself unto your fathers in eternal glory. . . . I will walk through the gate of heaven and claim what I seal, and those that follow me and my counsel.[40]

John Taylor took the same holistic view of the subject as did Joseph Smith and Wilford Woodruff. "We came here to be saviors," he said. And then he asked himself a series of questions:

---

[38] Brigham Young, DBY, 404–5.
[39] Wilford Woodruff, JD, 16:38.
[40] Joseph Smith Jr., MFP, 1:208.

"What, saviors?" "Yes." "Why, we thought there was only one Savior." "Oh, yes, there are a great many. What do the Scriptures say about it?" One of the old Prophets, in speaking of these things, says that saviors shall come up upon Mount Zion. Saviors? Yes. Whom shall they save? In the first place themselves, then their families, then their neighbors, friends and associations, then their forefathers, then pour blessings on their posterity.[41]

Of course, we cannot credit our role in all of this to any great virtue on our part. We simply do not know why we, of all the spirits who live or ever have lived upon this planet, have been given the priesthood and the ordinances of the temple and the responsibility of seeing that all receive them. We know, only, that we have been given these things and that we are accountable to God for what we do with what we have been given. "To us who have been born in this generation," George Q. Cannon commented,

> and who have beheld this glorious day, these blessings are given. We are chosen, as it were, to be the saviors of men, to be the saviors of our ancestors, and the saviors of a world that is perishing in sin; not for any merit of ours that we know anything about, but because of the grace of God and of His ineffable kindness and mercy that He has shown unto us, and that He is still willing to extend unto us.[42]

Whatever the reasons for our being placed in the circumstances in which we find ourselves, we should attempt to do our best. Our relationship with our Heavenly Father, and with his Son, and with our brothers and sisters of all nations and generations, depends upon it. "Let us try to live our religion," advised Wilford Woodruff,

> and try to be the friends of God; and let us make war against the works of the devil. Let us seek to overcome ourselves, and all our evil impressions, and bring our bodies in subjection to the law of Christ, that we may walk in the light of the Lord, gain power with him, and assist in sanctifying the earth and in building up temples, and in attending to the ordinances of

---

[41] John Taylor, JD, 15:290.
[42] George Q. Cannon, CD, 1:229

the house of God, that we may be saviors of men, both of the living and the dead.[43]

If we do so, and continue faithful to our covenants, our everlasting reward will be a transcendent one. As Elder Orson Pratt said, commenting upon the vision of the ancient prophet John the Revelator,

> On that occasion he saw one hundred and forty-four thousand standing upon Mount Zion, singing a new and glorious song; the singers seemed to be among the most happy and glorious of those who were shown to John. They, the one hundred and forty-four thousand, had a peculiar inscription in their foreheads. What was it? It was the Father's name. What is the Father's name? It is God—the being we worship. If, then, the one hundred and forty-four thousand are to have the name of God inscribed on their foreheads, will it be simply a plaything, something that has no meaning? or will it mean that which the inscriptions specify?—that they are indeed Gods—one with the Father and one with the Son . . . so far as carrying out the great purposes of Jehovah is concerned. No divisions will be there but a complete oneness; not a oneness in person but a perfect oneness in action in the creation, redemption, and glorification of worlds.[44]

---

[43] Wilford Woodruff, JD, 11:66.
[44] Orson Pratt, JD, 14:242–43.

Chapter 13

The Gentiles

And if some of the branches be broken off, and thou [the Gentiles], being a wild olive tree, wert graffed [i.e. grafted] in among them, and with them partakest of the root and fatness of the olive tree;

Boast not against the branches. But if thou boast, thou bearest not the root, but the root thee.

Thou [that is, the Gentiles] wilt say then, the branches were broken off, that I might be graffed in.

Well; because of unbelief they were broken off, and thou standest by faith. Be not high-minded, but fear:

For if God spared not the natural branches, take heed lest he also spare not thee.

Behold therefore the goodness and severity of God: on them which fell [meaning Israel], severity; but towards thee [the Gentiles], goodness, if thou continue in his goodness; otherwise thou also shalt be cut off.

And they [the house of Israel] also, if they abide not still in unbelief, shall be graffed in: for God is able to graff them in again.

For if thou [the Gentiles] wert cut out of the olive tree which is wild by nature, and wert graffed contrary to nature into a good olive tree: how much more shall these, which be the natural branches, be graffed into their own olive tree?

For I would not, brethren, that ye should be ignorant of this mystery, lest ye should be wise in your own conceits; that blindness in part is happened to Israel, until the fullness of the Gentiles be come in.

And so all Israel shall be saved: as it is written, There shall come out of Sion the Deliverer, and shall turn away ungodliness from Jacob:

For this is my covenant unto them, when I shall take away their sins.

As concerning the gospel, they are enemies for your sakes: but as touching the election, they are beloved for the fathers' sakes. . . .

For as ye in times past have not believed God, yet have now obtained mercy through their unbelief:

Even so have these also now not believed, that through your mercy they also may obtain mercy.[1]

THE TIMES OF THE GENTILES

The Church of Jesus Christ of Latter-day Saints was restored during what modern apostles and prophets have repeatedly called "the time of the Gentiles." This is the period, which commenced with the mission of Paul in the ancient Church, of the scattering of Israel and the dominance of foreign nations over the people of Israel. "We all know," explained Joseph Fielding Smith,

> that from the time of the destruction of Jerusalem in the year 70 a.d., until near the close of World War I, Jerusalem was trodden down of the Gentiles, and during all of that time the Jews were scattered and almost without privileges in the Holy Land. The Lord said they should remain scattered among the nations until the times of the Gentiles were fulfilled. Moroni said the times of the Gentiles were about to be fulfilled, Today we are living in the transition period; the day of the Gentiles has come in, and the day of Judah and the remnant of down-trodden Israel is now at hand. The sign for the fulfillment of this prophecy has been given.[2]

Thus, we find ourselves in a crucial time. The growth of The Church of Jesus Christ of Latter-day Saints throughout the world, and particularly among the descendants of Lehi in Latin America, and the reemergence of a Jewish state in Palestine tell us plainly that the ancient prophecies of a literal restoration of Israel are in the process of fulfillment. Yet we are still in a time when the gospel is preached to the Gentiles as well. The Twelve Apostles of the Church, in their great 1845 general epistle to the world, forthrightly declared to the Gentile nations what the Lord expected of them. It is what he still expects:

---

[1] Romans 11:17–28, 30–31. Compare the great Book of Mormon allegory of the olive tree in Jacob 5. A fine collection of essays on the historical background and the interpretation of Jacob 5, including its relationship to Romans 11, is Stephen D. Ricks and John W. Welch, eds., *The Allegory of the Olive Tree: The Olive, the Bible, and Jacob 5* (Salt Lake City: Deseret Book and FARMS, 1994).

[2] Joseph Fielding Smith, DS, 3:258–59.

And now, O ye kings, rulers, and people of the Gentiles: hear ye the word of the Lord; for this commandment is for you. You are not only required to repent and obey the gospel in its fulness, and thus become members or citizens of the kingdom of God, but you are also hereby commanded, in the name of Jesus Christ, to put your silver and your gold, your ships and steam-vessels, your railroad trains and your horses, chariots, camels, mules, and litters, into active use, for the fulfilment of these purposes. For be it known unto you, that the only salvation which remains for the Gentiles, is for them to be identified in the same covenant, and to worship at the same altar with Israel. In short, they must come to the same standard. For, there shall be one Lord, and his name one, and He shall be king over all the earth.[3]

Through the mechanism of adoption into the house of Israel, even those of purest Gentile lineage can receive all the blessings of Abraham as surely as if they were literal descendants of that great Patriarch.[4] "He has said," proclaimed the Twelve Apostles, speaking of the Lord,

that the Gentiles should come into the same gospel and covenant; and be numbered with the house of Israel and be a blessed people upon this good land for ever, if they would repent and embrace it.—And we know it. He has also said that, if they do not repent, and come to the knowledge of the truth, and cease to fight against Zion, and also put away all murder, lying, pride, priestcraft, whoredom, and secret abominations, they shall soon perish from the earth, and be cast down to hell.—And we know it.[5]

However, as might have been predicted, the reaction of the leaders of the world to the proclamation of the Twelve was a thunderous silence, where it was not one of deliberate hostility. But this, too, was foreseen in the ancient prophecies and was not unexpected by modern prophets. "The plain fact," said Joseph Smith,

---

[3] The Twelve Apostles, MFP, 1:255.
[4] See, for instance, the "oath and covenant of the priesthood," as it is found in Doctrine and Covenants 84:33–41.
[5] The Twelve Apostles, MFP, 1:263.

is this, the power of God begins to fall upon the nations, and the light of the latter-day glory begins to break forth through the dark atmosphere of sectarian wickedness, and their iniquity rolls up into view, and the nations of the Gentiles are like the waves of the sea, casting up mire and dirt, or all in commotion, and they are hastily preparing to act the part allotted them, when the Lord rebukes the nations, when He shall rule them with a rod of iron, and break them in pieces like a potter's vessel.[6]

It is this period, the "time of the Gentiles"—how it came to be, who is centrally involved in it, and how and why it will come to an end—that is the subject of this chapter.

WHO ARE THE GENTILES?

The English term *gentile* comes from the Latin word *gens,* which indicated a group who shared descent from a common male ancestor. (It is commonly translated as *clan.*) It gave rise to an adjective form, *gentilis* ("pertaining or belonging to the clan"), which in late Latin came to mean a non-Roman or a foreigner. In translations of the Bible into medieval Latin, *gentilis* came to represent the Hebrew *goy,* meaning a non-Jew. And from there, it came directly into English, where it has carried the same meaning and has sometimes even referred to non-Christians.

But who, exactly, are the Gentiles? Latter-day Saints have—especially, perhaps, in earlier generations—tended to refer to nonmembers of The Church of Jesus Christ of Latter-day Saints as "Gentiles," and there is a sense in which this is perfectly appropriate to the meaning and etymology of the word. But, as Joseph Fielding Smith said,

Let us also remember that we are of the Gentiles! By this I mean that the Latter-day Saints have come to their blessings through the Gentile nations. President Brigham Young . . . said that Joseph Smith was a pure Ephraimite. This is true; yet Joseph Smith came also of Gentile lineage. So do most all members of the Church. We may boast of our lineage, and rejoice in the fact that patriarchs have declared us to be of

---

[6] Joseph Smith Jr., HC, 1:314.

Ephraim, but at the same time let us not despise the Gentiles, for we are also of them. If it were not so the scriptures would not be fulfilled.[7]

Most members of the Church, even of those who can be considered to be literally descendants of Israel, come through the families of the Gentiles. This should hardly surprise us, since the scattered people of Israel, most of them lacking any consciousness of their identity, saw no objection over the centuries to intermarriage with those among whom they lived and with whom they shared culture, language, and religion. President George Q. Cannon explained that

> "As many of the Gentiles as will repent," the prophet says, "are the covenant people of the Lord." By virtue of this promise which God has made, we are His covenant people. Though of Gentile descent, and numbered among the Gentile nations, by and through our obedience to the Gospel of the Son of God we become incorporated, so to speak, among His covenant people and are numbered with them. We say frequently that we are descendants of the house of Israel. This is undoubtedly true. It is clear to any close observer that this people are Hebraic in their character and in their characteristics. We have the peculiarities of the Hebraic character. Our ancestors were of the house of Israel but they mingled with the Gentiles and became lost, that is, they became lost so far as being recognized as of the house of Israel, and the blood of our forefathers was mingled with the blood of the Gentile nations.[8]

Such mingling, of course, should not have happened. But the Lord of history is the Redeemer of history, just as he is of individual men and women. He is able to make even bad things into some form of good, even if it is not the good that his children might have had if they had continued faithful. "And we know that all things work together for good to them that love God."[9] Accordingly, Joseph Fielding Smith saw the hand of the Lord in the scattering of the people of the Lord:

---

7 Joseph Fielding Smith, WP, 140.
8 George Q. Cannon, CD, 2:2–3.
9 Romans 8:28.

For this purpose, which we see in the dispersion of Israel, many of the descendants of Jacob were led away from time to time to various parts of the earth. Because of transgression many went into captivity, and, at those early days, before they had become firmly impregnated with the teachings of their prophets, or fully understood that they were a people separate from the world, they saw no harm in mixing with other peoples. While much of this scattering was meted out to them as a punishment, yet the Lord turned it to the salvation of the Gentile nations. The scattering of Israel among the nations began almost as early as their national existence. It is a well known fact that some of the Greek tribes claimed kinship with Israel.[10]

THE GOSPEL IS RESTORED TO THE GENTILES

With this in mind, it should be understood that the occasional use of the term *gentile* by Latter-day Saints to describe nonmembers of the restored Church of Jesus Christ is not meant pejoratively. As Wilford Woodruff put it,

Sometimes our neighbors and friends think hard of us because we call them Gentiles; but, bless your souls, we are all Gentiles. The Latter-day Saints are all Gentiles in a national capacity.[11] The gospel came to us among the Gentiles. We are not Jews, and the Gentile nations have got to hear the gospel first. The whole Christian world has got to hear the gospel, and when they reject it, the law will be bound and the testimony sealed, and it will turn to the house of Israel. Up to the present day we have been called to preach the gospel to the Gentiles, and we have had to do it.[12]

"The gospel is now restored to us Gentiles," said President Woodruff,

for we are all Gentiles in a national capacity, and it will continue with us if we are faithful, until the law is bound, and the testimony sealed, and the times of the Gentiles are fulfilled, when it will again revert to the Jews, whom the Lord will have prepared

---

[10] Joseph Fielding Smith, WP, 138.
[11] This was spoken, of course, before the establishment of the state of Israel.
[12] Wilford Woodruff, DWW, 116.

to receive it. They will gather to their own land, taking with them their gold and silver, and will rebuild their city and temple, according to the prediction of Moses and the prophets.[13]

Joseph Fielding Smith's remark that, if we who form the predominant element in the modern Church were not Gentiles, "the scriptures would not be fulfilled," is completely true. Late in the nineteenth century, George Q. Cannon reminded his listeners that the Book of Mormon requires precisely this to have been the case:

> For nearly sixty years the Elders of this Church have been laboring which we who are here today are a part. We are designated Gentiles in the record which God has given unto us, the Book of Mormon. And it is predicted in that book that the Gentiles would receive the Gospel, that is, some of them, and that they would be the means in the hands of God of carrying this record, the Book of Mormon, to the descendants of the house of Israel, who should be in darkness at the time this record should come forth.[14]

President Smith, too, pointed to the Book of Mormon as evidence for a leading role being given to the Gentiles in the work of the latter days:

> When Moroni was about to hide up the abridgment of the Book of Mormon he prophesied that it would come forth to the convincing of both Jew and Gentile and to show the remnant of the house of Israel what great things the Lord has done for their fathers, and it was to come forth in the due time of the Lord, "by way of the Gentile" and the "interpretation thereof by the gift of God." Nephi in explaining his vision said that the "book of the Lamb of God, which had proceeded forth from the mouth of the Jew," should come forth from the Gentiles unto the remnant of the seed of his brethren. (1 Nephi 13:38–40.) Moreover, the Savior himself, when he came to the Nephites, informed them that when the Gospel should be revealed in the last days, and should come to the house of Israel, it would come from the Gentiles.[15]

---

13 Wilford Woodruff, DWW, 115.
14 George Q. Cannon, CD, 2:2.
15 Joseph Fielding Smith, WP, 145.

But the Bible also required that the restoration of the gospel come in a time of Gentile dominance. For instance, Jesus spoke to his apostles in Jerusalem about the last days and the day of final redemption that would come at the end of time. As Orson Pratt summarized it,

> Jesus said to his Apostles, When that day shall come, and the light shall begin to break forth among them that sit in darkness, when the fulness of my Gospel shall begin to break forth, that is the period when "the time of the Gentiles shall come in." Mark the expression; when the light shall begin to break forth, then at that period the time of the Gentiles shall have come in, and in that generation "the times of the Gentiles shall be fulfilled."[16]

FIRST TO THE GENTILES, THEN TO THE JEWS

As previously mentioned, the "time of the Gentiles" actually began when the apostle Paul and his fellow workers turned from the Jews, who had rejected their preaching in the synagogues of the diaspora. They began, instead, to teach the Gentile "God-fearers" who hovered around the edges of Judaism in the ancient world, but whose enthusiasm for the high moral teachings and doctrine of the religion of Israel was dampened by the ritualistic rigidity and ethnocentrism with which it had become encrusted. Christianity was, in a sense, made for just such people. "Thus," said the Prophet Joseph Smith,

> after this chosen family had rejected Christ and His proposals, the heralds of salvation said to them, "Lo we turn unto the Gentiles;" and the Gentiles received the covenant, and were grafted in from whence the chosen family were broken off: but the Gentiles have not continued in the goodness of God, but have departed from the faith that was once delivered to the Saints, and have broken the covenant in which their fathers were established (see Isaiah 24:5); and have become high-minded, and have not feared; therefore, but few of them will be gathered with the chosen family. Have not the pride,

---

16 Orson Pratt, JD, 2:261.

high-mindedness, and unbelief of the Gentiles, provoked the Holy One of Israel to withdraw His Holy Spirit from them, and send forth His judgments to scourge them for their wickedness? This is certainly the case.[17]

The ancient, largely Gentile church was destroyed by apostasy, and the dispensation of the meridian of time, the dispensation of the Savior himself, ended in the "time of the Gentiles." All of the intervening apostate centuries fell under this same description. The Jews were scattered and oppressed throughout the world; the people of Lehi destroyed themselves and lost virtually all awareness of their original identity. Thus, when the Lord restored his Church in the nineteenth century, it was still in the "time of the Gentiles."

Inspired seers understand that this is the time of the Gentiles' greatest opportunity for salvation. In the era of the Hebrew Bible, a true and saving knowledge of God was limited to a small number of people in a remote area of the globe who spoke a language understood by very few. In the days of the early Christian church, an effort was made to take the gospel to all who would listen, but this effort was frustrated by persecution, apostasy, and the sheer difficulty of communicating and administering the affairs of the movement over long distances. The restoration of the gospel in a Gentile nation and during a time of Gentile ascendancy means that peoples of Gentile heritage have a chance to hear the truths of God that they have never enjoyed before. Elder Orson Pratt saw the meaning in this:

> What would be the use of sending the Gospel to the Gentiles if their times were [already] fulfilled and there was no hope or chance for them to receive salvation? The very declaration—that an angel shall come forth with the Gospel in the latter days before the destruction of the wicked, and that that Gospel is to be preached to Gentiles as well as Jews, is proof and evidence to every reflecting mind that believes the Bible that the Gentiles will have an opportunity, until that message is delivered and the prediction concerning it fulfilled. When that is done the law is bound, the testimony is sealed, so far as they are concerned.[18]

---

17 Joseph Smith Jr., TPJS, 15.
18 Orson Pratt, JD, 14:62.

Wilford Woodruff commented upon this, explaining why the Jews lost (to the Gentiles, whom they despised) the place of precedence that they had long enjoyed with the God of heaven:

> They did not look for him to come as the Lamb slain from the foundation of the world. They had not the light, and consequently rejected Him and His message and put Him to death, and the Kingdom was given to the Gentiles—first to the Jews, then to the Gentiles. In these last days it came to the Gentiles first; and when they have proven themselves unworthy, it will be given to the Jews. It is to the Gentiles that we have been called to preach the Gospel.[19]

Joseph Fielding Smith, too, discussed this. "The Jewish Christians" of the ancient church, he said,

> were within their rights in the beginning in taking the message first to the Jews, for so it had been promised. The Gospel was then taken to the Gentiles. In this present dispensation it is to go first to the Gentiles and then to the Jews. The first are now last, according to the prophecy in the scriptures. (1 Nephi 13:42.)[20]

There is a marvelous symmetry to the divine plan. As the gospel was first revealed to the house of Abraham, and then taken by them to the Gentiles, so, in the last days, when Abraham's descendants have fallen victim to a spiritual amnesia, the gospel has been restored among the Gentiles, who will return it to house of Israel. In describing this, Elder Orson Pratt echoed the passage from Romans 11 that forms the epigraph to the present chapter:

> Through the mercy of the Gentiles, it is decreed that the house of Israel in the last days shall obtain mercy; that is, through the believing of the Gentiles, or, in other words, through the Saints of the living God who have embraced the covenant of peace from among the Gentiles, and have separated themselves from the wicked Gentile nations. It is through their mercy, through their long-suffering, patience,

---

[19] Wilford Woodruff, JD, 12:278.
[20] Joseph Fielding Smith, WP, 139–40.

and forbearance, that the house of Israel are to find salvation and mercy. And if we do not accomplish this work, we shall suffer.[21]

EPHRAIM MINGLED AMONG THE GENTILES

But contemporary prophets explain that among the Gentiles it is those with ties to one of the dispersed tribes of Israel who are expected to take the lead in the work of the Restoration and the gathering. "The Book of Mormon came to Ephraim," Brigham Young declared, "for Joseph Smith was a pure Ephraimite, and the Book of Mormon was revealed to him."[22] "Today," wrote Joseph Fielding Smith,

> the Gospel Standard is raised by Ephraim who has been gathered from the Gentiles and the scattered Israelites among the Gentiles have rallied unto it. The time has come when this same light shall go to the remnant on this land and to scattered Judah, that they too may have the privilege of being gathered into the fold.[23]

This is a premiere instance of the Lord's ability, mentioned above, to extract good from evil. For, as President Smith observed,

> Even in that exile and the scattering which followed, Ephraim has been blessed. We are led to believe by what has been revealed that Ephraim, more, perhaps, than those of the other tribes, "mixed himself with the nations." (See Hosea 7:8.) He was scattered far and near and for many generations lost his identity. This scattering was a punishment, yet as is often the case with punishment meted out by the Lord, it has turned to be a blessing. He became a blessing to the nations by giving to them the rights belonging to Israel.[24]

Because it springs from an Israelite lineage and because it is scattered throughout the nations of the Gentiles perhaps more fully than

---

[21] Orson Pratt, JD, 9:176.
[22] Brigham Young, JD, 2:268–69.
[23] Joseph Fielding Smith, WP, 141.
[24] Joseph Fielding Smith, WP, 120.

any other of the tribes sprung from Jacob, Ephraim is uniquely posi-
tioned to serve as a bridge between Israel and the non-Israelites.
President Smith saw this clearly and wrote of how Ephraim's work
will make it possible for Gentiles to enter into the house of Israel, be
adopted, and receive all the blessings of Abraham:

> These promises are given to the Gentiles on this land and they
> may assist in the building of Zion and the temple, and share
> in all the blessings of the house of Israel. It has been their priv-
> ilege to be honored and blessed in that they have been nurs-
> ing fathers to the remnant of the Lamanites, and they have
> been blessed with the Priesthood and with the privilege of
> organizing the Church in preparation for the return of all
> Israel. True it is, that these who have accomplished this, who
> are of the Gentiles, are also descendants of Israel through
> Ephraim. By virtue of their descent they have been entitled to
> these blessings; but others shall receive them, who may not be
> of Israel's blood, if they will only accept the promises made by
> the Lord to the Gentiles on this land. If they refuse, then
> when they are "lifted up in the pride of their hearts above all
> nations, and above all the people of the whole earth," the Lord
> will cut them off and will take the Gospel from them, and it
> shall go to the covenant people of the house of Israel. (3 Nephi
> 16:10–11.)[25]

The leading role that this tribe takes in the events and labors of
the last days has been an important theme of modern prophets and
apostles. "It is Ephraim that I have been searching for all the days of
my preaching," declared Brigham Young,

> and that is the blood which ran in my veins when I embraced
> the Gospel. If there are any of the other tribes of Israel mixed
> with the Gentiles we are also searching for them. Though the
> Gentiles are cut off, do not suppose that we are not going to
> preach the Gospel among the Gentile nations, for they are
> mingled with the house of Israel, and when we send to the
> nations we do not seek for the Gentiles, because they are dis-
> obedient and rebellious. We want the blood of Jacob, and that
> of his father Isaac and Abraham, which runs in the veins of the

---

25 Joseph Fielding Smith, WP, 148.

people. There is a particle of it here, and another there, blessing the nations as predicted.[26]

THE GRAFTED IN MAY BE CUT OFF

Both the apostle Paul and, in the Book of Mormon, the ancient
Old World prophet Zenos compared the house of Israel to an olive
tree. Those Gentiles who accept the gospel and seek membership in
the kingdom of God they compared to the branches of wild olive
trees, whose fruit is bitter and useless but who, when grafted into the
tame olive tree, miraculously produce tame fruit whose delicious
taste is indistinguishable from the natural fruit of the tree.

But such grafting need not be permanent. Gentiles can forfeit
their adoption into Israel, just the people of Israel, for a time at least,
forfeited their position as the blessed covenant people of God. "Jesus
offered his Gospel to the Jews in his day," said Wilford Woodruff,

> but in these latter days it has been offered first to the Gentiles,
> thus fulfilling the saying that the first shall be last and the last
> shall be first; and when the Gentiles count themselves unwor-
> thy of eternal life, the Gospel will go to the House of Israel
> and they will receive it. The Gentiles should heed the warn-
> ing given them by the Apostle Paul, lest they fall through the
> example of unbelief as did the Jews, who were broken off
> because they rejected the Messiah, and refused the message of
> salvation which he delivered unto them.[27]

---

[26] Brigham Young, JD, 2:268. President Young is using the term *Gentile* in a slightly different
sense, perhaps, than that in which we have used it above. For him, in this passage, *Gentile* and
rebellious appear to be equivalent terms. In the same discourse, on pp. 268–69, he seems to make
the equivalence even clearer: "Take a family of ten children . . . and you may find nine of them
purely of the Gentile stock, and one son or one daughter in that family who is purely of the
blood of Ephraim. It was in the veins of the father or mother, and was reproduced in the son or
daughter, while all the rest of the family are Gentiles. You may think that is singular, but it is
true. It is the house of Israel we are after, and we care not whether they come from the east, the
west, the north, or the south; from China, Russia, England, California, North or South America,
or some other locality." (President Young's usage here is similar to the sense in which *Latter-day
Saint* is opposed to *Gentile*, where no ethnic distinction is implied.) But, in another sense, we
know (and it should be clear from several of the statements cited in this chapter) that those who
are genealogically "Gentile" can still repent, just as those of Israel can and must, and can be
accepted on a basis of equality within the house of Israel.

[27] Wilford Woodruff, JD, 17:193.

Earlier, Orson Pratt sounded the same theme. "Now," he declared,

> here is a definite prediction: if ye continue in his goodness, the goodness of God will be extended to you, though you are Gentiles, though you are grafted, contrary to nature, into the tame olive tree, but if you do not continue in his goodness, if you lose your faith, as the house of Israel lost it; if you cease to bring forth the fruits of the kingdom, as they have done, you also shall be cut off.[28]

Accordingly, in line with his calling as an apostle and a prophet, Elder Pratt directed a solemn word of caution to those who have entered into the covenants of God and, by adoption, into the family of Abraham:

> A great warning to the Gentiles: the house of Israel—the branches of the tame olive tree—were broken off because they ceased to bring forth the fruits of the kingdom of God. As much as to say, Because they ceased to bring forth the fruit that pertains to the tame olive tree, they were broken off through unbelief; therefore you Gentiles, who are now grafted in, being branches of the wild olive tree, take heed and beware lest you fall after the same example of unbelief.[29]

THE END OF THE TIME OF THE GENTILES

God's servants have taught that, although many Gentiles have accepted and will accept the gospel of Jesus Christ, the time will come when the window of opportunity will close for those who remain obdurate. Orson Pratt described this event, with its serious consequences for those who have not yet repented:

> After the times of the Gentiles are fulfilled, which period is set in the mind of God, another scene will open up before the world, in the grand panorama of the last days. What is that? The downfall of the Gentile nations. Says one—"Whom do you call Gentiles?" Every nation excepting the literal

---

[28] Orson Pratt, JD, 14:63.
[29] Orson Pratt, JD, 14:63.

descendants of Israel. We, the Latter-day Saints, are Gentiles; in other words, we have come from among the Gentile nations, though many of us may have the blood of Israel within our veins. When God has called out the righteous, when the warning voice has been sufficiently proclaimed among these Gentile nations, and the Lord says "It is enough," he will also say to his servants—"O, ye, my servants, come home, come out from the midst of these gentile nations, where you have labored and borne testimony for so long a period; come out from among them, for they are not worthy; they do not receive the message that I have sent forth, they do not repent of their sins; come out from their midst, their times are fulfilled. Seal up the testimony among them and bind up the law."[30]

This time has not come yet. Not quite. And it is fortunate for many millions of people that it has not. Wilford Woodruff expressed his gratitude for the fact that the Gentiles still have the opportunity to hear and accept the gospel. "I rejoice," he said,

that the Lord still holds the door open, that we still have the privilege of sending the Elders to the nations; while this door remains open we shall continue to preach the Gospel to the Gentile world. When they reject it it will be taken from them and then we go to the Jews, and the ten tribes will come from the north to Zion to be crowned under the hands of the children of Ephraim. And the remnant of the Lamanites who are cursed below all humanity that we are acquainted with—who have been filled with the spirit of bloodshed which they have inherited from their fathers—they will embrace the Gospel in the due time of the Lord. They are of the house of Israel, and this spirit of war will be taken from them and they will become the children of God, but not until the Gentiles have entirely rejected the Gospel.[31]

Of course, the Lord's servants declare that the Lord's love for his children will never block the truly repentant from entry into his earthly kingdom and, ultimately, into his eternal rest. Even after the "day of the Gentiles" comes to its close, there will still be those who find their

---

30 Orson Pratt, JD, 18:64.
31 Wilford Woodruff, JD, 10:220.

way into the Church. But they will have to do so against great odds. Orson Pratt made this point quite well. "Will the Gentiles," he asked,

> be entirely cut off? Oh no, there will be a great many, even when Israel are gathering, who will come along and say, "Let us be numbered with Israel, and be made partakers of the same blessings with them; let us enter into the same covenant and be gathered with them and with the people of God." Though the testimony is bound, and though the law is sealed up, yet there will be an opening for you to come in. But you will have to come of your own accord, there will be no message sent to you, no ministration of the servants of God expressly directed to you. When the times of the Gentiles are filled, through the mercy of the believing Gentiles, the house of Israel must obtain mercy; that is, through the messengers that will then go forth.[32]

THE GOSPEL TO TURN TO THE HOUSE OF ISRAEL

In fact, the time of the Gentiles has probably lasted longer than Wilford Woodruff, Orson Pratt, and other leaders of the Church in the nineteenth century expected it to, and we can be grateful to the Lord for his mercy in extending the time before his angelic reapers descend upon us. But Elder Woodruff's warning still bears hearing, for, late or soon, the day will come when the window of opportunity for the Gentiles will close with a sudden and fearful sound:

> When this time arrives, which is nigh, even at our doors, let the Gentile nations who reject the gospel which is now sent to them, prepare to meet the judgments of an offended God! For when their cup is full even to the brim, the Lord will then remember the chastisements of the Jews, his favored people, and at whose hands they will have received double for their iniquities. Offenses must come, said the Savior, but woe unto them by whom they come. Woe unto the Gentiles, who have administered afflictions to the Jews for these many years! Woe unto them if they now reject this only means of salvation, for the awful calamities spoken of in these books, the Bible and Book of Mormon, will certainly befall them.[33]

---

32 Orson Pratt, JD, 14:64.
33 Wilford Woodruff, DWW, 115–16.

What then? "Then the word of the Lord," said Orson Pratt,

> will be—"O, ye, my servants, I have a new commission for
> you. Instead of going forth to convert the Gentile nations, go
> unto the remnants of the house of Israel that are scattered in
> the four quarters of the earth. Go and proclaim to them that
> the times of their dispersion are accomplished; that the times
> of the Gentiles are fulfilled; that the time has arrived for my
> people Israel, who have been scattered for generations in a
> dark and cloudy day, to gather unto their own homes again,
> and to build up old Jerusalem on its former heap. And then
> will commence the gathering of the Jews to old Jerusalem;
> then the ten tribes in the northern regions, wherever they may
> be, after having been concealed from the nations for twenty-
> five hundred years, will come forth and will return, as
> Jeremiah has said, from the north country. A great company
> will come, and they will sing in the height of Zion.[34]

The astonishing fact that, against all historical precedent and
expectation, the Jews have begun to gather again in Palestine, and that
a Jewish state rules from the ancient but now rebuilt city of Jerusalem,
should give serious observers pause. For, whether they acknowledge it
or not, they are watching the hand of the Lord at work.

"When the Gentiles reject the Gospel," said Wilford Woodruff
on the same subject,

> it will be taken from them, and go to the house of Israel, to
> that long suffering people that are now scattered abroad
> through all the nations upon the earth, and they will be gath-
> ered home by thousands, and by hundreds of thousands, and
> they will re-build Jerusalem their ancient city, and make it
> more glorious than at the beginning, and they will have a
> leader in Israel with them, a man that is full of the power of
> God and the gift of the Holy Ghost; but they are held now
> from this work, only because the fulness of the Gentiles has
> not yet come in.[35]

But it will. "The day is not far distant," declared Orson Pratt,

---

[34] Orson Pratt, JD, 18:64.
[35] Wilford Woodruff, JD, 2:200.

when young men, now living in these mountains, will be commissioned to go, not to the Gentiles, for their times will be fulfilled, but the Lord will say to them—"Go forth and fish and hunt up Israel in the four quarters of the earth. Go to the remnants of Joseph that are in South America, and scattered over this vast continent from the frozen regions of the north to Cape Horn in South America; go and teach them the Gospel, for they are a remnant of the tribe of Joseph: and his arm will be made bare in that day in such a manner that they will not reject the truth, and they will be grafted in again into their own olive tree, and become a righteous branch of the house of Israel."[36]

EPHRAIM WILL INTERCEDE FOR HIS BRETHREN

And, indeed, the swelling membership of the Church in Mexico and in Central and South America, where the children of Lehi live in great numbers, suggests the day is very near at hand.

We now turn to a discussion of the house of Israel, both in the Old World land of Palestine and in their scattered condition in the Americas. Their future is glorious, and it is a future in which all members of The Church of Jesus Christ of Latter-day Saints, whatever their own genealogical background, are summoned to play a role. As Wilford Woodruff expressed it,

I thank God that the day is at hand when the Jews will be restored. I have felt to pray for them; I feel interested in their behalf, for they are of the seed of Abraham and a branch of the house of Israel, and the promises of God still remain with them. It is true they fell through unbelief, and the kingdom was taken from them and given to the Gentiles, and when it came from them, it came clothed with all its gifts, powers, and glory, Priesthood and ordinances which were necessary for the salvation of men, and to prepare them to dwell in the presence of the Gods; and when the kingdom was given to the Gentiles, they for a while brought forth the natural fruits of the kingdom. But they, like the Jews, have fallen through the same example of unbelief, and now, in the last days, the kingdom of

---

[36] Orson Pratt, JD, 16:352–53.

God has to be taken from the Gentiles, and restored back to every branch and tribe of the house of Israel; and when it is restored to them, it must go back with all its gifts, and blessings, and Priesthood which it possessed when it was taken from them. But the Lord has said that in restoring these blessings to the children of Abraham, that He would be inquired of by the house of Israel, to do it for them. But from what branch or part of the house of Israel will the Lord look for this petition or request to issue, if not from the Latter-day Saints, for we are out of the tribe of Joseph through the loins of Ephraim, who have been as a mixed cake among the Gentiles, and are the first fruits of the kingdom, and the Lord has given unto us the kingdom and Priesthood and keys thereof. Hence the Lord will require us to ask for those blessings which are promised unto Israel, and to labour for their salvation.[37]

---

[37] Wilford Woodruff, JD, 4:232–33.

CHAPTER 14

THE HOUSE OF ISRAEL

THE DISPERSION AND GATHERING OF ISRAEL

Speaking of a time yet in the future, the ancient prophet Isaiah proclaimed nearly three thousand years ago that

> in that day there shall be a root of Jesse, which shall stand for an ensign of the people; to it shall the Gentiles seek: and his rest shall be glorious.
>
> And it shall come to pass in that day, that the Lord shall set his hand again the second time to recover the remnant of his people, which shall be left, from Assyria, and from Egypt, and from Pathros, and from Cush, and from Elam, and from Shinar, and from Hamath, and from the islands of the sea.
>
> And he shall set up an ensign for the nations, and shall assemble the outcasts of Israel, and gather together the dispersed of Judah from the four corners of the earth.[1]

The dispersion of Israel had not even occurred when Isaiah wrote, and a hundred generations have passed away since his death. Some have wondered, with reason, whether Isaiah's vision of the glorious future might not have been only a wishful dream. Modern prophets teach that it was a vision grounded in reality and the will of God, and, in fact, they have unanimously testified that the long yearned-for time is near. "A better day is dawning for the Jew and for the Lamanite," said President Joseph Fielding Smith. "The time is now at hand spoken by ancient prophets when the Lord shall feel after them. The words of Isaiah are now being fulfilled."[2] Speaking to a conference of the Church in April 1966, President Smith pointed to one of the unmistakable signs that this was indeed the case:

> Jesus said the Jews would be scattered among all nations and Jerusalem would be trodden down by the Gentiles until the times of the Gentiles were fulfilled. (Luke 21:24.) The prophecy in Section 45, verses 24–29, of the Doctrine and

---

[1] Isaiah 11:10–12.
[2] Joseph Fielding Smith, WP, 134.

Covenants regarding the Jews was literally fulfilled. Jerusalem, which was trodden down by the Gentiles, is no longer trodden down but is made the home for the Jews. They are returning to Palestine, and by this we may know that the times of the Gentiles are near their close.[3]

The fulfillment of the prophecies relating to the gathering and reestablishment of Israel will be public. The gathering will not be done—it is not *being* done—in a corner. Although undiscerning eyes will fail to recognize it for what it truly is, and although hearts not tuned to spiritual things will not see its spiritual significance, the process will be visible to all. Orson Pratt had this in mind when he explained,

> The prophet says, "All ye inhabitants of the world and dwellers on the earth, see ye, when he lifteth up an ensign on the mountains, and when he bloweth with a trumpet, hear ye" (Isaiah 18:3)—something that the Lord considered worthy of the attention of all the people of the earth. It was not to be sounded to one nation alone, not a work like that of ancient days—to be done among the Egyptian nation alone.[4]

Although it has gained little notice (and even less appreciation) from the world at large, the words of modern Church authorities make it obvious that the restoration of the Church and gospel of Jesus Christ was essential to set this process going and provides the key to the real meaning of much that is reported in today's newspaper headlines. "Would you suppose," asked Elder Pratt,

> that the House of Jacob, the ten tribes of Israel, can be gathered from the four quarters of the earth, and brought back to their own land, without the lifting of this ensign? No. Read the 11th chapter of Isaiah. There he says—"I will lift up an ensign for the nations, I will assemble the outcasts of Israel, and I will gather together the dispersed of Judah from the four quarters of the earth." Until the Lord God sends forth this proclamation to all the inhabitants of the world and dwellers on the earth, in vain may we look for the redemption of the outcasts of Israel and the dispersed of Judah.[5]

---

[3] Joseph Fielding Smith, CR, April 1966, 13.
[4] Orson Pratt, JD, 14:67.
[5] Orson Pratt, JD, 18:184.

THE ALLEGORY OF THE TWO STICKS

Treating the same theme on an earlier occasion, Elder Pratt pointed out that

> Ezekiel informs us . . . that prior to the great restitution of the House of Israel, never to be scattered or divided into two nations again, the Lord would bring forth the stick of Joseph, written upon for the tribe of Joseph, and the other, written upon for Judah, and cause them to grow together in His hand, and when this great event should take place, it should be the period when he would take Israel from among the heathen, whither they be gone, and gather them on every side, and bring them into their own lands, and when he had accomplished this work, he would make them one nation upon the mountains of Israel, and they should no more be two nations, neither should they, from that time forward, be two kingdoms any more at all.[6]

Given the essential connection between the gathering of Israel on the one hand and, on the other, the restoration of the Church and the priesthood and the revelation of that great lost record of a remnant of the house of Israel known as the Book of Mormon, it can scarcely be surprising that fresh prophetic references to the gathering began to appear from the very beginning of the Restoration. As President Ezra Taft Benson reminded us,

> In the first visit of Moroni to the Prophet Joseph (see Joseph Smith—History 1:40) mention was made that the "dispersed of Judah would be gathered from the four corners of the earth" (Isaiah 11:12). Thirteen years later, when Moses delivered the keys for the gathering of Israel and the Kirtland Temple was dedicated, the Prophet Joseph made further reference to the promises made to Judah and appealed to the Lord that the time may soon come when the children of Judah would return to the land promised to their father, Abraham (D&C 109:61–65).[7]

Taught by prophets and apostles who speak with divine authority, Latter-day Saints have confidently awaited the triumph of God's

---

[6] Orson Pratt, JD, 16:341.
[7] Ezra Taft Benson, TETB, 91.

purpose in the gathering of Israel since the establishment of the Lord's restored Church in 1830. Moreover, they have watched and, in fact, participated in the work of gathering. Their labors in settling the valleys of the West and in sending missionaries to the furthest reaches of the earth, though they have often been undertaken in the most humble of circumstances and have frequently involved very unromantic amounts of dirt and sweat, have been centrally important to the ultimate realization of the ancient visions of Isaiah and others. Today, as in earlier times, the Saints believe what the prophets have taught. As the First Presidency declared during the presidency of Brigham Young, "The promises of God, concerning the restoration of Israel, cannot fail, and nothing should divert our faith and our prayer from the constant expectation of their fulfillment."[8]

THE GENTILES INSTRUMENTAL IN GATHERING ISRAEL

As the Old Testament makes clear beyond mistake, God works through specific families and lineages. He did so anciently, and he does so today. Yet he does not do so because he loves any particular ethnic group more than he loves others. All human beings who have ever lived upon the earth are our Heavenly Father's children, and his deepest desire is that as many of them as possibly can will seek to return to his presence. "Behold," Nephi wrote, "the Lord esteemeth all flesh in one; he that is righteous is favored of God."[9] He chooses certain individuals, certain families, certain genealogical lines as his instruments in his work of "bringing to pass the immortality and eternal life" of all his children. Church authorities make it clear, however, that such choice should never be viewed as conferring greater value on one soul, or on one ethnic group, than another. "It is regrettable," said President Hugh B. Brown,

> that very few people in the world are free from the idea that they and their people and race are superior. The people on this continent were instructed that they should not hiss nor spurn nor make game of any remnant of the house of Israel,

8 Brigham Young, Heber C. Kimball, Willard Richards, MFP, 2:122.
9 1 Nephi 17:35.

"for behold, the Lord remembereth his covenant unto them, and he will do unto them according to that which he hath sworn." (3 Nephi 29:8.)[10]

Having stated that caution, we may now turn to the way in which the Lord works and will work with various groups of his children in these latter days.

It is clear from the teachings of both ancient scripture and the modern servants of God that the gospel was destined to come to the Gentiles first and, through their instrumentality, to go to the people of Israel only afterwards. "The proclamation which goes to Israel," said Orson Pratt, "must come through the Gentile nations; that is, through those whom God may select among the Gentiles, that through the mercy and kindness of the Gentiles, or those who receive the message in the latter days, the house of Israel may be saved."[11] Drawing, as subsequent prophets have often done, on the eloquent language of Isaiah, Elder Pratt noted:

In regard to this ensign, the Lord has never said that he will lift it up before the time comes to gather Israel. And now let us inquire where will it be lifted up; in what part of the earth will he commence the great work? He must begin it among the Gentiles, as I have already said, and as Isaiah tells us in the 49th chapter—a standard or ensign, to which the people will gather, will be reared among the Gentiles. Recollect this is something to be commenced among the Gentiles, not among the Jewish nation, not away yonder in Palestine or Jerusalem. "Thus saith the Lord God, behold I will lift up mine hand to the Gentiles and set up my standard to the people" (Isaiah 49:22)—the same ensign that Isaiah speaks of in the eleventh chapter—for a standard and an ensign are synonymous terms.[12]

This divine timetable, understood by the prophets who guide God's Church in these latter days, governs our missionary efforts in a very practical way. As Elder Pratt explained it,

---

10 Hugh B. Brown, CR, April 1966, 119.
11 Orson Pratt, JD, 14:64.
12 Orson Pratt, JD, 14:66-67.

> The Lord has a blessing in store for Jacob—the literal seed of
> Israel; but we cannot go to them until the Gentile fullness has
> come in, until their times are fulfilled, then all Israel will be
> saved, by a Deliverer sent out of Zion; in other words, there
> will be a Zion again on the earth.[13]

The prophets explain that the Gentiles have been given the responsibility of assisting in the restoration of the Jews to their ancient homeland and in their gathering into the unity of the Saints within the house of Israel. For instance, comparing the Book of Mormon to the Bible, Ezra Taft Benson observed that

> the prophets of the Book of Mormon even more clearly pre-
> dict the conditions under which they [the Jews] will gather.
> These prophets . . . foresaw the time when they would begin
> to believe in Jesus Christ, that the kings of the Gentiles would
> be as nursing fathers and their queens nursing mothers in
> helping to bring about their return. These prophets make it
> clear that eventually the fullness of the gospel will be carried
> to Jerusalem and to the descendants of Judah.[14]

Even within the process of gathering Israel, though, there is a differentiated schedule. For example, the time for preaching the gospel to the Jews will come very near to the end of the whole process. As Brigham Young said, "It is obligatory upon us to see that the House of Israel have the Gospel preached to them; to do all that is in our power to gather them to the land of their fathers, and to gather up the fulness of the Gentiles before the Gospel can go with success to the Jews."[15]

In all of this, however, it is not the undifferentiated "Gentiles" who will carry out this important assignment. Rather, according to the teachings of the modern prophets, it is the people of Ephraim, scattered among the nations of the earth for their unrighteousness, who have been given the responsibility. As they join the Church of God, they reclaim their ancient prominence, their ancient covenant relationship with the Lord, and their anciently prophesied mission. "We learn," wrote Joseph Fielding Smith,

---

13 Orson Pratt, JD, 14:63.
14 Ezra Taft Benson, CR, April 1950, 75.
15 Brigham Young, DBY, 437.

that when these glorious times shall come the children of Ephraim shall be "servants" of the Lord. Ephraim shall stand in the full glory of his birthright at the head, to minister to his fellow tribesmen. What a glory is his! What honor bestowed upon him now when he is no longer rebellious! And the Lord adds: "Behold, this is the blessing of the Everlasting upon the tribes of Israel, and the richer blessings upon the head of Ephraim and his fellows."[16]

THE EXTENT OF THE SCATTERING OF ISRAEL

But this responsibility bestowed on Ephraim is not merely an honor. It is a daunting challenge. For the dispersion of Israel has been virtually total, and the gathering of Israel will require vast labor in literally every area of the inhabited globe. "Israel are upon all the face of the earth," explained Orson Pratt.

> Some think that these American Indians are Israel, and we think that they are too; but they are only one part or portion of the twelve tribes; indeed, they are only a very small portion of the tribes of Joseph, the most of them being the descendants of Manasseh. But Israel dwell upon the islands of the sea, and in the countries and nations of Europe, in the various kingdoms and empires of Asia; some are scattered through Africa, and wherever you go you find the promised seed—the descendants of Jacob.[17]

Another early member of the Council of the Twelve, Orson Hyde, had this point made clear to him in a vivid and unforgettable way. In the period just preceding his famous journey to Palestine, during which he dedicated the Holy Land for the return of the Jews, he experienced a remarkable vision. "The cities of London, Amsterdam, Constantinople and Jerusalem," he reported in a letter to the Prophet Joseph Smith,

> all appeared in succession before me, and the Spirit said unto me, "Here are many of the children of Abraham whom I will gather to the land that I gave to their fathers; and here also is

---

16 Joseph Fielding Smith, WP, 125.
17 Orson Pratt, JD, 2:262.

the field of your labors. Take, therefore, proper credentials from my people, your brethren, and also from the Governor of your state, with the seal of authority thereon, and go ye forth to the cities which have been shown you, and declare these words unto Judah, and say, "blow ye the trumpet in the land; cry, gather together, and say, assemble yourselves, and let us go into the defensed cities. Set up the standard towards Zion—retire, stay not, for I will bring evil from the north and a great destruction. The lion is come up from his thicket, and the destroyer of the Gentiles is on his way—he is gone forth from his place to make thy land desolate, and thy cities shall be laid waste, without an inhabitant. Speak ye comfortably to Jerusalem, and cry unto her, that her warfare is accomplished—that her iniquity is pardoned, for she hath received of the Lord's hand doubly for all her sins. Let your warning voice be heard among the Gentiles as you pass; and call yet upon them in my name for aid and for assistance."[18]

THE GATHERING OF THE JEWS

Elder Hyde's prayer on the Mount of Olives was a divinely decreed action that ushered in the still ongoing gathering of the Jewish people to their ancient land in the Near East. This gathering had been foretold many times in the centuries preceding. The apostle Paul, for instance, predicted that the Jews, if they yielded up the unbelief that was, in his day, leading them to reject their Redeemer, would someday be grafted into the olive tree of covenant Israel again. For, he said, if even the Gentiles, who were cut, metaphorically, from a wild olive tree, could be grafted into Israel, how much more so could the repentant Jews be grafted in. It was the Jews who had belonged to the tame olive tree of Israel at their beginning; the tame olive tree was, therefore, their native environment.[19]

But, although Judah, or the Jews, are to be gathered together into the covenant family of Israel, the Lord's servants have prophesied that they will not be gathered, ultimately, to the same geographical location as the remainder of Israel. They have their own place, divinely

---

[18] Orson Hyde, HC, 4:376.

[19] See Romans 11:23-25; compare Jacob 5. Orson Pratt, JD, 14:63, offers a brief interpretation of this passage that is consistent with mine.

designated for them from ancient times. President Joseph Fielding Smith referred to this while testifying of the imminent fulfillment of the prophecies. "Judah also is to be gathered," he wrote,

> but to Jerusalem and Palestine. The tribes of Israel will come to Zion where they will be crowned and eventually many of them will find their way back to the land of their inheritance, for so it has been promised. (See Ether 13:10–11.) When Judah is gathered, and we may be happy in the knowledge that he is being gathered, he too must receive his blessings from his brother Ephraim. And the time will come—it is near at hand—when all Israel shall be cleansed. The covenants made with Abraham, Isaac, and Jacob in days of old, and renewed with Joseph Smith, in the present day, shall all be fulfilled.[20]

In so saying, President Smith reflected an understanding that is unique to the teachings of the restored gospel of Jesus Christ: Where others have recognized that a gathering of Israel is predicted in the scriptures, only those who also accept the words of God as given through the Prophet Joseph Smith and his successors understand that there will actually be two distinct centers or focuses of gathering. "The tribe of Judah will return to old Jerusalem," taught Wilford Woodruff, in a prediction that many other Christians would have found entirely acceptable. However, there is more. President Woodruff continued, saying that

> the city of Zion spoken of by David, in the one hundred and second Psalm, will be built upon the land of America, "And the ransomed of the Lord shall return, and come to Zion with songs and everlasting joy upon their heads." (Isaiah 35:10); and then they will be delivered from the overflowing scourge that shall pass through the land. But Judah shall obtain deliverance at Jerusalem. (See Joel 2:32; Isaiah 26:20–21; Jeremiah 31:12; Psalms 1:5; Ezekiel 34:11–13.) These are testimonies that the Good Shepherd will put forth His own sheep, and lead them out from all nations where they have been scattered in a cloudy and dark day, to Zion, and to Jerusalem; besides many more testimonies which might be brought.[21]

---

[20] Joseph Fielding Smith, WP, 126.
[21] Wilford Woodruff, DWW, 114.

THE GATHERING OF THE LAMANITES

The existence of a second gathering place, on this continent, is unknown to the world at large for the simple and obvious reason that they are unaware of, or do not recognize, the existence of another branch of Israel in the New World. But, of course, knowledge of this group of Israelites is among the most distinctive blessings bestowed by the Lord upon The Church of Jesus Christ of Latter-day Saints, and it was included among the earliest of their revelations. "The Book of Mormon," declared the Prophet Joseph Smith,

> is a record of the forefathers of our western tribes of Indians; having been found through the ministration of an holy angel, and translated into our own language by the gift and power of God, after having been hid up in the earth for the last four-teen hundred years, containing the word of God which was delivered unto them. By it we learn that our western tribes of Indians are descendants from that Joseph who was sold into Egypt, and that the land of America is a promised land unto them, and unto it all the tribes of Israel will come, with as many of the Gentiles as shall comply with the requisitions of the new covenant.[22]

Much more recently, President Spencer W. Kimball reiterated the inescapable necessity of bringing the descendents of the ancient Lamanites into the modern Church of God. "Of immense impor-tance to this work of gathering the scattered branches of the house of Israel," he insisted, "is the work of carrying the blessings of the restored gospel of Jesus Christ to the Lamanites, for the Lord's work in these latter days can in no wise be complete until these children of great promise are brought back into the fold."[23]

This has always been a central priority of the Lord's modern prophets and apostles, though sometimes the difficulty of the work has seemed overwhelming. Speaking in the nineteenth century, Wilford Woodruff expressed both deep faith that the prophecies would be fulfilled and, it would seem, considerable puzzlement about how that fulfillment would be achieved. "Not only will the Jews have blessings again," he said,

---

[22] Joseph Smith Jr., TPJS, 17.
[23] Spencer W. Kimball, TSWK, 595.

but these poor despised Indians will enjoy the light and glory of the gospel of Christ; their fathers proclaimed blessings upon them, by the spirit of prophecy and revelation, which are as assuredly to rest upon a remnant of that people as they exist, though they are now the most miserable beings that live upon the face of the earth. Nevertheless, a remnant of them will embrace the gospel, and their eyes will be opened and they will understand that they are of Israel. Our missionaries have labored among them, and what effect has it had? But little. Missionaries of different orders have labored among them, with little or no success.[24]

"I am looking for the fulfillment of all things that the Lord has spoken," he declared on another occasion,

and they will come to pass as the Lord God lives. Zion is bound to rise and flourish. The Lamanites will blossom as the rose on the mountains. I am willing to say here that, though I believe this, when I see the power of the nation destroying them from the face of the earth, the fulfillment of that prophecy is perhaps harder for me to believe than any revelation of God that I ever read. It looks as though there would not be enough left to receive the Gospel; but notwithstanding this dark picture, every word that God has ever said of them will have its fulfillment, and they, by and by, will receive the Gospel. It will be a day of God's power among them, and a nation will be born in a day. Their chiefs will be filled with the power of God and receive the Gospel, and they will go forth and build the new Jerusalem, and we shall help them. They are branches of the house of Israel, and when the fullness of the Gentiles has come in and the work ceases among them, then it will go in power to the seed of Abraham.[25]

Orson Pratt, a contemporary of President Woodruff, expressed the same faith in the face of huge political, cultural, and other obstacles. "That is the destiny of our Indian tribes," he said.

Many may yet suffer and perish, but when the time of their tribulation is past, when the Lord has rewarded unto them

---

[24] Wilford Woodruff, DWW, 120.
[25] Wilford Woodruff, JD, 15:282.

double for all the sins that were committed by their ancient fathers in their apostasy, and when he has visited them in judgment according to the prophecies that are contained in this Book of Mormon, and the times of the Gentiles who now occupy this land are fulfilled, then the Lord will make bare his arm, and he will redeem these remnants of Israel, that they may inherit the blessings promised to their ancient fathers.[26]

It would seem, though, that our nineteenth-century ancestors and forebears may have had too restricted a sense of where the flowering of the Lamanites would take place. They looked to the Iroquois and the Cheyenne and the Utes and the Apaches and the other Indian tribes of North America. But the dwelling places of the Lamanites are not limited to the territory north of the Rio Grande. Indeed, probably far more people of Lamanite descent live in Mexico and the lands southward than in the territory of today's United States of America. And, Church leaders have explained, many may live on the islands of the Pacific. "Those islanders and the natives of this country," said Brigham Young, speaking of the Polynesians and others, "are of the House of Israel—of the seed of Abraham, and to them pertain the promise; and every soul of them, sooner or later, will be saved in the Kingdom of God, or be destroyed root and branch."[27]

In fact, especially when viewed in the more geographically inclusive sense, the gathering of the Lamanites has not only begun, it is flourishing. "The Prophet Joseph Smith gave us the thought," remarked Spencer W. Kimball,

> that the Lord brought us out here from the East to bring the gospel to the Lamanites. One of the most important things that can possibly happen in this Dispensation of the Fulness of Times is to bring to the Lamanites a knowledge of God. He says: '. . . there will be tens of thousands of Latter-day Saints who will gather in the Rocky Mountains, and there they will open the door for establishing the gospel among the Lamanites, who will receive the Gospel and their endowments and the blessings of God.[28]

---

[26] Orson Pratt, JD, 16:353.
[27] Brigham Young, DBY, 437.
[28] Spencer W. Kimball, CR, October 1950, 65.

From its secure refuge in the Rocky Mountains, the Church and Kingdom of God has, in fact, expanded to include many hundreds of thousands of Lamanites in Mexico and in Central and South America. Many of that branch of covenant Israel now worship with their brothers and sisters of Ephraim, serving in stakes of the Church and working toward the redemption of their dead in the temples of the Lord. The prophets and apostles of the nineteenth century, whose efforts were so fully directed to the survival of the Kingdom in the face of brutal persecution that they had little to spare for the taking of the gospel to the lands southward, must be very pleased as they contemplate, from the heavens, the progress of the work that they did so much to begin. Elder Orson Pratt will serve well to represent the urgency with which they viewed this effort:

> Perhaps there is no subject that could be presented at the present time that is of so much importance and that has so great a bearing upon the human family, as the one set before us this forenoon. It is one on which the salvation of the Latter-day Saints depends. It is one, also, on which the salvation of the remnants of the tribe of Joseph upon this American continent depends. It is one that we must not only understand, or reason about, or think of, but one in which we must engage every faculty and power of our minds, if we would be blessed as a people. It is for this object, as has been plainly shown to you this forenoon, that the angels of God descended from the eternal world and spoke in the ears of mortal man. It is for this object that the heavens have been opened, and the everlasting Priesthood sent down and conferred upon chosen vessels. It is for this object—namely, the salvation and redemption of the poor, lost, degraded sons of the forest, that God has given the Urim and Thummim, and caused to be translated one of the most glorious sacred records, or histories that was ever introduced into the world by mortal man.[29]

THE GATHERING OF THE TEN LOST TRIBES

Latter-day Saints have also been taught by the prophets and apostles who lead them of yet another part of Israel that has been

---

[29] Orson Pratt, JD, 9:174–75.

taken away from its homeland but will return at some point in the future. "In the days of Peleg," explained President John Taylor,

> the Lord divided the earth, hence the eastern and western hemispheres, doubtless thinking by doing so he would have a better opportunity to preserve some of the human family from going down to perdition. But still the devil found ready access to the hearts of the people generally, and many became so corrupt that God had to destroy them. But before allowing his justice to overtake them, he saved unto himself certain good seed and planted it in different parts of his vineyard. He took away the ten tribes. We do not hear anything about them now, but we shall by and by.[30]

Joseph Fielding Smith also spoke of these absent descendents of Israel, candidly explaining that we know little about them but reminding us of what the scriptures teach concerning them. "The Ten Tribes were taken by force," he said,

> out of the land the Lord gave to them. Many of them mixed with the peoples among whom they were scattered. A large portion, however, departed in one body into the north and disappeared from the rest of the world. Where they went and where they are, we do not know. That they are intact we must believe, else how shall the scriptures be fulfilled? There are too many prophecies concerning them and their return in a body, for us to ignore this fact. . . . These lost tribes were in a body somewhere when the Savior visited the Nephites on this continent. We believe he went to them and established his Church among them with an organization similar to that given to the Nephites. They had their prophets and kept a record.[31]

While we know very little, to put it mildly, about the fate and whereabouts of the ten lost tribes after they were carried away from the defeated kingdom of Israel, tantalizing clues in the scriptures and in secular history suggest the outlines of a story. Unfortunately, this story is far beyond the scope of the present work. In his compendium

---

[30] John Taylor, JD, 18:331.
[31] Joseph Fielding Smith, WP, 130–31.

Mormon Doctrine, however, Elder Bruce R. McConkie quoted interesting information from the ancient apocryphal book of 2 Esdras that is consistent with the teachings of modern Church leaders:

> Those are the ten tribes, which were carried away prisoners out of their own land in the time of Osea the king, whom Salmanasar the king of Assyria led away captive, and he carried them over the waters, and so came they into another land. But they took this counsel among themselves, that they would leave the multitude of the heathen, and go forth into a further country, where never mankind dwelt, That they might there keep their statutes, which they never kept in their own land. And they entered into Euphrates by the narrow passage of the river. For the most High then shewed signs for them, and held still the flood, till they were passed over. For through that country there was a great way to go, namely, of a year and a half: and the same region is called Arsareth. Then dwelt they there until the latter times; and now when they shall begin to come, The Highest shall stay the stream again, that they may go through.[32]

Reflecting not the uncertainties of their past history and present location but the prophetic certainty of their future, President Wilford Woodruff offered a useful sketch of what will happen in connection with the ten tribes and how it will relate to the other works of gathering that will characterize the last days. "The Jews," he said,

> will be moved upon by and by, and they will return to the land of their fathers, and they will rebuild Jerusalem. These Lamanites here will receive the gospel of Christ in fulfillment of the revelations of God. The prophets which have been shut up in the north country with the nine and a half tribes led away by Shalmanezer, King of Assyria, thousands of years ago, will come in remembrance before God; they will smite the rocks and mountains of ice will flow down before them, and those long lost tribes will come forth in your day and mine, if we live a few years longer, and they will be crowned under the hands of the children of Ephraim—the elders of Israel who dwell in the land of Zion. And by and by the testimony of the

---

[32] 2 Esdras 13:40–47, as cited by Bruce R. McConkie, MD, 455–56.

gospel will be sealed among the Gentiles, and the gospel will turn to the whole house of Israel, and the judgments of God will back up the testimony of the elders of this Church, and the Lord will send messengers who will go forth and reap down the earth.[33]

EPHRAIM'S ROLE TOWARD THE TEN TRIBES

On an earlier occasion, President Woodruff spoke in similar terms about the subject:

Here are the ten tribes of Israel; we know nothing about them only what the Lord has said by his prophets. There are prophets among them, and by and by they will come along, and they will smite the rocks, and the mountains of ice will flow down at their presence, and a highway will be cast up before them, and they will come to Zion, receive their endowments, and be crowned under the hands of the children of Ephraim, and there are persons before me in this assembly today who will assist to give them their endowments. They will receive their blessings and endowments, from under the children of Ephraim, who are the first fruits of the kingdom of God in their dispensation, and the men will have to be ordained and receive their priesthood and endowments in the land of Zion, according to the revelations of God.[34]

Now, it seems apparent in this latter passage that President Woodruff, when he spoke those words, was overly optimistic about the timetable for the return of these lost Israelites. (It is probably significant that, in the passage immediately preceding it, which comes from very nearly two decades later, he regards it as only a possibility that those in the audience will participate in the restoration of the lost tribes.) The possibility cannot be ruled out, however, that some of those present in President Woodruff's audience will, in fact, be involved in the return of the ten tribes in a resurrected state. Whether or not he himself intended such a proposition, his statement, if inspired, could well have had a meaning that he did not suspect.

---

[33] Wilford Woodruff, DWW, 114.

[34] Wilford Woodruff, DWW, 119. The notion that the ten tribes will have to be ordained and receive their endowments at the hands of Ephraim seems to suggest that they do not, now, have the fulness of the gospel. Given their history, of course, that would be unsurprising.

Inspired foretellings not infrequently come to pass in a way that not even the person foretelling could have visualized.

But let us grant the possibility that this great prophet's hopes for an early consummation may have led him to an unrealistic expectation that was simply not in the Lord's will. We have had occasion before to comment on the fact that we mortals, with our brief lifespans and our consequent impatience, have often wanted to hurry the Lord and have frequently expected to see the prophecies of the last days wholly fulfilled during our own brief sojourns on earth. And perhaps there is no subject more suited to awaken such desires to hasten the process along than that of the lost tribes of Israel, precisely because we know so little about them. Nonetheless, and despite the paucity of our knowledge about the ten tribes—they have, after all, been deliberately and divinely hidden from us—there are things that we can know about them with considerable certainty because the testimony of modern prophets on these matters has been consistent and of long duration. For instance, in their great proclamation to the world following the martyrdom of Joseph Smith, the Quorum of the Twelve Apostles bore united and strong testimony to the eventual fulfillment of the ancient prophecies concerning the lost tribes. The Lord, they declared,

> **has said that the Ten Tribes of Israel should also be revealed in the North country, together with their oracles and records, preparatory to their return, and to their union with Judah, no more to be separated.—And we know it.**[35]

And today's latter-day seers and prophets know, as well, upon whom the responsibility will rest of bringing these separated brothers and sisters into a covenant relationship with the Lord. For as the words of Joseph Fielding Smith make clear, such a covenant relationship is made possible by, and only by, the restored gospel of Jesus Christ and is to be found in, and only in, The Church of Jesus Christ of Latter-day Saints:

> **It is Ephraim, today, who holds the Priesthood. It is with Ephraim that the Lord has made covenant and has revealed the**

---

[35] The Twelve Apostles, MFP, 1:263.

fulness of the everlasting Gospel. It is Ephraim who is building temples and performing the ordinances in them for both the living and the dead. When the "lost tribes" come—and it will be a most wonderful sight and a marvelous thing when they do come to Zion—in fulfillment of the promises made through Isaiah and Jeremiah, they will have to receive the crowning blessings from their brother Ephraim, the "first-born" in Israel.[36]

Once again, it will fall to those of us who, thus far, constitute the largest group within the Church to take the gospel to the remnants of scattered Israel. Once again, we see that acceptance of membership in the restored Church is not an invitation to rest among our blessings, but an opportunity to work and to serve. The Lord's power will bring all the events of the last days to pass as he sees fit, but Ephraim holds a central place among the human instruments that he will use to do so. We cannot know precisely when they will occur, and we do not know precisely how, but we must be prepared to play our assigned role.

---

[36] Joseph Fielding Smith, WP, 125.

CHAPTER 15

THE JEWS

"The Jews," remarked Wilford Woodruff, "have been a hiss and a bye-word among the Gentiles since the death of the Savior, eighteen hundred years ago." Nevertheless, he continued, "Their redemption is at the door today; it has been proclaimed by inspired men to their own tribe. It is left on record that the Jews will return home, that Jerusalem will be rebuilt; their temple will be established, and all those great and mighty promises given by inspiration and revelation will come to pass."[1]

In so saying, Wilford Woodruff was simply restating what has been the doctrine of The Church of Jesus Christ of Latter-day Saints from its inception. "Judah must return," the Prophet Joseph Smith taught.

> Jerusalem must be rebuilt, and the temple, and water come out from under the temple, and the waters of the Dead Sea be healed. It will take some time to rebuild the walls of the city and the temple, etc.; and all this must be done before the Son of Man will make His appearance.[2]

It would also, ancient and modern prophets have taught, require the people of Judah to endure almost indescribable suffering. And few prophecies have been so obviously (and painfully) fulfilled. Still, the Lord has not forgotten this important group of his ancient covenant people. As President Woodruff explained,

> The Jews will fulfill and realize all that has been said respecting them and all that has been promised and predicted upon their heads by their father Jacob and by the prophets. It was foretold by the prophet Moses that they should be driven and despised by their enemies, and that they should be cursed of God, and that his curse should follow them until Christ came; and that they would reject him, and then they would be scattered as corn is sifted in a sieve, etc. But hear it all Israel, after your sorrow and pain and distress and after the days of your tribulation,

---

[1] Wilford Woodruff, CD, 2:202.
[2] Joseph Smith Jr., HC, 5:337.

your great Elohim will stretch out his hand and gather you from every nation wherever you are driven, and he will bring you home to your own land, and you shall rebuild your temple and city, and you shall be delivered by Shiloh when he comes.[3]

Other prophetic statements indicate that it would be a mistake, even after the pogroms of eastern Europe and the Holocaust and the other horrific events that Judah has passed through, to imagine that their testing is fully at an end. "The Jews will have to perform quite a role in these last times," wrote John Taylor.

They also will have to endure a large amount of trials, persecutions and difficulties which have yet to come upon them. They will in due time be gathered together to their own lands as we are gathered here; and nations will go up against them, and then too will certain nations come against us.[4]

There remain, still, difficult passages ahead for Judah.

THE MISSION OF ORSON HYDE

As we have noted, Latter-day Saint concern with the people of Judah goes back to the very opening of this dispensation. When Moroni visited the young prophet Joseph Smith, part of his message involved the citation of Joel 2:28–32, a passage that clearly refers to the redemption of the Jews in their ancient Palestinian home. "He . . . said," Joseph later recalled, "that this was not yet fulfilled, but was soon to be. And he further stated that the fulness of the Gentiles was soon to come in."[5]

Mormon interest in the gathering of the Jews was not altogether unusual in the nineteenth century, nor is it completely unparalleled today. After all, other Christians also have the biblical prophecies, and these are rather clear. But Latter-day Saint commitment to the restoration and redemption of Judah is perhaps unusual among Christians for its intensity, and quite unique for the basis on which it rests. "Historically," observed Ezra Taft Benson,

we must recognize that interest in the restoration of the Jews to their homeland is older than modern Zionism and the great

---

[3] Wilford Woodruff, JD, 21:300–1.
[4] John Taylor, GK, 349.
[5] Joseph Smith—History 1:41.

work of Theodor Herzl and others. There were a number of Christian sects in the nineteenth century that held millennial views and saw the return of the Jews to their homeland as a "sign of the times" that would precede the second advent of Jesus Christ. The Mormon interest was and is more than this. Our concern and interest are a kinship to our Jewish brothers.[6]

The words of modern prophets remind us that Latter-day Saint feelings of kinship with the Jews, rooted in the conviction that the Saints, too, by either birth or adoption, are of Israel, have been strengthened since the beginnings of the Restoration by their own history and experiences. "There is a great affinity for the Jews by the Mormons," observed Ezra Taft Benson.

> The Jews have endured great persecution and suffering. This we understand, for our people have also undergone severe persecution and extermination. Indeed, the man we revere as a modern prophet, Joseph Smith, was martyred for his testimony in 1844. In 1846 our people had to leave the United States in exodus because of the threat of annihilation. We settled in a desert region similar to the topography around the Dead Sea and the Sea of Galilee. There we developed our "land of promise." Yes, we can empathize with the suffering of the Jews, for we have co-suffered with them. But our affinity toward modern Judah is not prompted out of mutual suffering; it is prompted out of a knowledge of our peculiar heritage. Jeremiah has prophesied that in the latter times, "the house of Judah shall walk with the house of Israel, and they shall come together" (Jeremiah 3:18).[7]

At its base, the Latter-day Saints' sense of kinship with Judah rests upon a shared biblical heritage. Again, Ezra Taft Benson, who had a deep and abiding interest in the subject, summarizes the state of the matter well and draws from it advice for both members of the Church and the descendants of Judah:

> We need to know more about the Jews, and the Jews ought to know more about the Mormons. When we understand one another, perhaps we will understand why David Ben-Gurion

6 Ezra Taft Benson, TETB, 91–92.
7 Ezra Taft Benson, TETB, 94.

said to me on one of my visits to Tel Aviv, "There are no people in the world who understand the Jews like the Mormons." Among the kindred doctrines of the Mormons and the Jews is our mutual belief in Jehovah, a God of revelation. We share a common belief in prophets. We hold a common commitment to the return of the Jews to the "land of Jerusalem," in fulfillment of the words of the ancient prophets. There are many other doctrinal and social similarities.[8]

And, in fact, Latter-day Saints have closely watched and, to a certain extent, have sought to participate in the destiny of Judah in the last days. Under divine direction given to their prophets, they have not been content to wait passively for God to unfold his purposes, but have actively prayed and worked for the return of the Jews to the ancient land of the Bible. They have a remarkable record, only a small part of which can be discussed here, of direct involvement in the gathering of Judah to Palestine. Ezra Taft Benson recalled the beginnings of this involvement:

> Before the Prophet was killed, he dispatched an Apostle by the name of Orson Hyde to dedicate the land of Palestine for the return of the Jews. This concern for a homeless people and the sending of this Apostle were done at a time when the Mormons themselves were virtually homeless, having been dispossessed of their lands and possessions in Missouri. Orson Hyde left on his assignment in the fall of 1840 and arrived in Palestine in October 1841.[9]

Upon his entry into Jerusalem, Elder Hyde carried out the mission that he had been assigned. He climbed to the top of the Mount of Olives, overlooking the Temple Mount and the Old City, and offered a magnificent prayer, dedicating the land for the return of the Jews. One important paragraph of the prayer reads as follows:

> Thou, O Lord, did once move upon the heart of Cyrus to show favor unto Jerusalem and her children. Do Thou now also be pleased to inspire the hearts of kings and the powers of the earth to look with a friendly eye towards this place, and

---

8 Ezra Taft Benson, TETB, 97–98.
9 Ezra Taft Benson, TETB, 95.

with a desire to see Thy righteous purposes executed in relation thereto. Let them know that it is Thy good pleasure to
restore the kingdom unto Israel—raise up Jerusalem as its
capital, and constitute her people a distinct nation and government, with David Thy servant, even a descendant from the
loins of ancient David to be their king.[10]

SUBSEQUENT DEVELOPMENTS IN PALESTINE

Even during their own time of exodus and gathering to the Great
Basin of the American West, the prophets and apostles of this last dispensation did not forget Judah. In the great declaration of the Twelve
Apostles to the world, the leaders of the Church after the assassination of Joseph Smith spoke forthrightly and with authority of what
was to take place. "We . . . testify," they wrote,

> that the Jews among all nations are hereby commanded, in the
> name of the Messiah, to prepare, to return to Jerusalem in
> Palestine; and to rebuild that city and temple unto the Lord:
> And also to organize and establish their own political govern-
> ment, under their own rulers, judges, and governors in that
> country. For be it known unto them that we now hold the
> keys of the priesthood and kingdom which is soon to be
> restored unto them. Therefore let them also repent and pre-
> pare to obey the ordinances of God.[11]

Once securely and solidly established in the West, the leaders of
the Church again turned their attention to Palestine and the decreed
destiny of the Jews. Among others, they dispatched George A. Smith
of the First Presidency, Lorenzo Snow of the Quorum of the Twelve
Apostles, and Eliza R. Snow, the president of the Relief Society, to
travel to Jerusalem and rededicate Palestine. In modern times, Ezra
Taft Benson recalled the story for a Latter-day Saint audience:

> The land was again dedicated by President George A. Smith
> in 1873. And so, we have been looking forward as Latter-day
> Saints for a hundred years, confidently expecting that in the
> Lord's own due time these prophecies made in the dedicatory

---

[10] Orson Hyde, HC, 4:457.
[11] The Twelve Apostles, MFP, 1:254–55.

prayers as well as in the scriptures would be fulfilled; and the promises made that this land would again become a fruitful land, that the sterility would be removed and the springs of living water would burst forth; that these too would be fulfilled. We knew that kings of the earth would be inspired to look with a friendly eye, as Brother Hyde prayed on that visit to the Holy Land, that the powers of the earth would look with a friendly eye upon the gathering of Judah.[12]

Have these prayers, offered up by modern prophets and apostles, had any effect? Manifestly, yes. Speaking of President Smith's visit to Jerusalem, Ezra Taft Benson continued the story:

It was shortly after this dedication that the first organization sprang up, dedicated to the promotion of the return of the Jews to Palestine. And about this time also President Wilford Woodruff made his remarkable prophecy and statement regarding Judah when he said: "The Lord has decreed that the Jews should be gathered from all the Gentile nations where they have been driven, into their own land . . . and this is the will of your great Elohim, O house of Judah, and whenever you shall be called upon to perform this work, the God of Israel will help you. You have a great future and destiny before you and you cannot avoid fulfilling it; you are the royal chosen seed, and the God of your father's house has kept you distinct as a nation for eighteen hundred years, under all the oppression of the whole Gentile world. You may not wait until you believe on Jesus of Nazareth but when you meet with Shiloh your king, you will know him; your destiny is marked out, you cannot avoid it."[13]

As the ancient prophecies indicated would happen, and as the supplication of Orson Hyde asked, the nations of the earth joined together in enabling representatives of scattered Judah to return to the land about Jerusalem. James E. Talmage indicated that

in the work of gathering, the Gentiles are destined to take a great and honorable part, as witness the . . . words of Nephi: "But behold, thus saith the Lord God: When the day cometh that

---

[12] Ezra Taft Benson, TETB, 95–96.
[13] Ezra Taft Benson, TETB, 96.

they shall believe in me, that I am Christ, then have I covenanted with their fathers that they shall be restored in the flesh, upon
the earth, unto the lands of their inheritance. And it shall come
to pass that they shall be gathered in from their long dispersion,
from the isles of the sea, and from the four parts of the earth;
and the nations of the Gentiles shall be great in the eyes of me,
saith God, carrying them forth to the land of their inheritance.
Yea, the kings of the Gentiles shall be nursing fathers unto them,
and their queens shall become nursing mothers; wherefore, the
promises of the Lord are great unto the Gentiles, for he hath
spoken it, and who can dispute?" (2 Nephi 10:7-9.)[14]

Ezra Taft Benson, from a somewhat later vantage point, could see
that what the prophets had predicted was being fulfilled:

Elder Orson Hyde dedicated the land of Palestine for the return
of the Jews and made great promises concerning their going
there. The British nation is playing a great part in making these
promises come true. General Allenby of the British forces,
helped open that land for the return of the Jews in 1918. We
know that the leaders of the nations do not fully realize why
they are doing this, but we as Latter-day Saints know. It has
been one of the missions that this great nation has had—the
bringing about of the return of the Jews to Palestine in fulfillment of the Bible prophecies that are very clearly made concerning this event. We know they will gather there. They will
become a strong nation. They will have their wars with outside
nations. They will have their prophets (Revelation 11).[15]

THE ZIONIST MOVEMENT

The gathering of the Jews to Palestine, which commenced in the
nineteenth century, picked up speed in the early twentieth century
and surged to a flood following Hitler's rise to power in Germany. Yet
this gathering was not, by and large, a gathering of religiously obser-
vant people, let alone a movement of converts to Christianity. This
was what the apostles and prophets of this dispensation expected. As
Orson Pratt put it,

---

[14] James E. Talmage, AF, 18:334–35.
[15] Ezra Taft Benson, TETB, 99.

The Jews dispersed among the Gentiles will not come and sing in the height of Zion, or but very few of them, they will go to Jerusalem. Some of them will believe in the true Messiah, and thousands of the more righteous, whose fathers did not consent to the shedding of the blood of the Son of God, will receive the Gospel before they gather from among the nations. Many of them, however, will not receive the Gospel, but seeing that other[s] are going to Jerusalem they will go also; and when they get back to Palestine, to the place where their ancient Jerusalem stood, and see a certain portion of the believing Jews endeavoring to fulfill and carry out the prophecies, they also will take hold and assist in the same work.[16]

Brigham Young knew that "Jerusalem is not to be redeemed by our going there and preaching to the inhabitants. It will be redeemed by the high hand of the Almighty. It will be given into the possession of the ancient Israelites by the power of God, and by the pouring out of his judgments."[17] And so it has been. "One of the living miracles of the ages," Bruce R. McConkie rightly said,

is the preservation of the Jewish people as a distinct race and the restless anxiety in the hearts of so many of them to return to the land of their fathers. This modern movement to resettle the house of Judah in Palestine is called Zionism. It gains impetus from the many Old Testament prophecies which tell of the latter-day return of Judah to their homeland.[18]

The establishment of the modern state of Israel is one of the most remarkable events in human history. Whereas the far greater empires that oppressed them and repeatedly dispersed them, empires such as Babylonia and Rome, have vanished, leaving behind only ruins and dead languages, representatives of the people of Judah have returned to the ancient land from which they were carried away nearly two thousand years ago. They have resurrected their ancient language, and have begun to plant anew the hillsides that repeated sieges had left barren. They enjoy a political independence that they had lost, seemingly forever, in the early second-century revolt of Simeon bar Kokhba

---

[16] Orson Pratt, JD, 18:64.
[17] Brigham Young, DBY, 121.
[18] Bruce R. McConkie, MD, 855.

against Rome, when the city of Jerusalem was obliterated, then rebuilt with a new and pagan Latin name and declared off limits to Jews. We should not permit the work-a-day reality of Israel, and its daily presence in the newspaper headlines, to dull the astonishment that that nation's rebirth should awaken in us. It is dramatic evidence of the power of God and the truth of the ancient prophecies.

THE CONVERSION OF THE JEWS

But much remains to be done before the story of Judah is complete. They must still, someday, accept the gospel of Jesus Christ. The leaders of The Church of Jesus Christ of Latter-day Saints have always taught that the time of their conversion would come, but that it would come late in the events of the last days. And they knew that control of the schedule was not in their hands, but in God's. "Jerusalem," said Brigham Young,

> is not to be redeemed by the soft, still voice of the preacher of the Gospel of peace. Why? Because they were once the blessed of the Lord, the chosen of the Lord, the promised seed. They were the people from among whom should spring the Messiah; and salvation could be found only through that people. The Messiah came through them, and they killed him; and they will be the last of all the seed of Abraham to have the privilege of receiving the New and Everlasting Covenant. You may hand out to them gold, you may feed and clothe them, but it is impossible to convert the Jews, until the Lord God Almighty does it.[19]

Wilford Woodruff agreed. Great missionary though he was, his extensive travels and his study of the scriptures had taught him that it was not yet the time to take the gospel to the Jews.

> Here is Judah, which is the tribe of Israel from whom Jesus sprang; how many times have I seen them among the nations of the earth, standing in their synagogues, even gray-haired rabbis, with their faces to the east, calling on the great Elohim to open the door for them to go back to Jerusalem, the land of their fathers, and to send their Shiloh, their king of deliverance. When I have seen this my soul has been filled with a

---

[19] Brigham Young, DBY, 121.

desire to proclaim unto them the word of God unto eternal life, but I knew I could not do this, the time had not come, I could not preach to them. I might have stood in their midst for a month and preached unto them Jesus Christ or their Shiloh and king, but I should have failed to establish one particle of faith in their minds that he was the true Messiah.[20]

With a trace of (perhaps pardonable) exaggeration—for some descendants of Judah have, in fact, embraced the gospel—Wilford Woodruff insisted that, so long as the proper time has not come,

> you cannot convert a Jew, you may as well try to convert this house of solid walls as to convert them into the faith of Christ. They are set in their feelings, and they will be until the time of their redemption. They are looking forward to the time when they will go home and rebuild Jerusalem. They have looked for it many hundreds of years. They are looking for the coming of their king. They do not suppose for a moment that he has already come, but they are looking for him to come as the Lion of the tribe of Judah, not as a lamb led to the slaughter and as a sheep that is dumb before his shearers; they are looking for him to come with power and great glory.[21]

"You have not heard of our trying to convert the Jews," Orson Pratt reminded his hearers.

> Why? Because God has decreed and determined that he will fulfill the times of the Gentiles first, in accordance with ancient prophecy. When that time arrives, the Lord will have prepared some of the Jewish nation to receive the Gospel, and then they will gather to their own land, and rebuild their city upon its former site.[22]

Modern scripture likewise clearly teaches that unbelieving Jews will be upon the land of Palestine when the Lord returns.

> And then shall the Lord set his foot upon this mount, and it shall cleave in twain . . . And then shall the Jews look upon me

[20] Wilford Woodruff, DWW, 116–17.
[21] Wilford Woodruff, DWW, 117.
[22] Orson Pratt, JD, 18:225.

and say: What are these wounds in thine hands and in thy feet? Then shall they know that I am the Lord; for I will say unto them: These wounds are the wounds with which I was wounded in the house of my friends. I am he who was lifted up. I am Jesus that was crucified. I am the Son of God. And then shall they weep because of their iniquities; then shall they lament because they persecuted their king.[23]

SPIRITUAL CONVERSION BEFORE PHYSICAL GATHERING

It can be argued, in fact, that Judah will not truly be gathered, whatever its geographical whereabouts, until the people of Judah have accepted the Savior, Jesus Christ, and the fulness of his gospel. "It is," observed James E. Talmage, "evident . . . that the time of the full recovery or redemption of the Jews is to be determined by their acceptance of Christ as their Lord. When that time comes, they are to be gathered to the land of their fathers."[24] Bruce R. McConkie shed a great deal of light on this question when he explained that "the gathering of Israel consists of joining the true Church, of coming to a knowledge of the true God and of his saving truths, and of worshiping him in the congregations of the Saints in all nations and among all peoples."[25] Consistent with this understanding, the Book of Mormon, too, seems to indicate that the true gathering of the Jews will commence only after, and not before, they have received the gospel. Consider, for example, the following passages:

> And after they have hardened their hearts and stiffened their necks against the Holy One of Israel, behold, the judgments of the Holy One of Israel shall come upon them. And the day cometh that they shall be smitten and afflicted. Wherefore . . . they shall be scattered, and smitten, and hated; nevertheless, the Lord will be merciful unto them, that when they shall come to the knowledge of their Redeemer, they shall be gathered together again to the lands of their inheritance.[26]

---

[23] Doctrine and Covenants 45:48, 51–53.
[24] James E. Talmage, AF, 18:334–35.
[25] Bruce R. McConkie, in *Official Report of the First Mexico and Central America Area General Conference* (Salt Lake City: The Church of Jesus Christ of Latter-day Saints, 1973), 45.
[26] 2 Nephi 6:10–11.

When the day cometh that they shall believe in me, that I am Christ, then have I covenanted with their fathers that they shall be restored in the flesh, upon the earth, unto the lands of their inheritance.[27]

And I will remember the covenant which I have made with my people; and I have covenanted with them that I would gather them together in mine own due time, that I would give unto them again the land of their fathers for their inheritance, which is the land of Jerusalem, which is the promised land unto them forever, saith the Father. And it shall come to pass that the time cometh, when the fulness of my gospel shall be preached unto them; and they shall believe in me, that I am Jesus Christ, the Son of God, and shall pray unto the Father in my name . . . Then will the Father gather them together again, and give unto them Jerusalem for the land of their inheritance.[28]

Thus, although it does not appear to meet the full requirements for "gathering" to Israel, the amazing return of the Jews to Palestine may perhaps be a kind of preparatory gathering, designed to play a part in their eventual acceptance of Jesus Christ. As it so frequently does, the Book of Mormon sketches the future of Judah in Palestine with notable clarity:

Wherefore, he will bring them again out of captivity, and they shall be gathered together to the lands of their inheritance; and they shall be brought out of obscurity and out of darkness; and they shall know that the Lord is their Savior and their Redeemer, the Mighty One of Israel.[29]

And the prophets' teachings leave no room to doubt that the process of gathering Judah to its ancient home is underway at this very moment, leading to the time when Judah will, in large numbers, return to its rightful place in covenant Israel.

Yes, my brethren and sisters, this great drama goes on before our very eyes, in large measure unnoticed by the

---

[27] 2 Nephi 10:7.
[28] 3 Nephi 20:29–31, 33.
[29] 1 Nephi 22:12.

Christian world. One hardly ever hears reference to the prophecies regarding Judah's return. Yet, the promises are clear that it would be one of the great events of the last days. And, of course, we know from modern revelations and prophecies that much more is yet to occur. Read the fourteenth chapter of Zechariah and the eleventh chapter of Revelations with reference to other great events that are yet to come, affecting directly this chosen people, the House of Judah. Eventually their city will be encompassed by Gentile armies. Yes, during their last great struggle, the Master will make his appearance as the Mount of Olives cleaves in twain for their protection.[30]

THE GREAT FUTURE BATTLE

Modern and ancient prophets have made it clear that, even after the Jews have gathered to Palestine, their trials will not be completely behind them. As Orson Pratt explained it,

> When tens of thousands of them have gathered and rebuilt their Temple, and re-established Jerusalem upon its own heap, the Lord will send forth amongst them a tremendous scourge. What will be the nature of that scourge? The nations that live in the regions round about Jerusalem will gather up like a cloud, and cover all that land round about Jerusalem. They will come into the Valley of Jehoshaphat, east of Jerusalem, and they will lay siege to the city. What then? The Lord will raise up two great Prophets, they are called witnesses, in the Revelations of St. John. Will they have much power? Yes, during the days of their prophesying they will have power to smite those who undertake to destroy them, and until their testimonies are fulfilled they will be able to keep at bay all those nations besieging Jerusalem, so that they will not have power to take that city. How long will that be? Three and a half years, so says John the Revelator. If any man hurt them, they shall have power to bring upon that man, nation or army, the various plagues that are there written. They will have power to smite the earth with plague and famine, and to turn the rivers of water into blood.[31]

---

[30] Ezra Taft Benson, CR, April 1950, 78–79.
[31] Orson Pratt, JD, 18:65.

Bruce R. McConkie read the scriptures in the same way. "There are to be," he explained,

> "two witnesses, . . . two prophets that are to be raised up to the Jewish nation in the last days, at the time of the restoration." They are "to prophesy to the Jews after they are gathered and have built the city of Jerusalem in the land of their fathers." (D&C 77:15.) "And I will give power unto my two witnesses," the Lord says, "and they shall prophesy a thousand two hundred and threescore days, clothed in sackcloth." (Revelation 11:3.)[32]

Even here, though, it would seem that the active involvement with Judah of the modern prophets and apostles of The Church of Jesus Christ of Latter-day Saints may well continue—and in a spectacular way. And their mission, though ultimately crowned with triumphant success, will be a difficult and painful one. Orson Pratt laid out the story to come:

> And when they have fulfilled their prophecy, then the nations that have been lying before Jerusalem so long, waiting for an opportunity to destroy the city, will succeed in killing these two Prophets, and their bodies, says John's revelations, will lie in the streets of Jerusalem three days and a half after they are killed. What rejoicing there will be over the death of these men! Those who have been waiting so long and anxiously for this to take place, will no doubt send gifts one to another, and if the telegraph wires are not destroyed, they will telegraph to the uttermost parts of the earth that they have succeeded in killing the two men who had so long tormented them with plagues, turning the waters into blood, etc. But by and by, right in the midst of their rejoicing, when they think the Jews will now certainly fall a prey to them, behold there is a great earthquake, and in the midst of it these two Prophets rise from the dead, and they hear a voice up in the heavens saying— "Come up hither;" and they immediately ascend in the sight of their enemies.[33]

---

32 Bruce R. McConkie, MD, 733.
33 Orson Pratt, JD, 18:65.

CHRIST'S COMING TO THE JEWS

Even so, the story is not over. Elder Pratt continued, asking,

What next? Notwithstanding all this, those nations will be so infatuated, and so determined to persecute the people of God—as much as Pharaoh and his army in ancient days—that they will say—"Come, now is the time to pitch into the Jews and destroy them." And they will commence their work of destruction, and they will succeed so far as to take one half the city, and while they are in the very act of destroying Jerusalem, behold the heavens are rent, and the Son of God with all the heavenly hosts appears, and he descends and rests upon the summit of Mount Olives, which is before Jerusalem on the east. And so great will be the power of God that will then be made manifest, that the mountain will divide asunder, half going towards the south, and half towards the north, producing a great valley going east and west, from the walls of Jerusalem eastward.[34]

This astonishing event will put an end not merely to the war against Judah, but to the unbelief of the Jews and, effectively, to the world's longstanding rebellion against its rightful ruler. Looking to that future time, the Quorum of the Twelve Apostles under the leadership of Brigham Young announced:

In that day the Lord will pour upon the inhabitants of Jerusalem the spirit of grace and supplication, and they shall look upon the Messiah whom they have pierced. For lo! he will descend from heaven, as the defender of the Jews, and to complete their victory. His feet will stand in that day upon the Mount of Olives, which shall cleave in sunder at his presence, and remove one half to the north, and the other to the south; thus forming a great valley where the mountain now stands. The earth will quake around him, while storm and tempest, hail and plague, are mingled with the clash of arms, the roar of artillery, the shouts of victory, and the groans of the wounded and dying. In that day all who are in the siege, both against Judea and against Jerusalem, shall be cut in pieces; though all the people of the earth should be gathered together against it.[35]

---

[34] Orson Pratt, JD, 18:65.
[35] The Twelve Apostles, MFP, 1:258.

What will be the effect? It will be incalculable. Again, the proclamation of the Twelve speaks eloquently of a future world order that will be vastly different from the one under which we now live and which will be inaugurated by the Savior's appearance on the east side of Jerusalem:

> This signal victory on the part of the Jews, so unlooked for by the nations, and attended with the personal advent of Messiah, and the accompanying events, will change the whole order of things in Europe and Asia, in regard to political and religious organization, and government. The Jews as a nation become holy from that day forward; and their city and sanctuary becomes holy. There also the Messiah establishes his throne, and seat of government. Jerusalem then becomes the seat of empire, and the great centre and capital of the old world.[36]

---

[36] The Twelve Apostles, MFP, 1:258.

CHAPTER 16

THE LAMANITES

We also bear testimony that the "Indians" (so called) of North and South America are a remnant of the tribes of Israel; as is now made manifest by the discovery and revelation of their ancient oracles and records. And that they are about to be fathered, civilized, and made one nation in this glorious land. They will also come to the knowledge of their forefathers, and of the fulness of the gospel; and they will embrace it, and become a righteous branch of the house of Israel.[1]

So spoke the Council of the Twelve Apostles in their proclamation to the world only a short time after the martyrdom of their great leader, the Prophet Joseph Smith. In doing so, they sounded one of the most prominent themes of the Restoration, a theme virtually unique to those who accept the divine authenticity of the Book of Mormon. "The Book of Mormon," said Joseph Smith, "has made known who Israel is, upon this continent. And while we behold the government of the United States gathering the Indians, and locating them upon lands to be their own, how sweet it is to think that they may one day be gathered by the Gospel!"[2]

THE LOWLY CONDITION OF THE LAMANITES

From the beginning, Latter-day Saint theologians have expressed unusual concern for the Indian populations of the New World, a concern that grows out of the information that they have been given in the Book of Mormon about some of the ancestors of the Indians. That history, as readers of the ancient record know, is deeply tragic. As Spencer W. Kimball remarked, "Only the most brazen soul could fail to weep when contemplating the fall of this people, and yet it was the decree of the Lord that the Lamanites should be preserved in the land, that this remnant of Joseph should again come into their promised inheritance."[3]

---

[1] The Twelve Apostles, MFP, 1:254.
[2] Joseph Smith Jr., TPJS, 93.
[3] Spencer W. Kimball, TSWK, 595.

But the Book of Mormon also informs the Indians of the Americas—and notice that they include the people of North, Central, and South America, a fact that those of us who live in the United States occasionally forget—of the promises made to some of their ancestors and, thus, exalts them to a high and important place in the providence of God. Elder Delbert L. Stapley of the Council of the Twelve had this in mind in April conference of 1956. "In a sense," he said,

> I do not feel sorry for the Indian people because they are children of promise, belonging as they do to the house of Israel and are the posterity of Abraham, the father of the faithful, through whose lineage the Lord promised that all nations of the earth are to be blessed; therefore, they are a chosen race and people unto God, possessing a divine and royal heritage. However, I do feel sorry about the lack of privileges, denial of citizenship rights, and insufficient opportunities for schooling and culture which continue to shroud them in darkness and despair. There are too many of them in our modern day, living under most primitive conditions and circumstances which destroy faith, initiative, ambition, and confidence. That it required hundreds of years for the Indians to reach their low state of degeneracy does not allow the Church or the nation unlimited time to return them to the high civilization and spiritual activation they once enjoyed nor the opportunities and blessings of our present enlightened era of scientific knowledge, productive achievement and culture.[4]

THE SAINTS' RESPONSIBILITY TOWARD THE LAMANITES

Modern prophets and apostles have consistently taught that we, the predominantly Ephraimite members of The Church of Jesus Christ of Latter-day Saints, have a duty not only to bring the gospel to our Lamanite brothers and sisters but also to help them overcome the temporal disadvantages that the transgressions of their ancient ancestors and the oppressions of the Gentiles have brought upon them. As the Twelve Apostles declared in their 1845 proclamation to the world,

[4] Delbert L. Stapley, CR, April 1956, 56.

The sons and daughters of Zion will soon be required to devote a portion of their time in instructing the children of the forest. For they must be educated, and instructed in all the arts of civil life, as well as in the gospel. They must be clothed, fed, and instructed in the principles and practice of virtue, modesty, temperance, cleanliness, industry, mechanical arts, manners, customs, dress, music, and all other things which are calculated in their nature to refine, purify, exalt and glorify them, as the sons and daughters of the royal house of Israel, and of Joseph; who are making ready for the coming of the bridegroom.[5]

Successive presidents and apostles of the Church have continued to emphasize our responsibility in this regard. For example, the First Presidency under Brigham Young advised the early Utah Saints to

be merciful, therefore, and be patient to the poor, degraded, and ignorant children of the mountains and the plains. They are the seed of Abraham, unto whom pertain the promises; seek to enlighten and bring them back unto a knowledge of the Lord God of their fathers; remember that He is their God to-day, as well as anciently, and that He witnesses, with equal interest, the movements of the children of Israel, as when He gave them instructions from Sinai's consecrated mount, the Temple of Solomon, or Calvary's blood-stained soil.[6]

"Brigham Young seemed to catch the vision of it," observed Spencer W. Kimball.

He said that the Lord could not have devised a better plan than to put us where we are in order to accomplish that very thing of educating and teaching the Lamanites. Our ancestors came a thousand miles across the desert, under terrific persecutions and hardships, to locate where the Gentiles had scattered the Lamanites. They had pretty well "reservationed" them here in the western states. They were in our every county, and the Lord brought us out here that we might teach them the gospel.[7]

---

5 The Twelve Apostles, MFP, 1:256.
6 Brigham Young, Heber C. Kimball, Jedediah M. Grant, MFP, 2:178.
7 Spencer W. Kimball, CR, October 1950, 66.

In a joint statement, President Young and his counselor, Heber C. Kimball, advised the priesthood of the Church on the manner in which they should interact with the surviving descendants of the ancient Book of Mormon peoples. "Remember, brethren," they counseled,

> that they are the remnants of Israel, and although they may apparently continue for a time to waste away and sink deeper and deeper into the depths of sin, misery, and woe, that unto them pertain the promises made to faithful Abraham, and they will be fulfilled. Be diligent, therefore, to do them good, and seek in all of your intercourse with them to bring them back to a knowledge of the Lord God of their fathers. Preserve yourselves from their savage ferocity; never condescend to their level, but always seek to elevate them to a higher, purer, and consequently, a more useful and intelligent existence.[8]

The great nineteenth-century apostle Orson Pratt felt strongly and spoke repeatedly and passionately about the duty of the Saints toward the Lamanites. Indeed, he was critical of his fellow members of the Church for what he viewed as their neglect of that duty. "It almost seems sometimes," he lamented,

> that the people are determined to take their rest and be at ease before their great labour is accomplished or their day of rest comes. They build houses, they plant vineyards, they sow their fields, they gather together large flocks and herds, they multiply their goods and substance, they surround themselves with the comforts and luxuries of this life, and say to themselves, "We will enjoy ourselves and be at ease in Zion; we will remain upon our farms and in our fine houses; we will engage in our merchandize and in various occupations; we will let the Lamanites take care of themselves, and we will let the purposes of the Almighty roll round without our help." And after all these things, they will pray every day that the Lord will roll round events, accomplish his purposes, and fulfill the covenants made with the house of Israel, and yet not lift one solitary finger to facilitate the answer to their prayers.[9]

---

[8] Brigham Young, Heber C. Kimball, MFP, 2:205.
[9] Orson Pratt, JD, 9:176.

Shall we, therefore, dwell at ease upon our farms and in our habitations, and suffer these sons of the forest to remain in eternal ignorance of the great truths that we are in possession of? If so, woe be unto this people, or any other people that are intrusted with the sacred things committed to our charge, and who do not use them according to the mind and will of God; for it is his mind that they should be used for the redemption of those that are unacquainted with these principles by which alone salvation can be obtained.[10]

A COMMON BROTHERHOOD AS ISRAELITES

Others among the prophets and apostles called by God to lead his Church in the latter days have spoken similarly. In particular, they have cautioned those of European extraction, mostly Ephraimites, against the serious and crippling sin of what we nowadays call "racism"—a sin that disregards the image of God present in every one of the Father's children, and that interferes with our assigned task of taking the gospel to all peoples. Spencer W. Kimball, for instance, reminded his audience of the humble status of their own ancestors before the Lord:

Truly our paths have met once more—we, a mixed remnant of Israel, principally Ephraim, even referred to as Gentiles, now come forth out of captivity (see, e.g., 1 Nephi 13:19, 39), a people with a long history of apostasy and darkness and persecution, now only through the grace of Almighty God restored to the blessings of the gospel, that we in turn might be a blessing to the nations of the earth; and the Lamanites, also a people of disobedience now returned to the fold, whose sufferings have been sore, and punishment severe, and humiliation complete, whose affliction these many centuries must certainly be fruit meet for repentance. And what should be the nature of our reunion? We are relatives. We are brothers and sisters under the skin. We should receive each other with great joy.[11]

President George Albert Smith likewise insisted that feelings of racial superiority not enter in among the Latter-day Saints to justify their slothfulness in attending to their mission to the Lamanites. "These Indians in the western world," he explained,

---

[10] Orson Pratt, JD, 9:176–77.
[11] Spencer W. Kimball, TSWK, 596.

are the descendants of Father Lehi who left Jerusalem, centuries ago at the direction of our Heavenly Father. They are
His children, and I hope that there will be no member of the
Church, in any department, who will feel that because it is the
Indians, they are not important. They are just as important as
are the whites. They are entitled to the priesthood if they live
to be worthy of it, and our Heavenly Father is anxious that
they should have that blessing.[12]

THE SAINTS INDEBTED TO LEHI'S DESCENDANTS

Indeed, Orson Pratt reminded his Ephraimite listeners that they
owed a deep debt of gratitude to the peoples of the Book of
Mormon—a debt that should be, and can only be, repaid to their
modern descendants. If anybody in this relationship is entitled to
feelings of ethnic pride, he almost seemed to say, it is not the Saints
who have entered the Church from among the nations of the
Gentiles. Speaking of the Lamanites, he declared:

> It is a great privilege indeed (and we are indebted to their
> fathers for it,) that we enjoy being associated with them in the
> accomplishment of so great a work. It is to their fathers and
> to God that we are indebted for the enjoyment of such great
> blessings in fulfillment of the prophecies. Their ancient
> Prophets among their ancestry looked with interest upon
> their children, and they interceded day and night for their
> redemption. In answer to their prayers, an angel has flown
> through the midst of heaven to preach the everlasting Gospel
> to the nations; and it is therefore to them that we are indebt-
> ed for many of the privileges that we now enjoy. If we are thus
> indebted as a people, woe be unto us who are gathered from
> among the Gentiles, if we neglect to pay the debt by our exer-
> tions to save them! Woe to us who have contracted the debt!
> for a day of judgment and retribution will come, and there
> will be no escape! No lawyers will be there to quibble and
> bring up technicalities of law; but the debt will have to be
> paid, for to their forefathers are we indebted for the light and
> knowledge that we possess.[13]

---

[12] George Albert Smith, CR, April 1950, 185.
[13] Orson Pratt, JD, 9:179.

Elder Delbert L. Stapley observed that Brigham Young's successor was also deeply committed to carrying out the Church's mission to the Indians. "President John Taylor," he said,

> was greatly concerned about an active Lamanite program, for he declared: "The work of the Lord among the Lamanites must not be postponed, if we desire to retain the approval of God. Thus far we have been content simply to baptize them and let them run wild again, but this must continue no longer; the same devoted effort, the same care in instructing, the same organization of priesthood must be introduced and maintained among the house of Lehi as amongst those of Israel gathered from gentile nations. As yet, God has been doing all, and we comparatively nothing. He has led many of them to us, and they have been baptized, and now we must instruct them further and organize them into churches with proper presidencies, attach them to our stakes, organizations, etc. In one word, treat them exactly in these respects, as we would and do treat our white brethren."[14]

President Spencer W. Kimball bore powerful testimony of the destiny of the Lamanites, as well as of the role that Ephraimite members of the Church have been assigned in these latter days. His conviction was that the purposes of God will be fulfilled whatever we do. The Lord works through human servants, and we have been called to work as his servants, but God will find other, more willing, more faithful disciples if we reject his summons to assist in the great task before us. "The day of the Lamanite is surely here," he declared,

> and we are God's instrument in helping to bring to pass the prophecies of renewed vitality, acceptance of the gospel, and resumption of a favored place as part of God's chosen people. The promises of the Lord will all come to pass; we could not thwart them if we would. But we do have it in our power to hasten or delay the process by our energetic or neglectful fulfillment of our responsibilities.[15]

---

[14] Delbert L. Stapley, CR, April 1956, 56.
[15] Spencer W. Kimball, FPM, 349.

A GLORIOUS FUTURE AWAITS THE LAMANITES

God's modern servants have spoken with one voice about the glorious destiny that awaits the descendants of the peoples of the Book of Mormon. "This remnant of the house of Israel or Jacob, which we term the American Indians," Orson Pratt testified,

> are eventually to become a righteous branch of the house of Israel; when the times of the Gentiles are fulfilled, they will be numbered among the people of the covenant made with ancient Israel, they will be a branch of the Lord, beautiful and glorious, excellent and comely, and the power of the Lord will be upon them. In that day Jesus will come to them, they being a remnant of the tribe of Joseph. Then will be fulfilled that which was predicted by the Patriarch Jacob upon the descendants of Joseph. Speaking of Joseph he says, "Joseph is a fruitful bough, a fruitful bough by a well, whose branches run over the wall. The archers have sorely grieved him and shot at him and hated him, but his bow abode in strength, and the arms of his hands were made strong by the hands of the mighty God of Jacob, from thence is the Shepherd, the stone of Israel." (Genesis 49:22-24.)[16]

From his standpoint in the nineteenth century, Elder Pratt saw the apparent unlikelihood of this destiny for the Indians of the Americas, who had suffered much, and were continuing to suffer, from poverty, superstition, lack of education, military defeats, and the extraordinary ravages of imported diseases to which they had no immunity. "It will," he said on another occasion,

> be astonishing to us when the time comes for the Lord to gather in, from every part of this great continent, these poor, miserable, degraded Lamanites, that his servants may have power over them in order to bring them to civilization. It looks impossible to us, but remember that that is the day of the Lord's power, and that then will be fulfilled the saying in the Book of Doctrine and Covenants, that the Spirit of the Lord shall be shed forth upon the hearts of those who are ordained to that power; then every man among these remnants

---

[16] Orson Pratt, JD, 14:354.

of Joseph will hear the Gospel in his own tongue, by the power of the Holy Ghost shed forth upon those who are ordained unto this power. There is such a saying as that in the Book of Covenants, and when that day comes the Lord God will work mightily by signs, wonders and miracles in various ways that will have an influence over these remnants of Joseph to convert them and bring them to a knowledge of the truth, that the prayers of their ancient fathers, and of the Prophets and Elders who once dwelt on this American continent, may be fulfilled upon their heads.[17]

The Twelve Apostles under Brigham Young saw a role for the federal government of the United States in bringing the Lamanites under its jurisdiction to a better condition:

Let the Government of the United States also continue to gather together, and to colonize the tribes and remnants of Israel (the Indians), and also to feed, clothe, succor, and protect them, and endeavor to civilize and unite; and also to bring them to the knowledge of their Israelitish origin, and of the fulness of the gospel which was revealed to, and written by, their forefathers on this land; the record of which has now come to light. . . . They would then begin to know and understand what was to be done with these remnants, and what part they have to act in the great restitution of Israel, and of the kingdom of God.[18]

The Twelve knew, nonetheless, that the principal responsibility for raising the status of the Lamanites rests upon the Latter-day Saints, for they alone have the knowledge of the true past and true future, and therefore of the true stature, of the Book of Mormon peoples. And they knew what effect that knowledge would have upon those Lamanites who accepted the gospel and entered into and kept its covenants and ordinances. It was that knowledge alone, they insisted, that would restore to the Indians their dignity and allow them to confront their tormentors and oppressors as equals (or more than equals). "The despised and degraded son of the forest," they declared,

---

[17] Orson Pratt, JD, 17:306.
[18] The Twelve Apostles, MFP, 1:261.

who has wandered in dejection and sorrow, and suffered reproach, shall then drop his disguise, and stand forth in manly dignity, and exclaim to the Gentiles who have envied and sold him: Joseph: does my father yet live?" Or, in other words: I am a descendant of that Joseph who was sold into Egypt. You have hated me, and sold me, and thought I was dead. But lo! I live, and am heir to the inheritance, titles, honors, priesthood, sceptre, crown, throne, and eternal life and dignity of my fathers who live for evermore.[19]

They knew of the priestly splendor and dignity that God holds ready for those who will accept his revelations and do his will, a status far above anything the world can offer. And they offered a memorable picture of the Lamanite who, through repentance and conversion to the gospel of Jesus Christ, rejoins covenant Israel:

He shall then be ordained, washed, anointed with holy oil and arrayed in fine linen, even in the glorious and beautiful garments and royal robe of the high priesthood, which is after the order of the Son of God; and shall enter into the congregation of the Lord, even into the Holy of Holies, there to be crowned with authority and power which shall never end. The Spirit of the Lord shall then descend upon him, like the dew upon the mountains of Hermon, and like refreshing showers of rain upon the flowers of Paradise. His heart shall expand with knowledge, wide as eternity; and his mind shall comprehend the vast creations of his God, and His eternal purpose of redemption, glory, and exaltation, which was devised in heaven before the worlds were organized; but made manifest in these last days, for the fulness of the Gentiles, and for the exaltation of Israel. He shall also behold his Redeemer and be filled with his presence, while the cloud of his glory shall be seen in his temple.[20]

THE LAMANITES TO ASSUME THEIR RIGHTFUL ROLE

It is interesting to note the recurrence of temple imagery in connection with this theme of the reintegration of the Lamanites into a covenant relationship with the Lord God of Israel. Somewhat before

---

[19] The Twelve Apostles, MFP, 1:260.
[20] The Twelve Apostles, MFP, 1:260.

the dedication of the great temple in Salt Lake City, President Wilford Woodruff had an experience that again connected the Lamanites with the redemptive work of the House of the Lord. "I had a dream one night about our temple in Salt Lake City," he reported.

> I thought the temple was dedicated and organized, and we as the elders of Israel were laboring there for the redemption of our dead, and suddenly there was a door opened in the west, and an Indian chief came into the temple, leading a vast host of his tribe, and took possession of the temple, and I thought they performed more work in one hour than we could do in a day. This made a strong impression on my mind. I am satisfied that, although we have done a little for the Lamanites, we have got to do a great deal more. . . . I believe the day will come when these Lamanites, with the dark skin that rests upon them, will enter into these temples of the Lord in these mountains and do a great deal of work. They will come to an understanding of the redemption of the dead. They will have wisdom given unto them. They will have light and truth given unto them, and the spirit of their forefathers will be manifest unto them.[21]

The words of God's spokesmen in this dispensation are explicit: the Lamanites will be—and, with the rapid growth of the Church in areas of predominantly Lamanite population, they increasingly are—full partners in the great tripartite mission of the Church, which is to perfect the Saints, to proclaim the gospel, and to redeem the dead. "The Lamanites must rise again in dignity and strength," Spencer W. Kimball announced,

> to fully join their brethren and sisters of the household of God in carrying forth his work in preparation for that day when the Lord Jesus Christ will return to lead his people, when the Millennium will be ushered in, when the earth will be renewed and receive its paradisiacal glory and its lands be united and become one land.[22]

In fact, according to the words of the prophets, the Lamanites will be more than mere partners with the people of Ephraim, and far

---

[21] Wilford Woodruff, DWW, 296–97.
[22] Spencer W. Kimball, TSWK, 567.

more than merely subservient assistants. They have their own role to play, and it is a central one. The Utah pioneer Mosiah Hancock remembered what Brigham Young had to say about the steadfastness and commitment of the Lamanites, once they are truly converted:

> Said he, "Our hope lies in the Lamanites. I hope that you brethren who labor among the Indians will be kind to them. Remember that someday they will take their position as the rightful heir to the principles of life and salvation, for they never will give up the principles of this Gospel. Many of this people for the sake of riches and popularity, will sell themselves for that which will canker their souls and lead them down to misery and despair. It would be better for them to dwell in wigwams among the Indians than to dwell with the gentiles and miss the glories which God wishes them to obtain."[23]

Orson Pratt called the attention of his audience to the prophecies of the Book of Mormon, which stress that the Lamanites will not be subordinate players in the important events of the latter days. "Do you know," he asked,

> that they will be the principal actors in some of the grand events of times to come? What says the Book of Mormon in relation to the building up of the New Jerusalem on this continent—one of the most splendid cities that ever was or ever will be built on this land? Does not that book say that the Lamanites are to be the principal operators in that important work, and that those who embrace the Gospel from among the Gentiles are to have the privilege of assisting the Lamanites to build up the city called the New Jerusalem? This remnant of Joseph, who are now degraded, will then be filled with the wisdom of God; and by that wisdom they will build that city; by the aid of the Priesthood already given, and by the aid of Prophets that God will raise up in their midst, they will beautify and ornament its dwellings; and we have the privilege of being numbered with them, instead of their being numbered with us.[24]

---

[23] Mosiah Hancock, Autobiography, 73.
[24] Orson Pratt, JD, 9:178–79.

And, of course, in the building of the city of the New Jerusalem their most important task will be the construction of its great temple, to which the Lord will come, and from which he will reign, and in which the millennial work of the redemption of the dead will be carried forward by the dedicated and inspired labors of the righteous Saints.

We still await the full realization of these prophecies. But the spectacular progress of the Church among the Lamanites, which has really begun only in recent decades, unmistakably suggests that they are in process of fulfillment even now. Those who are attuned to the prophecies relating to the last days cannot fail to note this fact and to ponder its significance. Elder Bruce R. McConkie's words are worth recalling here:

> Indeed, that day—the day of the Lamanite—shall dawn before the Second Coming. Its arrival will be one of the signs of the times, and all those who can read the promised signs will thereby know that the coming of their Lord is nigh at hand. Pending that day, the Lord's command to his people is: "Be not deceived, but continue in steadfastness, looking forth for the heavens to be shaken, and the earth to tremble and to reel to and fro as a drunken man, and for the valleys to be exalted, and for the mountains to be made low, and for the rough places to become smooth—and all this when the angel shall sound his trumpet." (D&C 49:23.)[25]

[25] Bruce R. McConkie, MiM, 210.

CHAPTER 17

THE GATHERING OF ISRAEL

THE SOCIALITY OF THE GOSPEL

The restored gospel of Jesus Christ is a gospel of relationships. It is embodied in and carried forth by a Church, an organized society made up of a multitude of different personalities who come from a vast variety of backgrounds, and the gospel cannot be found in its fulness apart from that Church. Furthermore, although we are encouraged to pray and to ponder the scriptures individually as well as with others, there is clearly no room in the gospel for a purely private spirituality. We are commanded to join with others to perfect the Saints, to proclaim the gospel to those who have not yet received it, and to work for the redemption of the hosts of the dead. We live in families, and we worship in congregations. Furthermore, we are assured by modern revelators that such relationships will continue into the eternities. The Prophet Joseph Smith taught, concerning the life of the righteous in the world to come, that "that same sociality that exists among us here will exist among us there, only it will be coupled with eternal glory, which glory we do not now enjoy."[1]

Brigham Young fully agreed and insisted that the "sociality" of the Saints was to be strengthened and cultivated in this life, too. "A gathering and social spirit seems," he said,

> to be the order of heaven—of the spirit that is in the Gospel we have embraced. Though it may be esteemed as a fault—as an unwarrantable act to separate ourselves from those who do not believe as we believe, yet such is the nature of a portion of our religion pertaining to the performance of outward duties. If the Latter-day Saints can associate together, free from the contaminating influences that are in the world, it is a blessing and a great privilege. What would induce a child to grow up in the wickedness of the wicked world, if it never saw or heard any of it?[2]

---

[1] Doctrine and Covenants 130:2.
[2] Brigham Young, DBY, 237.

It is this spirit of sociality, and the desire to separate, as Zion, from the wicked influences of Zion's archetypal enemy, Babylon, that undergirds the practice of "gathering." And "gathering" has been characteristic of the Lord's Saints in all dispensations. But the notion of "gathering" seems to include far more than merely assembling a large number of individuals in one place, or in one organization. For it seems to be the Lord's intent to unify and to harmonize many things, to the extent that they will hearken to his voice. As John Taylor, Brigham Young's successor in the presidency of the Church, said,

> He has designed to gather together his people into one, and his spirit into one, and his power into one. The Scriptures say that God will gather together all things, whether they are things in the heavens or things on the earth; he will gather them all into one, and his people will be gathered into one, and his word will be gathered into one.[3]

In some ways, therefore, it is apparent that the threefold mission of the Church—the perfecting of the Saints, the proclamation of the gospel, and the redemption of the dead—is itself a single mission of unification, albeit with three facets. For the Lord wishes to bring all his children into a covenant relationship with himself and with each other, uniting all peoples and all generations into a harmonious kingdom led by one Spirit and based upon one consistent, revealed doctrine, made possible through and only through the Atonement—the "at-one-ment"—wrought by the Holy One of Israel.[4] Missionary service, the work of the temples, and the teaching of the gospel in chapels and homes—all aim at this single, transcendent goal.

A LITERAL GATHERING FORETOLD

Instrumental in the accomplishment of this task, though, is a literal gathering of the Saints together so that they may instruct one another, organize for the preaching of the gospel, and build temples. Joseph Smith stated this clearly in the early days of the Church:

---

[3] John Taylor, JD, 18:282.
[4] "At-one-ment" is not merely a cute folk-etymology. It represents the actual origin of the theological term *atonement*.

One of the most important points in the faith of the Church of the Latter-day Saints, through the fullness of the everlasting Gospel, is the gathering of Israel (of whom the Lamanites constitute a part) that happy time when Jacob shall go up to the house of the Lord, to worship Him in spirit and in truth, to live in holiness; when the Lord will restore His judges as at the first, and His counselors as at the beginning; when every man may sit under his own vine and fig tree, and there will be none to molest or make afraid; when He will turn to them a pure language, and the earth will be filled with sacred knowledge, as the waters cover the great deep.[5]

The ultimate gathering of Israel was foretold by ancient prophets from the earliest days of Israel's existence. The prophet Moses, for example, knew that Israel would be dispersed and would then be brought together again through the power of God. Even as he was bringing his people through the desert toward their promised home in Canaan, he knew that they would not yet be settling there permanently. "And it shall come to pass," he said,

> when all these things are come upon thee, the blessing and the curse which I have set before thee, and thou shalt call them to mind, among all the nations whither the Lord thy God hath driven thee, and shalt return unto the Lord thy God, and shalt obey His voice, according to all that I command thee, this day, thou and thy children, with all thine heart, and with all thy soul, that then the Lord thy God will turn thy captivity, and have compassion upon thee, and will return and gather thee from all the nations whither the Lord thy God hath scattered thee. If any of thine be driven out unto the outmost parts of heaven, from thence will the Lord thy God gather thee, and from thence will He fetch thee.[6]

Manifestly, this has not yet happened. The people of Israel have been driven out of Palestine on several occasions—by the Assyrians, by the Babylonians, by the Romans—and a few have even returned (only, sometimes, to be driven out yet again). Yet it is the testimony of modern prophets that the gathering is now underway, definitively

---

5 Joseph Smith Jr., TPJS, 92–93.
6 Deuteronomy 30:1–4, as cited by Joseph Smith Jr., TPJS, 84–85.

this time, never again to be undone. Orson Pratt looked forward to the completion of the process in this, our dispensation:

> Has this been fulfilled? Has He done this for the house of Israel, scattered among the heathen, bringing them back and making them one nation in the land and upon the mountains, with one king to reign over them all? Has there ever been a period since the twelve tribes lived, some two thousand five hundred years ago, that the house of Israel has been made one? It is very well known that such things have not yet taken place. But the prophecy will be fulfilled, and that too in our day. The Lord will gather the ten tribes from the north, and the house of Judah from the four quarters of the earth whither they be gone, and will gather them on every side, and bring them into their own land, making of them one nation under one king never more to be divided.[7]

This regathering of ancient, scattered peoples will not come about through natural processes alone, although its true significance and the true agent behind it will not be apparent to everybody. It can only happen through the mighty power of God, acting in and through the forces of history. "Though smitten of men, a large part of them gone from a knowledge of the world," James E. Talmage wrote,

> Israel are not lost unto their God. He knows whither they have been led or driven; toward them His heart still yearns with paternal love; and surely will He bring them forth, in due time and by appointed means, into a condition of blessing and influence befitting His covenant people. In spite of their sin and notwithstanding the tribulations that they were bringing upon themselves, the Lord said: "And yet for all that, when they be in the land of their enemies, I will not cast them away, neither will I abhor them, to destroy them utterly, and to break my covenant with them: for I am the Lord their God." (Leviticus 26:44.) As complete as was the scattering, so shall be the gathering of Israel.[8]

---

7 Orson Pratt, JD, 19:173.
8 James E. Talmage, AF, 328–29.

TWO CENTERS OF GATHERING

And it will be just as completely literal. Further, for those who have eyes to see, it will be a historical event of such magnitude that the scriptures say it will supplant the miraculous exodus of the children of Israel from Egypt as a reminder of the power of God.

Two geographical centers have been designated by scripture and by modern apostles and prophets as the centers of the gathering in the latter days. "It may be proper here to remark," said John Taylor,

> that there will be two places of gathering, or Zion; the one in Jerusalem, the other in another place; the one is a place where the Jews will gather to, and the other a mixed multitude of all nations. Concerning the house of Israel, Jeremiah says, "Therefore, behold, the days come, saith the Lord, that it shall no more be said, The Lord liveth, that brought up the children of Israel out of the land of Egypt; but, the Lord liveth, that brought up the children of Israel from the land of the north, and from all the lands whither he had driven them: and I will bring them again into their land that I gave unto their fathers." (Jeremiah 14:14-15.) According to this passage, and many others, there will evidently be a great display of the power of God manifested towards the house of Israel in their restitution to their former habitations.[9]

Lorenzo Snow, too, taught that

> there will be a universal gathering to America and Palestine. Mormonism teaches that prior to the Millennial reign of peace, there is to be a universal gathering of scattered Israel, the lineal descendants of Abraham, Isaac, and Jacob; meaning not only the Jews, but also the "lost tribes" and such of the chosen seed as have for generations been mixed with other peoples. This gathering, which includes the converted Gentiles, is preliminary to the glorious advent of the King of kings, and the resurrection of those who are Christ's at His coming. The places of assembly are America and Palestine, the former taking chronological precedence as the gathering place of "Ephraim and his fellows," while the "dispersed of Judah" will migrate to and

---

[9] John Taylor, GG, 98.

rebuild Jerusalem. Here, upon the American continent, will be reared Zion, a new Jerusalem, where the Saints will eventually assemble and prepare for the coming of the Messiah.[10]

ISRAEL'S GATHERING PRECEDES THE SECOND COMING

The gathering must precede, and will be an important step toward, the coming of the Lord Jesus Christ in glory. This has been a favorite theme of the apostles and prophets of this final dispensation. Orson Pratt cited scriptural passages that seem to allude to that great day:

> After they are all gathered, "then shall the powers of heaven come down and be in the midst of this people, and I also will be in your midst." Now I do not say that this will be a period after his second coming in the clouds of heaven, but I believe that it will be a coming prior to that time, when he comes to manifest himself to all the nations and kindreds of the earth. It will be a fulfillment of that saying in the Psalms of David— "Give ear, O shepherd of Israel, thou that leadest Joseph like a flock. Stir up thy strength and come and save us." He is called, in a peculiar manner, the shepherd of Israel.[11]

So, likewise, did the Prophet Joseph Smith:

> Enoch was in good company in his views upon this subject: "And I heard a great voice out of heaven, saying, Behold, the tabernacle of God is with men, and He will dwell with them, and they shall be His people and God Himself shall be with them, and be their God." I discover by this quotation, that John upon the isle of Patmos, saw the same things concerning

---

[10] Lorenzo Snow, TLS, 153. Note that President Snow mentions "converted Gentiles." It is, of course, possible for righteous non-Israelites to enter into the same covenants with God that Israelites can enter. Indeed, by adoption they themselves become members of the house of Israel. This must be borne in mind when looking at passages like the following, from Orson Hyde: "When the secret is fully out, the seed of the blessed shall be gathered in, in the last days; and he who has not the blood of Abraham flowing in his veins, who has not one particle of the Savior's in him, I am afraid is a stereotyped Gentile, who will be left out and not be gathered in the last days; for I tell you it is the chosen of God, the seed of the blessed, that shall be gathered" (Orson Hyde, JD, 2:82). Nobody will be excluded from entry into the kingdom of God on the basis of mere ethnicity.

[11] Orson Pratt, JD, 17:302.

the last days, which Enoch saw. But before the tabernacle can be with men, the elect must be gathered from the four quarters of the earth.[12]

Alluding to a parable given by the Savior, the Prophet explained that

> the Kingdom of Heaven is like a grain of mustard seed. The mustard seed is small, but brings forth a large tree, and the fowls lodge in the branches. The fowls are the angels. Thus angels come down, combine together to gather their children, and gather them. We cannot be made perfect without them, nor they without us; when these things are done, the Son of Man will descend, the Ancient of Days sit; we may come to an innumerable company of angels, have communion with and receive instructions from them.[13]

The prophets and apostles of the latter days have insisted, quite rightly, that their teachings on this subject are only those of the apostles and prophets who preceded them in ancient times. Certainly their hopes and dreams are those of all the righteous Saints who have ever spoken about the matter. Joseph Smith himself will serve as a representative of his fellow-servants:

> In speaking of the gathering, we mean to be understood as speaking of it according to scripture, the gathering of the elect of the Lord out of every nation on earth, and bringing them to the place of the Lord of Hosts, when the city of righteousness shall be built, and where the people shall be of one heart and one mind, when the Savior comes: yea, where the people shall walk with God like Enoch, and be free from sin. The word of the Lord is precious; and when we read that the veil spread over all nations will be destroyed, and the pure in heart see God, and reign with Him a thousand years on earth, we want all honest men to have a chance to gather and build up a city of righteousness, where even upon the bells of the horses shall be written "Holiness to the Lord."[14]

---

12 Joseph Smith Jr., TPJS, 84, citing Revelation 21:3.
13 Joseph Smith Jr., MFP, 1:114.
14 Joseph Smith Jr., TPJS, 93.

EPHRAIM RECEIVES THE KEYS OF GATHERING

But the searching out and reestablishment of the house of Israel has not been merely a matter of words and dreams. From its beginnings, the Church and its leaders have, by divine decree, been actively involved with the gathering. Their involvement commenced, as Joseph Fielding Smith noted, when

> the keys of the gathering of Israel, including the return of the Ten Tribes from the north, were given to Joseph Smith and Oliver Cowdery by Moses in the Kirtland Temple, April 3, 1836. In these words Joseph Smith has reported this visitation: ". . . the heavens were again opened unto us; and Moses appeared before us, and committed unto us the keys of the gathering of Israel from the four parts of the earth, and the leading of the ten tribes from the land of the north."[15]

This visitation to a prophet of Ephraim, among a people largely of Ephraim, was completely consistent with the ancient prophecies of the Hebrew Bible. Jeremiah, for example, announced many centuries before Christ that Ephraim would play a central role in the gathering of Israel as a whole:

> For there shall be a day, that the watchmen upon the Mount Ephraim shall cry, Arise ye, and let us go up to Zion unto the Lord our God. For thus saith the Lord: Sing with gladness for Jacob, and shout among the chief of the nations: publish ye, praise ye, and say, O Lord, save thy people, the remnant of Israel. Behold I will bring them from the north country, and gather them from the coasts of the earth, and with them the blind and the lame, the woman with child and her that travaileth with child together: a great company shall return thither. They shall come with weeping, and with supplications will I lead them: I will cause them to walk by the rivers of waters in a straight way, wherein they shall not stumble: for I am a father to Israel, and Ephraim is my firstborn.[16]

Accordingly, as Joseph Fielding Smith put it,

---

[15] Joseph Fielding Smith, WP, 131.
[16] Jeremiah 31:6-9., as cited by Joseph Fielding Smith, WP, 123.

Today the Gospel Standard is raised by Ephraim who has been gathered from the Gentiles and the scattered Israelites among the Gentiles have rallied unto it. The time has come when this same light shall go to the remnant on this land and to scattered Judah, that they too may have the privilege of being gathered into the fold.[17]

THE ELECT COVENANT WITH THE LORD BY SACRIFICE

It should not be thought, simply because the gathering will represent a massive intervention of divine power in the affairs of God's children, that it will come about without the cooperative efforts of at least some of them. Ephraim's participation in the process was not only foreordained, it is essential. And it has been, and will often be, costly. Orson Pratt, for example, knew this from wrenching personal experience. His service in the nineteenth-century Church cost him several homes and thousands of miles of travel as a missionary, under conditions that few in the twentieth century would be willing to endure. His devotion to the kingdom cost him the leisure time that he, an extraordinarily talented man, would have loved to have devoted to his mathematical and astronomical studies. His own brother died an apostolic martyr. Elder Pratt taught that

> to prepare the people for that great day it is necessary that the Saints should be gathered together . . . when he should give this great and grand revelation in the last days, when the mighty God, even the Lord, shall speak. He will call to the heavens to assist in the great latter-day work; and all the angels and the heavenly host, who do his bidding, will go forth as swift messengers to execute his decrees and fulfil his purposes in bringing about this grand gathering of his elect from the four quarters of the earth. Who will they be? Those who have made a covenant with him by sacrifice. What kind of a sacrifice? The sacrifice of every earthly thing required, their native countries, their fathers and mothers, for in many instances those who obey the Gospel are compelled to sever the nearest earthly ties—parents from their children, children

---

17 Joseph Fielding Smith, WP, 141.

from their parents and kindred from their kin, in order that they may come forth and be gathered into one grand body preparatory to the coming of the Son of God in flaming fire.[18]

Elder Pratt lived the principle laid out by the founder of this final dispensation. "It was in offering sacrifices," the Prophet Joseph Smith had taught,

> that Abel, the first martyr, obtained knowledge that he was accepted of God. And from the days of righteous Abel to the present time, the knowledge that men have that they are accepted in the sight of God is obtained by offering sacrifice. And in the last days, before the Lord comes, He is to gather together His saints who have made a covenant with him by sacrifice. Psalms 1:3-5: "Our God shall come, and shall not keep silence: a fire shall devour before Him, and it shall be very tempestuous round about Him. He shall call to the heavens from above, and to the earth, that He may judge His people. Gather my saints together unto me; those that have made a covenant with me by sacrifice."[19]

And, of course, Joseph Smith himself gave his life for the cause of the Lord, illustrating for us the extent of the sacrifice that may sometimes be required of those who serve God. For Joseph, sacrifice was no merely theoretical principle. And he knew it would not be merely a lofty ideal, an airy abstraction, in the lives of any of those who sought to establish Zion in the last days:

> To illustrate more clearly this gathering: We have another parable — "Again, the Kingdom of heaven is like a treasure hid in a field, the which, when a man hath found, he hideth, and for joy thereof, goeth and selleth all that he hath, and buyeth that field!" The Saints work after this pattern. See the Church of the Latter-day Saints, selling all that they have, and gathering themselves together unto a place that they may purchase for an inheritance, that they may be together and bear each other's afflictions in the day of calamity.[20]

---

[18] Orson Pratt, JD, 15:56.
[19] Joseph Smith Jr., Sidney Rigdon, LF, 6:59.
[20] Joseph Smith Jr., MFP, 1:68.

A DIVISION WILL OCCUR

Not unexpectedly, the prophets warn that there will be those who are unwilling to pay the price required to be gathered with the Saints. Indeed, some will have no interest whatever in the ancient prophetic dream of a covenant community led by revelation from the heavens, or they will refuse to recognize that that is precisely what Zion is. So there will be a great division between Zion and Babylon. Joseph Smith spoke clearly of this:

> "Again, the Kingdom of Heaven is like unto a net that was cast into the sea, and gathered of every kind, which when it was full they drew to shore, and sat down, and gathered the good into vessels, but cast the bad away." For the work of this pattern, behold the seed of Joseph, spreading forth the Gospel net upon the face of the earth, gathering of every kind, that the good may be saved in vessels prepared for that purpose, and the angels will take care of the bad. So shall it be at the end of the world—the angels shall come forth and sever the wicked from among the just, and cast them into the furnace of fire, and there shall be wailing and gnashing of teeth.[21]

"We understand," he said, drawing upon yet another New Testament parable,

> that the work of gathering together of the wheat into barns, or garners, is to take place while the tares are being bound over, and preparing for the day of burning; that after the day of burnings, the righteous shall shine forth like the sun, in the Kingdom of their Father. Who hath ears to hear, let him hear.[22]

Indeed, we might almost see a kind of mirror image of the gathering of Israel—a countergathering, comprised of those who refuse to submit to the will of God and to join with his Saints in building the kingdom. Orson Hyde recognized this already in his time, and surely it is worse today than it was in the nineteenth century. "If you want to see the gathering of the ungodly," he remarked,

---

21 Joseph Smith Jr., TPJS, 102.
22 Joseph Smith Jr., TPJS, 101.

look at the combined armies of the world assembling for bloody conflict. Look at the meteors in the heavens: they cannot be silent; they must speak the language they are designed to speak in the last days. The nations are perplexed, in distress, wretchedness, and misery. They are clothed in mourning, for the demon of war is let loose, blood is flowing, and the Saints are gathering to the valleys of the mountains to be taught and instructed in the ways of the Almighty.[23]

A PRELIMINARY GATHERING TO STAKES OF ZION

Initially in this dispensation, when the Church was securely established in the valleys of the mountains of the American West, Church authorities admonished members to come from whatever country they inhabited and to join in the building of communities of the Saints and in the erecting of temples. This continued until relatively recent times. In fact, Joseph Fielding Smith could still speak of the gathering to Utah:

> While the work of preparation is going on and Israel is being gathered, many people are coming to the land of Zion saying: "Come ye, and let us go up to the mountain of the Lord, to the house of the God of Jacob." The Latter-day Saints are fulfilling this prediction, since they are being gathered from all parts of the earth and are coming to the house of the Lord in these valleys of the mountains. Here they are being taught in the ways of the Lord through the restoration of the gospel and by receiving blessings in the temples now erected. Moreover, before many years have passed away, the Lord will command the building of the City Zion, and Jerusalem in Palestine will in due time be cleansed and become a holy city and the habitation of the Jews after they are cleansed and are willing to accept Jesus Christ as their Redeemer.[24]

In more recent times, however, and until the order is given to build the city of the New Jerusalem, the Saints have been counselled to remain in their countries of origin. This has become possible because, through the offerings of money and labor and missionary

[23] Orson Hyde, JD, 6:340.
[24] Joseph Fielding Smith, DS, 3:71.

service made by devoted Saints, the Church can now provide its full programs of instruction and ordinances (including the ordinances of the house of the Lord) around the world. We can build temples on every continent. Moreover, we have now attained such numbers that we can no longer gather in one place. This does not mean, however, that the doctrine of the gathering is obsolete. For, as Bruce R. McConkie explained,

> The gathering of Israel is both spiritual and temporal. The lost sheep gather spiritually when they join the Church, and they gather temporally when they come to a prepared place—that is, to Zion or one of her stakes. There they can strengthen each other in the Lord; there they can receive for themselves, in holy houses built for that very purpose, the covenant made in days of old with Abraham, Isaac, and Israel. There they can redeem their dead through the vicarious ordinances of the temples. Speaking of places and locales, Zion itself (the New Jerusalem) has not as yet been established in our day, but it will be in due course. For the present, the Lord's people, who are Zion, are called to gather in the stakes of Zion as these are established in the lands of their inheritance.[25]

The Prophet Joseph Smith had taught many years before that there would come a time when there would be multiple centers of gathering:

> There will be here and there a Stake [of Zion] for the gathering of the Saints. Some may have cried peace, but the Saints and the world will have little peace from henceforth. Let this not hinder us from going to the Stakes; for God has told us to flee, not dallying, or we shall be scattered, one here, and another there. There your children shall be blessed, and you in the midst of friends where you may be blessed. The Gospel net gathers of every kind.[26]

But the function of gathering remains unchanged. God's prophets instruct the Saints to come together to strengthen one another in the face of the increasing wickedness of the world; to provide model

---

[25] Bruce R. McConkie, NWAF, 569.
[26] Joseph Smith Jr., TPJS, 160.

communities that will, in their mutual caring, be lights to the world; to organize themselves for service to one another and for carrying out the three-part mission of the Church; and to take refuge against the approaching storm. As Joseph Smith said,

> The holy word also affirms that Israel gathers to Zion to escape the abomination of desolation that shall be poured out upon a wicked world in the last days. In Zion there will be safety; in the world, naught but sorrow and tribulation and desolation. To all the members of The Church of Jesus Christ of Latter-day Saints the Lord commands: "Arise and shine forth that thy light may be a standard for the nations; and that the gathering together upon the land of Zion, and upon her stakes, may be for a defense, and for a refuge from the storm, and from wrath when it shall be poured out without mixture upon the whole earth." (D&C 115:5-6.)[27]

---

[27] Bruce R. McConkie, NWAF, 574.

CHAPTER 18

AN INCREASE IN WICKEDNESS

One of the chief missions of a prophet is to warn the people to whom he has been sent, to call upon them to repent.[1] Modern apostles and prophets have done precisely that. Consistently, since the founding of The Church of Jesus Christ of Latter-day Saints, its appointed leaders have rebuked the sins and evils they recognized in the world about them. "I need not stop to tell you," said Wilford Woodruff,

> that we live in a day of darkness, wickedness, unbelief, and transgressions of every kind; I need not tell you this; the heavens know it, the earth knows it, the devils know it, all men know it who are acquainted with the human family in the day and age in which we live.[2]

"The Lord is not pleased with wickedness and sin," he said at another time.

> Let any man look at our own beloved country. There is more crime now committed in ten years in it, than used to be in a century. Will the Lord bear with this? No, he will not. He has already destroyed two great and powerful nations that dwelt on this continent, and the remnants of another are scattered over the country in the miserable few who bear the marks of the curse of God upon them—the Indians. If men shed innocent blood, do wickedly, and work iniquity, the seed that they sow they must reap the harvest thereof.[3]

THE DETERIORATION OF SOCIETY

Probably no serious observer would argue that things have improved since Wilford Woodruff spoke in the nineteenth century. So the prophetic warnings have continued. More recently, for example, Harold B. Lee commented on some of the evils that he observed:

---

[1] See Ezekiel 33:1-11; Doctrine and Covenants 88:81.
[2] Wilford Woodruff, DWW, 225.
[3] Wilford Woodruff, JD, 11:248.

Many questions are asked today as the disturbed conditions in the world become more confusing and appalling to our people and to others who are shocked by the continuance of undeclared wars and by the spectacle of government affairs and some private and public businesses being dominated, in many instances, by official mandate rather than by due legislative processes. We see rebellion against the law, which approaches anarchy when leaders openly incite riots against law and order; we are witnessing the constant parading of ugly and soul-destroying, lewd, and provocative literature, theatricals and radio and television shows. We hear vicious attacks on public officials without the opportunity being given to them to make a defense or a rebuttal to the evil diatribes and character assassinations that tend to discourage worthy men from accepting appointments to public offices. These are but a few of the ills that afflict us in our so-called modern age.[4]

"We constantly hear or read of wars and rumors of wars," observed Ezra Taft Benson.

Atheism, agnosticism, immorality, and dishonesty are flaunted in our society. Desertion, cruelty, divorce, and infidelity have become commonplace, leading to a disintegration of the family. Truly we live in the times of which the Savior spoke, when "the love of men shall wax cold, and iniquity shall abound" (D&C 45:27).[5]

None of this, of course, should be surprising. The prophets have predicted the wickedness of the latter days for many, many years. Joseph Fielding Smith had those prophecies on his mind when he commented on the trajectory that our world is following toward greater and greater evil:

Let me call your attention to the fact that this world is not growing better. If I may be pardoned for the expression: We need not "kid" ourselves into thinking that this world is growing better. If so, then the prophecies have failed. This world today is full of wickedness. That wickedness is increasing. True, there are many

---

[4] Harold B. Lee, CR, April 1966, 64.
[5] Ezra Taft Benson, TETB, 105–6.

righteous people scattered throughout the earth, and it is our duty to search them out and give unto them the gospel of Jesus Christ and bring them out of Babylon. The Lord has said to them: "Go ye out from Babylon," which is the world.[6]

As with their ancient counterparts, modern prophets and apostles have refused to limit their admonitions to "private" religion. Rather, they have recognized that the social order, too, needs to be brought into line with the mandates of God and that justice and the care of the poor are legitimate targets of inspired, prophetic critique. Hugh B. Brown offers an eloquent example, calling attention to some of the temporal problems which cry out for gospel-oriented solutions. "We have all felt," he said,

> the impact of war and economic depression, the dehumanizing influence of industrialization, the overcrowding of our cities, the ever-present and ominous threat of nuclear war with its total destruction, and the myriad social forces that complicate our lives and affect our values. We share the conscience of a world in which mass murder has been real and in which millions go to bed hungry every night in the presence of abundance.[7]

Joseph Fielding Smith also spoke out on economic issues, noting the strife that is engendered by material rivalry. "Today," he remarked,

> the whole world is in the slough of wickedness. Bitterness and hate have entered the hearts of the mighty; their hearts are failing them, and fear has overtaken them. Surely the word of the Lord is true: "The whole world groaneth under sin and darkness even now." In our own fair land, said by the Lord to be choice above all other lands, dissatisfaction, distress, and turmoil reign. Strikes have for many months crippled industry. Capital and labor are at cross purposes. Property is being wantonly and maliciously destroyed. Force is being used to accomplish selfish ends. Legislation is advocated to help to reach such ends. Discontent and hatred are born of such conditions.[8]

---

[6] Joseph Fielding Smith, DS, 3:30.
[7] Hugh B. Brown, AL, 17.
[8] Joseph Fielding Smith, DS, 3:22–23.

YIELDING TO SELFISH INTERESTS

Very much in the spirit of ancient prophets like Isaiah and Amos, President Smith pointed directly to greed as a root cause of many of our modern maladies. "The world today is full of selfishness, greed, the desire to possess," he lamented.

> For many years we have been living extravagantly. Our wants have been supplied—not our needs alone, but our wants—and we have wanted much. Most of us have been able to obtain them, and now a time comes when we find ourselves somewhat curtailed, hedged around about, not having so many privileges, and our desires are not so fully granted, and so we begin to complain. But we should get rid of our selfishness and greed, our desire to possess that which is beyond the needs and blessings which are really ours.[9]

"As long as they have in their hearts selfishness and greed," President Smith insisted,

> and the desire for power and for wealth, and for all of the other things that belong to this world, and forget the things of the kingdom of God, there will be no peace, and there will be no contentment. There will be quarreling and contention, strife and war, and in the midst of all their labor, trouble will come which they could avoid, and that very easily, by repentance, getting contrite spirits and broken hearts, and loving their neighbors; but this they will not do.[10]

But money and the lust for it leads not only to the amassing of material possessions. Already in the nineteenth century, Church leaders were pointing to what they saw as an obsession with leisure entertainment that, they felt, distracted people from important responsibilities and brought them into harmful habits. John Taylor and his counselor George Q. Cannon contended that

> the mania for recreations of various kinds which has seized upon many of the people is harmful in several ways. It unfits them for the regular duties of life. It renders them restless and

---

9 Joseph Fielding Smith, DS, 3:24.
10 Joseph Fielding Smith, DS, 3:49–50.

impatient of proper restraint. It obstructs business. It tends to contract habits of dissipation. It throws our young folks into the company of persons whose society should be shunned. It cultivates worldliness. It conduces to many evils, and the spirit of purity, temperance, holiness and peace will not abide in resorts such as have been established for the purpose of enticing the Saints into folly. Many thousands of dollars have been worse than wasted during the past summer on excessive amusements and sometimes unseemly diversions. The influential men and women of the Church should discountenance this evil, and with all wisdom and prudence endeavor to check it and prevent its increase among the Saints.[11]

A Time for Soul Searching

Who can doubt that the problem they noted has, if anything, grown much worse since their day. With our compact discs and jet skis and painless travel methods and videotapes and omnipresent television sets—none of them unworthy things in and of themselves—we have vastly greater opportunities to waste money and to use our time frivolously than did the Saints of the nineteenth-century West. We have access in our homes to great music and drama and to world news in a way that they could scarcely have imagined, but we are also able to bring into our homes wickedness and decadence that would have been even more unimaginable to them. Ironically, the Zion that early Latter-day Saints sought to establish in the isolation of the Rocky Mountains now can summon Babylon into its very living rooms at the speed of light. The mountains are no longer our gatekeepers. We ourselves must guard the portals of our minds and hearts. In this regard, Ezra Taft Benson's words are immensely important: "Great nations," he explained, "are never conquered from outside unless they are rotten inside. Our greatest national problem today is erosion, not the erosion of the soil, but erosion of the national morality—erosion of traditional enforcement of law and order."[12]

Already in the nineteenth century, the Lord's prophets warned the Saints against bringing the values of the world with them into the Church and kingdom of God. John Taylor, for example, said that

---

[11] John Taylor, George Q. Cannon, MFP, 3:85.
[12] Ezra Taft Benson, CR, April 1968, 50.

in regard to our temporal affairs, these are the things which seem to perplex us more or less. We have been brought up in Babylon, and have inherited Babylonish ideas and systems of business. We have introduced, too, among us, all kinds of chicanery, deception, and fraud. It is time that these things were stopped, and that matters assumed another shape. It is time that we commenced to place ourselves under the guidance and direction of the Almighty. You can not talk in any places about temporal matters, but everybody is on the alert at once, and the idea is—Do you want my property? No. Do you want my possessions? No, no; there is no such feeling, but we do want men and women to give God their hearts; we do want people, while they profess to fear God, not to be canting hypocrites and to depart from every principle of right.[13]

Much more recently, N. Eldon Tanner advised us to examine ourselves, to monitor carefully just how we are doing in our effort to carry out the commandments of God. He reminded the Saints that we must watch our own stewardships—rather than worrying about other stewards (which virtually all of us would prefer to do). "If," he advised,

we are to stop the onslaught of immorality, divorce and family disintegration, lawlessness, strife, riots, burglaries, murders, crime, and deception, we must not ask what are they doing about it. We must ask and answer the question, "What am I doing?" Let us examine ourselves, acknowledge our faults, and repent where we should.[14]

REJECTING FALSE SOLUTIONS

Despite this counsel, however, many modern people have sought to solve the problems brought by wickedness upon our societies not by means of personal repentance and individual reformation, but through turning to supposed external solutions. By having others fix things for us. But these "solutions" have often worsened the situation, or created new evils undreamed of previously. Modern prophets and apostles have spoken repeatedly of this.

---

[13] John Taylor, GK, 261.
[14] N. Eldon Tanner, CR, October 1966, 49.

In the economic realm, for example, leaders of the Church have warned against coercive measures ostensibly designed to solve the problems of poverty and class strife that we have previously noted. "We have . . . gone a long way," Marion G. Romney observed,

> on the road to public ownership and management of the vital means of production. In both of these areas the free agency of Americans has been greatly abridged. Some argue that we have voluntarily surrendered this power to government. Be this as it may, the fact remains that the loss of freedom with the consent of the enslaved, or even at their request, is nonetheless slavery. . . . We here in the United States, in converting our government into a social welfare state, have ourselves adopted much of socialism. Specifically, we have to an alarming degree adopted the use of the power of the state in the control and distribution of the fruits of industry.[15]

As one of the principal architects of the welfare plan of the Church, Marion G. Romney can hardly be charged with lack of concern for the poor or the needy. But he feared the loss of individual agency to an overly powerful government, which, by means of economic control, might eventually be able to compel its citizens to virtually any evil. Ezra Taft Benson shared the same worry and gave specific advice to his American audience to help them avoid it. "Great care should be taken," he counselled,

> not to accept grants from the federal government. Along with federal money, inevitably there will come federal controls and guidelines that not only may get local police embroiled in national politics, but may even lead to the eventual creation of a national police force. Every despotism requires a national police force to hold the people in line. Communism is no exception. Our local police should remain free from federal control.[16]

THE SPREAD OF SECRET COMBINATIONS

One of the false and coercive "solutions" to perceived economic problems that have arisen in the modern period has drawn special

---

[15] Marion G. Romney, CR, April 1966, 98.
[16] Ezra Taft Benson, CR, October 1967, 38–39.

and repeated attention from leaders of the Church. Their study of the Book of Mormon and their understanding of the plan of salvation has led modern prophets and apostles to oppose communism, or Marxism-Leninism, as an unacceptable threat to the freedom of the individual, and they have not hesitated to link it with the "secret combinations" depicted in the Book of Mormon and with the rival plan of Lucifer, which was rejected in the great antemortal Council in Heaven. And, indeed, it is a powerful counterfeit gospel, a counterfeit that has done immense damage and taken the lives of tens of millions of people. "The object of the Gadiantons, like modern communists," observed Ezra Taft Benson, "was to destroy the existing government and set up a ruthless criminal dictatorship over the whole land."[17]

"One of the most urgent, heart-stirring appeals made by Moroni as he closed the Book of Mormon," Elder Benson recalled,

> was addressed to the gentile nations of the last days. He foresaw the rise of a great world-wide secret combination among the gentiles which " . . . seeketh to overthrow the freedom of all lands, nations, and countries" (Ether 8:25). He warned each gentile nation of the last days to purge itself of this gigantic criminal conspiracy which would seek to rule the world. . . . The Prophet Moroni seemed greatly exercised lest in our day we might not be able to recognize the startling fact that the same secret societies which destroyed the Jaredites and decimated numerous kingdoms of both Nephites and Lamanites would be precisely the same form of criminal conspiracy which would rise up among the gentile nations in this day.[18]

"The threat of communism is sinister and its dangers are imminent," warned President Hugh B. Brown.

> Hundreds of millions of our fellow beings are being relentlessly imbued with the satanic ideology that the Fatherhood of God, the Saviorhood of Christ, and the brotherhood of man are stupid myths, that religion is nothing but a tranquilizing opiate. They seek to deprive men of physical, mental, and spiritual freedom while endowing the state with monstrous supremacy. This relentless indoctrination is but a continuation

---

[17] Ezra Taft Benson, CR, October 1961, 71.
[18] Ezra Taft Benson, CR, October 1961, 71–72.

of the war that began when Satan's plan of force was rejected by the Father. We live in the most dangerous period of all history. The sixth chapter of Ephesians was never more applicable than today: "For we wrestle not against flesh and blood, but against principalities, against powers, against the rulers of the darkness of this world, against spiritual wickedness in high places." (Ephesians 6:12.)[19]

Drawing on the Book of Mormon, Ezra Taft Benson pointed out that

when all of the trappings of propaganda and pretense have been pulled aside, the exposed hard-core structure of modern communism is amazingly similar to the ancient Book of Mormon record of secret societies such as the Gadiantons. In the ancient American civilization there was no word which struck greater terror to the hearts of the people than the name of the Gadiantons. It was a secret political party which operated as a murder cult. Its object was to infiltrate legitimate government, plant its officers in high places, and then seize power and live off the spoils appropriated from the people. . . . The Prophet Moroni described how the secret combination would take over a country and then fight the work of God, persecute the righteous, and murder those who resisted. Moroni therefore proceeded to describe the workings of the ancient "secret combinations" so that modern man could recognize this great political conspiracy in the last days: "Wherefore, O ye Gentiles, it is wisdom in God that these things should be shown unto you, that thereby ye may repent of your sins, and suffer not that these murderous combinations shall get above you, which are built up to get power and gain—and the work, yea, even the work of destruction come upon you."[20]

"The prophets have said that these threats are among us," said President Benson. "The Prophet Moroni, viewing our day, said, 'Wherefore the Lord commandeth you, when ye shall see these things come among you that ye shall awake to a sense of your awful situation.'"[21] At the time of this writing, with the apparent decline of

---

[19] Hugh B. Brown, CR, April 1963, 7.
[20] Ezra Taft Benson, CR, October 1961, 71.
[21] Ezra Taft Benson, CR, October 1961, 71, citing Ether 8:24.

communism around the world, we may be tempted to relax our guard. But the words of the apostles and prophets do not authorize us to do so. We should not assume that modern "secret combinations" will always present themselves to us as expressly Leninist movements. They can take many forms. And while institutional communism seems to be on the decline, many of its worst elements—including its atheism, its materialism, its penchant for coercion, its denial of objective truth and its willingness to deceive, its principle that a supposedly noble end justifies virtually any means chosen to achieve it—survive in other guises and continue to pose serious threats to the well-being and even to the salvation of God's children.

GOD'S JUDGMENTS ARE INEVITABLE

In keeping with his biblically attested practice, our Heavenly Father has communicated his displeasure with human misbehavior to chosen and inspired servants and has told them to warn the people that he will not tolerate unrighteousness forever. "For the Spirit of the Lord will not always strive with man," wrote the prophet Nephi. "And when the Spirit ceaseth to strive with man then cometh speedy destruction."[22] But that destruction will not arrive without advance notice. "Surely the Lord God will do nothing, but he revealeth his secret unto his servants the prophets."[23] "Did you," asked Wilford Woodruff,

> ever know the Lord to bring his judgments upon any nation, from the days of Adam in the Garden of Eden until the present time, before he had warned them of their sins? No; the Lord has always warned the people before he has punished them for their wickedness.[24]

But the promised punishment will come. It must come, in order to put an end to evil and rebellion against the Lord. "God will not be mocked," declared Ezra Taft Benson.

---

[22] 2 Nephi 26:11. This warning is recorded frequently in the scriptures, in similar wording. See, for example, Genesis 6:3; Ether 2:15; Doctrine and Covenants 1:33; Moses 8:17. Even as individuals, the time allowed us to repent is not infinite (Alma 34:32–35). The Book of Mormon admonishes us with actual examples of peoples with whom the Spirit ceased to strive (as at 1 Nephi 7:14; Mormon 5:16–18; Ether 15:19; Moroni 8:28; 9:4) and summons us to learn wisdom from contemplating their fates (Mormon 9:31).

[23] Amos 3:7.

[24] Wilford Woodruff, DWW, 223.

He will not permit the sins of sexual immorality, secret murderous combinations, the killing of the unborn, and disregard
for all His holy commandments and the messages of His servants to go unheeded without grievous punishment for such
wickedness. The nations of the world cannot endure in sin.
The way of escape is clear. The immutable laws of God
remain steadfastly in the heavens above. When men and
nations refuse to abide by them, the penalty must follow.
They will be wasted away. Sin demands punishment.[25]

Indeed, if God failed to punish the wickedness of the latter days,
he could truly be charged with partiality and inconsistency, for the
Bible and other ancient scriptures clearly record that because of his
justice he chastised the peoples of antiquity. "The Gentile or
Christian world today," Wilford Woodruff said,

can no more commit sins, and be guilty of lying, stealing,
blasphemy, whoredom or murder, or committing abominations, and escape the wrath of God, than could Sodom and
Gomorrah, or the antediluvian world, or ancient Israel. The
word of the Lord has been proclaimed against the Gentiles
and all the inhabitants of the earth in the last days who commit sin, and it will as assuredly be fulfilled as in ancient days.
The Lord has a controversy with this generation, and he will
judge the inhabitants according to the deeds done in the body,
and none can stay his hand.[26]

But the prophets have always taught that much of the punishment that will fall upon the wicked will come, as it always does, from
the intrinsic consequences of their own sins. Unchastity, violations of
the Word of Wisdom, strife and rivalry, insatiable greed, lack of
love—these carry with them their own natural penalties and bring
with them unavoidable suffering. "The wicked will destroy themselves," testified Lorenzo Snow.

Our object is the temporal salvation of the people as much as
it is for their spiritual salvation. By and by the nations will be
broken up on account of their wickedness. The Latter-day

---

[25] Ezra Taft Benson, TETB, 74.
[26] Wilford Woodruff, DWW, 223–24.

Saints are not going to move upon them with their little army;
they will destroy themselves with their wickedness and
immorality. They will contend and quarrel one with another,
state after state and nation after nation, until they are broken
up, and thousands, tens of thousands, and hundreds of thousands will undoubtedly come and seek protection at the hands
of the servants of God, as much so as in the days of Joseph
when he was called upon to lay a plan for the salvation of the
house of Israel.[27]

REPENTANCE IS THE ONLY SOLUTION

In the meantime, modern prophets and apostles summon both
the Saints and nonmembers of the Church to repent. They call upon
them to accept and keep the covenants and ordinances of the Lord,
to listen to the voice of modern revelation, and, thereby, to enter the
only path that will dependably spare them the suffering that always
comes with rebellion against God. For that suffering is promised to
be especially sharp and particularly destructive in the last days. "We
are living," announced Wilford Woodruff,

> in the dispensation and generation to which Jesus referred—
> the time appointed by God for the last six thousand years,
> through the mouths of all the prophets and inspired men who
> have lived and left their sayings on record, in which his Zion
> should be built up and continue upon the earth. These
> prophecies will have their fulfilment before the world; and all
> who will not repent will be engulfed in the destructions which
> are in store for the wicked. If men do not cease from their
> murders, whoredoms, and all the wickedness and abomina-
> tions which fill the black catalogue of the crimes of the world,
> judgment will overtake them; and whether we are believed or
> not, these sayings are true, and I bear my testimony as a ser-
> vant of God and as an Elder in Israel to the truth of the events
> which are going to follow very fast on each other.[28]

"Judgments await the world, and they await this nation," Elder
Woodruff testified,

---

[27] Lorenzo Snow. TLS, 150.
[28] Wilford Woodruff, JD, 14:5.

and the day is as hand when the Lord will sweep the earth as with a besom of destruction. In the vision which the Lord gave to Enoch, he saw the heavens weeping over the earth because of the fall of man; and when Enoch asked the Lord—"When will the earth rest from under the curse of sin?" the Lord told him that in the last days the earth should rest, for then it should be redeemed from the sin, wickedness and abominations that were upon it. The earth is now pretty near ripe, and when ripened the Lord will cut them off. These things are before the Latter-day Saints, but the world do not believe in them any more than they believed in the message of Noah or Lot.[29]

Joseph Fielding Smith bore the same witness and cautioned us that the time of the fulfillment of the terrible prophecies relating to the unrighteous and rebellious in the latter days is not far off. "The world is rapidly coming to its end," he said,

that is, the end of the days of wickedness. When it is fully ripe in iniquity the Lord will come in the clouds of heaven to take vengeance on the ungodly, for his wrath is kindled against them. Do not think that he delayeth his coming. Many of the signs of his coming have been given, so we may, if we will, know that the day is even now at our doors.[30]

Amidst all of this, however, the righteous need not fear. For they have been assured of ultimate victory. But the message of the prophets and apostles is that the righteous must be careful to separate themselves from the world, to gather with the Saints, and to place themselves under the protection of the atoning sacrifice of the Savior, much as the ancient Israelites were required to mark their homes with the blood of the sacrificed lamb of the Passover in order to escape the destruction God had decreed upon the inhabitants of Egypt. Orson Pratt spoke of the clear distinction that will exist between Zion and Babylon in the latter days:

What condition do you suppose the wicked will be in in those days, even all the inhabitants of the earth except Zion? "For behold darkness shall cover the earth and gross darkness the

---

[29] Wilford Woodruff, JD, 18:38.
[30] Joseph Fielding Smith, DS, 3:2.

people; but the Lord shall arise upon thee, and his glory shall be seen upon thee." What a difference between Zion and the rest of mankind! Darkness covering the whole four quarters of the globe. Why darkness? Because the salt of the earth is gathered out; the children of light are gathered together to Zion, and those who are left behind are in darkness, that is, a great many of them. No doubt there will be honest ones, and vast numbers who will come to Zion, notwithstanding the darkness that covers the earth.[31]

It is those who come to Zion who will have security, whatever the appearances may seem to be. "There may be circumstances arise in this world," John Taylor assured the Saints,

to pervert for a season the order of God, to change the designs of the Most High, apparently, for the time being. Yet they will ultimately roll back into their proper place—justice will have its place, and so will mercy, and every man and woman will yet stand in their true position before God.[32]

[31] Orson Pratt, JD, 14:355.
[32] John Taylor, GK, 346.

CHAPTER 19

APOSTASY AMONG GOD'S PEOPLE

DARKNESS COVERS THE EARTH

As we discussed in the previous chapter—and it hardly requires the reading of a book to realize this—we live in a time of rampant wickedness and immorality. Accordingly, inspired Church leaders admonish us to gather with the Saints and to take refuge in the Church as if it were the ark of Noah. "Go ye out from among the nations," said the Lord, "even from Babylon, from the midst of wickedness, which is spiritual Babylon."[1] The Prophet Joseph Smith offered a chilling but by no means exhaustive list of the evils of the nineteenth century, which could easily be repeated and, indeed, expanded as we approach the end of the twentieth. "Consider for a moment, brethren," he said,

> the fulfillment of the words of the prophet; for we behold that darkness covers the earth, and gross darkness the minds of the inhabitants thereof—that crimes of every description are increasing among men—vices of great enormity are practiced— the rising generation growing up in the fullness of pride and arrogance—the aged losing every sense of conviction, and seemingly banishing every thought of a day of retribution—intemperance, immorality, extravagance, pride, blindness of heart, idolatry, the loss of natural affection; the love of this world, and indifference toward the things of eternity increasing among those who profess a belief in the religion of heaven, and infidelity spreading to commit acts of the foulest kind, and deeds of the blackest dye, blaspheming, defrauding, blasting the reputation of neighbors, stealing, robbing, murdering; advocating error and opposing the truth, forsaking the covenant of heaven, and denying the faith of Jesus—and in the midst of all this, the day of the Lord fast approaching when none except those who have won the wedding garment will be permitted to eat and drink in the presence of the Bridegroom, the Prince of Peace![2]

---

[1] Doctrine and Covenants 133:14. Compare 133:5, 7.
[2] Joseph Smith Jr., TPJS, 47.

Bruce R. McConkie explained the situation by noting that

> that spirit which enlightens every person born into the world,
> which is poured out in abundant measure to guide in bring-
> ing about latter-day progress and advancements, is now ceas-
> ing to strive with the wicked. "I, the Lord, am angry with the
> wicked; I am holding my Spirit from the inhabitants of the
> earth" (D&C 63:32), "for my Spirit shall not always strive
> with man, saith the Lord of Hosts." (D&C 1:33.)[3]

This is not at all surprising, of course, to those who understand
the scriptures, for it was predicted many centuries before. And, having been foreseen by God and his prophets, it has also been worked
into the divine plan, which provides an avenue of escape. "The
Apostle Paul saw our day," Ezra Taft Benson taught.

> He described it as a time when such things as blasphemy, dis-
> honesty, cruelty, unnatural affection, pride and pleasure seek-
> ing would abound (see 2 Timothy 3:1-7). He also warned that
> "evil men and seducers would wax worse and worse, deceiving
> and being deceived" (2 Timothy 3:12). Such grim predictions
> by prophets of old would be cause for great fear and discour-
> agement if those same prophets had not, at the same time,
> offered the solution. In their inspired counsel we can find the
> answer to the spiritual crises of our age.[4]

There are and will be many, though, who will not accept divine
counsel. What will happen to and among those who reject the word
of the Lord as revealed by his latter-day prophets and apostles?
Wilford Woodruff offered a rather depressing answer to the question.
"When this Gospel was first proclaimed to the world," he recalled,

> darkness covered the earth; and wherever this doctrine is
> preached by those having authority and it is rejected, that peo-
> ple become more dark than they were before, and go blindly
> along like the ox to the slaughter, and they will sooner or later
> be overtaken by the judgments of the Almighty.[5]

---

[3] Bruce R. McConkie, MD, 727.
[4] Ezra Taft Benson, TETB, 88.
[5] Wilford Woodruff, JD, 10:16.

Zion and Babylon will draw further and further apart, and safety will be found only in the society of the righteous. But this safety comes from active commitment to righteousness, from the faithful keeping of covenants, from seeking to do the will of the Lord as it is revealed in the scriptures and through his modern servants. Mere membership in the Church will not suffice. The standard works of the Church offer ample and eloquent testimony that even believers, even those who have once accepted the gospel, can fall away. As John Taylor noted, "The children of Israel, formerly, after seeing the power of God manifested in their midst, fell into rebellion and idolatry, and there is certainly very great danger of our 'doing the same thing.'"[6]

THE EARLY CHRISTIAN APOSTASY

The early Christian Church also departed from the purity of the revelations of God. As Ezra Taft Benson pointed out,

> Jesus said that the kingdom established in His time would be "given to a nation bringing forth the fruits thereof" (Matthew 21:43). In other words, Jesus knew, as did the Apostles, that an apostasy would take place before His kingdom would be finally established as a prelude to and preparation for His second coming. The Apostle Paul wrote to members of the Church at Thessalonica that the second coming of Jesus Christ "shall not come, except there come a falling away first" (2 Thessalonians 2:3).[7]

The earliest revelations of this dispensation declare that the world into which The Church of Jesus Christ of Latter-day Saints was restored was a world in the grip of apostasy. And, with all respect to our brothers and sisters of other Christian faiths and beyond, it still is. "I will refer you to another ancient prophecy," said Orson Pratt,

> contained in the 4th chapter of second Timothy—"For the time will come when they will not endure sound doctrine; but after their own lusts shall they heap to themselves teachers, having itching ears; and they shall turn away their ears from the truth, and shall be turned unto fables;" and who, he says,

---

6 John Taylor, HC, 2:489.
7 Ezra Taft Benson, TETB, 85.

in the previous chapter, shall "have a form of godliness, but denying the power thereof; from such turn away." It seems, then, that this people, whom Paul speaks of, were to have a form of godliness; they were, in other words, to be a pious people, professedly a very religious people, but were only to possess a form, lacking all power.[8]

FURTHER DANGERS AHEAD

There is much in this apostate world that is attractive, and a great deal of it really is both good and true. We need not reject beauties and truths because they reside outside the Church; rather, we should embrace them and take them with us into Zion. But, God's servants reminds us, much that is attractive is false. For instance, Joseph Fielding Smith warned against incorrect ideas that conflict with essential doctrines of the restored gospel. "These are perilous times," he declared.

This is a day when we are in grave danger—danger because of the teachings of men, danger because of the lack of faith in the hearts of men, because the philosophies of the world have a tendency to undermine the fundamental things of the gospel of Jesus Christ. These are things we must contend against. There is a spirit of indifference in the world toward religion today. People are not worshiping in spirit and truth, but the Lord expects us, members of the Church of Jesus Christ of Latter-day Saints, to worship in spirit and truth, to walk in righteousness, and to stand in this liberty which will make us free, spoken of in these revelations.[9]

But it is not only—and, perhaps, not especially—false ideas that threaten us. Rather, it is the natural man, the urge to seek one's pleasure at the expense of more important things, the temptation to take the path of ease, the road of least resistance. Again, Joseph Fielding Smith vigorously warned us against this error:

The people of this nation, and the people of other nations, have forsaken the Lord. We have violated his laws. We have failed to hearken to his promises. We have not considered that we were under obligation to keep his commandments, and the

[8] Orson Pratt, JD, 18:226.
[9] Joseph Fielding Smith, DS, 3:56.

laws of the land as well as the laws of God are not respected. The Sabbath day has become a day of pleasure, a day of boisterous conduct, a day in which the worship of God has departed, and the worship of pleasure has taken its place. I am sorry to say that many of the Latter-day Saints are guilty of this. We should repent.[10]

In their predictions of the punishments that will come upon those who reject or ignore the will of God, modern prophets and apostles have not exempted the members of the Church. In the very early days of the Restoration, for example, the Prophet Joseph Smith, speaking for himself as well as for Frederick G. Williams and Oliver Cowdery, warned the members of the Church of the consequences of failing to sustain its leaders in their divinely ordained responsibilities. "If this Church, which is essaying to be the Church of Christ, will not help us," he declared,

> when they can do it without sacrifice, with those blessings which God has bestowed upon them, I prophesy—I speak the truth, I lie not—God shall take away their talent and give it to those who have no talent, and shall prevent them from ever obtaining a place of refuge, or an inheritance upon the land of Zion; therefore they may tarry, for they might as well be overtaken where they are, as to incur the displeasure of God, and fall under His wrath by the way side, as to fall into the hands of a merciless mob, where there is no God to deliver, as salt that has lost its savor, and is thenceforth good for nothing, but to be trodden under foot of men.[11]

Brigham Young, too, cautioned the members of the Church that their acceptance with God was not automatic merely because their names were on the records of the organization. "I tell you," he said,

> that this people will not be suffered to walk as they have walked, to do as they have done, to live as they have lived. God will have a reckoning with us ere long, and we must refrain from our evils and turn to the Lord our God, or He will come out in judgment against us.[12]

---

[10] Joseph Fielding Smith, DS, 3:24–25.
[11] Joseph Smith Jr., Frederick G. Williams, Oliver Cowdery, MFP, 1:45.
[12] Brigham Young, JD, 4:44.

UPON THE LORD'S HOUSE IT WILL BEGIN

Orson Pratt prophesied that the membership of the Church, if it turned against the covenants it had made, would find its gathering together not a blessing, but a curse. The Lord, he announced, would commence his punishments with his rebellious Saints rather than with those who had broken no covenants because they had never entered into any:

> But if you Latter-day Saints who have received the message of the everlasting gospel, and who have, in obedience to the voice of heaven, gathered out of Babylon, if you pollute yourselves by turning again to the vanities, wickedness, and corruptions of the people from whose midst you have been delivered, then, says the Lord, "Behold, judgment shall begin at the house of God," it shall begin with you Latter-day Saints, and then will go forth to the nations and kingdoms of the earth, with weeping, wailing and lamentations among all people.[13]

The Church as a whole, the prophets assure us, will not go astray. But that does not protect individuals, and even large numbers of individuals, from the consequences of their individual choices. Wilford Woodruff sought to impress upon the minds of his hearers the seriousness of the choices that they would make:

> If this people with the light they have, the teachings they have, and the examples they have had set before them inter-mingled with chastisement—if they still will go on and be neglectful of their duties, with regard to their salvation they will have to pay the debt, for the sinner in Zion will be cut off from the Church of God, and will have to pay the penalty whether it be small or great. It is of the utmost importance that we should guard ourselves against sin as the tree of life is guarded. We have no time to throw away in the service of sin, in committing iniquity and grieving the Holy Spirit of God.[14]

Those who deliberately choose to ignore or reject the counsels of God and his servants have only themselves to blame. "If condemnation follows the rejection of the Gospel," Orson F. Whitney explained,

---

13 Orson Pratt, JD, 18:227.
14 Wilford Woodruff, JD, 4:229.

God cannot help it, His servants cannot help it. If we invite men to come out into the sunlight and they prefer to stay in the shade, who is to blame but themselves? They prefer darkness to light. They have their choice. Light has burst forth in the midst of darkness, but the darkness comprehendeth it not. Men love darkness rather than light, because their deeds are evil. If, however, we extend the message of mercy and of peace, our responsibility ends. Men will be judged by the light they possess. The heathen nations will be redeemed and will obtain a higher exaltation than those who receive the truth and turn away from it, or refuse to accept it when it is offered to them. God is merciful to ignorance and lack of opportunity; but responsibility rests like a mountain upon those who hear the truth and then reject it.[15]

However, God's judgment will not always be immediate, and it may not always be instantly clear. One of the great challenges of the latter days will be learning to discern between truth, on the one hand, and falsehoods that look very much like truth, on the other. This will be complicated by the fact that not all of those who reject the prophets will actually leave the Church. As Ezra Taft Benson indicated,

The Lord strengthened the faith of the early Apostles by pointing out Judas as a traitor, even before this Apostle had completed his iniquitous work (see Matthew 26:23-25; Luke 13:21-26). So also in our day the Lord has told us of the tares within the wheat that will eventually be hewn down when they are fully ripe. But until they are hewn down, they will be with us, amongst us. (See D&C 86:6-7.)[16]

Perhaps sensing that some members of the Church might be surprised at the thought of enemies or "traitors" among the membership, Elder Benson reiterated his point with emphasis:

Yes, within the Church today there are tares among the wheat and wolves within the flock. As President J. Reuben Clark, Jr., stated: "The ravening wolves are amongst us, from our own membership, and they, more than any others, are clothed in

---

15 Orson F. Whitney, JD, 26:268–69.
16 Ezra Taft Benson, TETB, 89.

sheep's clothing because they wear the habiliments of the priesthood. We should be careful of them." (CR, April 1949, 163.) The wolves amongst our flock are more numerous and devious today than when President Clark made this statement.[17]

Harold B. Lee pointed out that this is, sadly, nothing new. "It seems curious," he said,

> that in all dispensations, our worst enemies have been those within, those who have betrayed the works of the Lord. There were the sons of Mosiah and the younger Alma before their miraculous conversions. It was so in the days of the Master, who said of His betrayer, Judas, "Have not I chosen you twelve, and one of you is a devil?" (John 6:70.) Likewise did Joseph Smith have his betrayers. We may well expect to find our Judases among those professing membership in the Church, but, unfortunately for them, they are laboring under some kind of evil influences or have devious motives.[18]

HEARTS SET UPON THINGS OF THE WORLD

Why would some members of the Church, who have tasted the light of the gospel, choose to reject it? Bruce R. McConkie had pondered the matter. "The children of Zion fail in their great mission for two reasons," he suggested.

> (1) Oftentimes they set their hearts upon temporal things and are more concerned with amassing the things that moth and rust corrupt, and that thieves break through and steal, than in laying up for themselves treasures in heaven. Hence the divine direction: "But the laborer in Zion shall labor for Zion; for if they labor for money they shall perish." (2 Nephi 26:31.) (2) Others fail to live by the high standards of belief and conduct imposed by the gospel. Of them the divine word says: "Your minds in times past have been darkened because of unbelief, and because you have treated lightly the things you have received—which vanity and unbelief have brought the whole church under condemnation. And this condemnation resteth upon the children of Zion, even all. And they shall remain

---

[17] Ezra Taft Benson, TETB, 89.
[18] Harold B. Lee, SYHP, 21.

under this condemnation until they repent and remember the new covenant, even the Book of Mormon and the former commandments which I have given them, not only to say, but to do according to that which I have written—that they may bring forth fruit meet for their Father's kingdom; otherwise there remaineth a scourge and judgment to be poured out upon the children of Zion." (D&C 84:54-58.)[19]

Modern prophets have certainly warned against greed as one of the major stumbling blocks for members of the Church in the latter days. Some become so obsessed with obtaining and enjoying material possessions that they have little time or energy left over for prayer, for service, for gospel study, for temple worship. This was a great concern of the second president of the Church, Brigham Young. In his autobiography, Mosiah Hancock recalled that

> in the summer of 1862, President Brigham Young came through Dixie. . . . He conversed freely on the situation of the Saints in the mountains, and said that he dreaded the time when the Saints would become popular with the world; for he had seen in sorrow, in a dream, or in dreams, this people clothed in the fashions of Babylon and drinking in the spirit of Babylon until one could hardly tell a Saint from a black-leg. And he felt like shouting, "To your tents, O Israel!" because it was the only thing that could keep the people pure.[20]

Lorenzo Snow, who had lived through some of the most trying days in the early history of the Church, feared that those days would return, and for the same reason. "The spirit of speculation will affect the Saints in the last days," he predicted.

> I remember very clearly the troublous times which were experienced in Kirtland some fifty-three years ago. At that time a spirit of speculation pervaded the minds of the people of this nation. There were money speculations, bank speculations, speculations in lands, speculations in city lots, speculations in numerous other directions. That spirit of speculation rose out of the world, and swept over the hearts of the Saints like a

---

[19] Bruce R. McConkie, NWAF, 580–81.
[20] Mosiah Hancock, Autobiography, 73.

mighty wave or rushing torrent, and many fell, and apostatized. Singular as it may appear, this spirit of speculation pervaded the Quorum of the Twelve Apostles and the Quorum of the Seven Presidents of Seventies; indeed, there was not a quorum in the Church but was more or less touched with this spirit of speculation. As that spirit increased, disunion followed. Brethren and sisters began to slander and quarrel one with the other, because their interests were not in harmony. Will this be the case with the Latter-day Saints I am now addressing? I fear it is coming, but how far it will affect you it is not for me to say.[21]

Greed or materialism is just one species of what might be called devotion to inappropriate objects. In ancient times, it often took the form of explicit idolatry. In our time, by contrast, overt idolatry is relatively rare. But that does not mean that we do not often grant our highest devotion to things other than God. These might include careers and wealth, status and prestige, learning, pleasure, youthfulness or fitness, power, or any number of similar objects. Each is a good thing in its place, used for the right ends, but each becomes idolatrous when it supplants the proper reverence we owe to our Father in Heaven. "In the Church," said Harold B. Lee,

> men who have been elevated to high positions have betrayed us, and some have wondered why others have not been called to fill certain positions. The Lord tells us why men fail. He said, "Because their hearts are set so much upon the things of this world, and [they] aspire to the honors of men." (D&C 121:35.)[22]

MODERN IDOLATRY AND FALSE IDEAS

Brigham Young spoke out forcefully on this subject. "Whether you can see it or not," he told the Saints of his day,

> I know that this people are more or less prone to idolatry; for I see that spirit manifested every day, and hear of it from nearly every quarter. We must stop worshipping idols. We are in the possession of the keys of the kingdom; the eternal Priesthood

---

[21] Lorenzo Snow, TLS, 151–52.
[22] Harold B. Lee, CR, October 1965, 128.

is committed to this people, and we are blessed as are no other people of which we have any knowledge. This people have the words of life—the way of life and salvation: they know how to save themselves and all that will cleave to them.[23]

Another class of improper objects of devotion apostles and prophets have warned against is made up of false ideas. Incorrect theories and inaccurate perceptions, often borrowed from the world, often carrying with them the prestige of fashion or academic respectability, can lead us into idolatry if they lead us away from the constituted oracles of God. In some cases, they may even take the place in our devotions that ought to belong to the Lord. As Ezra Taft Benson put it,

> Not only are there apostates within our midst, but there are also apostate doctrines that are sometimes taught in our classes and from our pulpits and that appear in our publications. And these apostate precepts of men cause our people to stumble. As the Book of Mormon, speaking of our day, states: ". . . they have all gone astray save it be a few, who are the humble followers of Christ; nevertheless, they are led, that in many instances they do err because they are taught by the precepts of men." (2 Nephi 28:14.)[24]

Sometimes, competing theories and ideologies encourage the growth of factions, groups of Saints who, warring against one another and against the divinely-appointed leadership of the Church, damage the unity of the kingdom of God. Such factions are every bit as devilish in their origin as those that originate in petty jealousies and ambitions, and they have been known to cripple branches and wards of the Church. The prophets condemn factionalism of all kinds. As John Taylor noted,

> There are those in our midst, who, although they have a name and a standing in the church, disregard the authority of the priesthood, both local and general. I hear sometimes of parties, and of cliques, and of rings in our midst. What! a party in the church and kingdom of God? What! rings associated with the principles of eternal truth—associated with the celestial law

---

23 Brigham Young, JD, 6:197.
24 Ezra Taft Benson, CR, April 1969, 11.

that emanates from our Heavenly Father? The devil got up a ring and was cast out of heaven for getting it up, as also a third part of the spirits who associated themselves with him. They were cast out because they devised principles that were in opposition to the word and will and law of God, and every man who follows in their footsteps, unless he speedily repent, will be placed in the same position—will also be cast out. The law of God must be put in force against the transgressor. No man who professes to be a Latter-day Saint can transgress with impunity. The priesthood of God cannot be disregarded with impunity.[25]

YIELDING TO MURMURING AND GOSSIP

One of the worst consequences of factionalism, and one of the chief contributors to and reinforcers of it, is gossip. When such gossip is aimed at the leaders of the Church, it becomes murmuring. The Book of Mormon offers us a striking case study of murmuring and its consequences in the persons of Laman and Lemuel. Millions of people have lived and died without the light of the gospel because of their constant complaints against their father, Lehi, and their brother, Nephi. Their endless cynicism, and their eagerness to read others' motives in the worst possible way, made it virtually impossible for them to commit themselves to the way of the Lord, even after an angelic manifestation, and have influenced nearly a hundred generations for ill.

John Taylor and George Q. Cannon strongly warned the Saints of their day against gossip. "Many stories go from mouth to mouth," they remarked,

> concerning the truth of which those who repeat them know nothing. But it seems as though the constant repetition of a falsehood impresses many people as though it were a fact. Where Latter-day Saints, so-called, are found telling that which is untrue, they should be called to an account. It is written that whosoever loveth and maketh a lie shall not be permitted to enter into the Holy City, nor to have a right to the tree of life, but they are to be without, with dogs, sorcerers, whoremongers, murderers and idolaters. The Lord has said, "He that telleth lies shall not tarry in my sight." Latter-day

25 John Taylor, GK, 173–74.

Saints should be warned upon these points, that they may not grieve the Spirit of the Lord, nor do injury to their friends and neighbors, by indulging in this pernicious habit of repeating and attaching credence to every slander and false rumor that may be put in circulation.[26]

Continuing with their theme, President Taylor and President Cannon cautioned the Saints specifically against the form of gossip that we have called murmuring. "Every one should be careful," they admonished,

> when they hear a story about their brethren and sisters, to refrain from repeating it until they know it to be true, and then not to do so in a way to injure the person about whom it is told. The reputation of our neighbors and the members of our Church should be as dear to us as our own, and we should carefully avoid doing anything to another or saying anything about another that we would not wish done or said about ourselves. We testify that those who give way to this influence, who take delight in reading lies which are published about us in papers circulated in our midst or outside of our Territory, who delight in listening to the false and malicious representations which are made concerning the servants and people of God or His work, or who themselves gossip about and aid in the dissemination of these things to the injury of their fellows, will, unless they speedily repent, lose the Spirit of God and the power to discern between truth and falsehood, and between those who serve God and those who serve Him not. Their own minds will become so darkened by the spirit of falsehood that the Spirit of God will cease to have power with them and will flee from them.[27]

In the twentieth century, Joseph Fielding Smith warned against the same evil practice, which separates those Saints who fall into it from the Spirit of God, as well as from those who have been called to communicate the will of the Lord to them. "Are we guilty," he asked,

> of finding fault with those who preside over us? Are we willing to listen to the counsels that they give to us, and receive

---

26 John Taylor, George Q. Cannon, MFP, 3:83.
27 John Taylor, George Q. Cannon, MFP, 3:83–84.

the voice of God as it comes through the one who stands to represent him as his mouthpiece upon the face of the earth? How many of us are willing to do that? We stood upon our feet here this morning and sang, "We Thank Thee, O God, for a Prophet," and yet there are some among us who criticize him, who find fault with him. When he speaks by the power of the inspiration of Almighty God, we are ready to condemn him, as we have done in times past.[28]

PERSECUTION BY FORMER CHURCH MEMBERS

Harold B. Lee warned of the terrible consequences that will confront those who persist in criticizing the prophets the Lord has placed in his Church. "There are those among us," Elder Lee observed,

> who would set themselves up as critics of the Church, saying that the Church has gone out of the way. Some splintered apostate clans even from the beginning of this dispensation have made fictitious claims to authority. We should warn these, as well as those who are in danger of being led astray, of what the Prophet predicted. He said "That man who rises up to condemn others, finding fault with the Church saying they are out of the way, while he himself is righteous, then know assuredly that that man is way to apostasy and if he does not repent, [he] will apostatize, as God lives."[29]

Notwithstanding prophetic warnings, some have fallen away from the Church and have either lost or renounced their membership in it. They have cut themselves off from the authority of the priesthood, from the ordinances of the temple, and from the messages that the Lord reveals through his servants. Especially in recent years, many of these apostates have become highly vocal and visible critics of the Church. But they are nothing new. President Wilford Woodruff was driven from state to state with the Saints until they found refuge together in the Great Basin West. He saw mobs and burned buildings, experienced violent opposition, and lost his prophet-leader, Joseph Smith, to a murderous conspiracy that had been urged on to its fatal action by virulent apostates. "There are two things which have always

---

[28] Joseph Fielding Smith, DS, 3:33.
[29] Harold B. Lee, CR, October 1965, 129–30.

followed apostates in every age of the world, and especially in our day," he remarked, reflecting on his own experiences.

> In the early days of the Church, in Kirtland, as soon as men apostatized from the church and kingdom of God, they immediately began to fear their fellow men, and to fancy their lives were in danger. Another peculiarity common to apostates was that they desired to kill those who had been their benefactors. This was the case with the Higbees, Laws, and others with regard to the Prophet Joseph, when they turned against him, they sought with all their powers to take away his life. Not only were they afraid of their own lives, but they sought to take his, and they eventually succeeded, and woe is their doom. What would they not give in exchange for their souls? But no matter, they cannot redeem them. This spirit also accompanies the apostates. What are they afraid of? There is something they do not understand or comprehend; they walk in the dark, and by and by they will unite with the wicked and try to overthrow the very work they have been trying to build up.[30]

Indeed, it has frequently been observed of apostates from The Church of Jesus Christ of Latter-day Saints that, though they leave the Church, they can rarely leave it alone. Anti-Mormon agitation from the days of Philastus Hurlbut to the present has drawn its strength from this fact. These enemies of the work of God should be numbered among the trials to be expected in the last days. As Joseph Smith testified,

> The scripture is ready to be fulfilled when great wars, famines, pestilence, great distress, judgments, etc., are ready to be poured out on the inhabitants of the earth. John saw the angel having the holy priesthood, who should preach the everlasting Gospel to all nations. God had an angel—a special messenger—ordained and prepared for that purpose in the last days. Woe, woe be to that man or set of men who lift up their hands against God and His witness in these last days: for they shall deceive almost the very chosen ones![31]

---

30 Wilford Woodruff, DWW, 279–80.
31 Joseph Smith Jr., HC, 6:364.

THE SAINTS OF GOD WILL PREVAIL

Still, although the critics will undoubtedly cause some of the Saints to stumble and to fall, the words of God's servants assure us that their dream of destroying the work of God will come to nothing. "The Lord has warned us of those who fight against Zion or who betray their sacred trust as holders of the priesthood," Harold B. Lee said. And then, continuing, he suggested that

> we would do well to remember what the Lord has promised to this people. The Lord declared, "How long can rolling waters remain impure? What power shall stay the heavens? As well might man stretch forth his puny arm to stop the Missouri river in its decreed course, or to turn it up stream, as to hinder the Almighty from pouring down knowledge from heaven upon the heads of the Latter-day Saints." (D&C 121:33.)[32]

So the enemies of the Church will fail. But as they do, they will also bring upon themselves destruction and the punishment of the Lord. As Heber C. Kimball declared,

> God says judgment shall come, and it shall commence at the house of God first, and then it will come upon those that have rebelled in the house of God; and . . . all the suffering that ever fell upon men and women will fall upon the apostates. They have got to pay all the debt of the trouble that they have brought upon the innocent from the days of Joseph to this day, and they cannot get rid of it.[33]

Pending that time, the safety of the Saints lies in their maintaining unity with each other and, even more importantly, with God and with the prophets through whom he speaks. They must resist the temptation to give their loyalty to objects other than the Lord. They must reject factionalism. They must not import into the Church the values and priorities of Babylon. After all, as Wilford Woodruff (to whom these were not merely theoretical questions) asked,

---

[32] Harold B. Lee, CR, October 1965, 129.
[33] Heber C. Kimball, JD, 5:94.

What are the things of this world? What are houses and lands, goods and chattels, and the treasures of the earth generally, to us? What are they to any Saints of God compared with eternal life? We should certainly be as well off to unite ourselves and our interests together in the things of God as to be separate. There have been too much selfishness and division and every man for himself amongst us, and the devil for us all.[34]

The Saints' security consists in remaining close to the great caravan of the kingdom, as it moves toward its destiny in the last days. If they wander away into strange paths, if they fall behind or attempt to run ahead, they will be vulnerable in their isolation. What is more, they will hinder the work of the Church. Lorenzo Snow knew this, and he implored the Saints to manifest to the world the unity and harmony that characterizes the Godhead and that should characterize the kingdom of God. It is a unity and a harmony, he knew, for which many, caught up in the strife of the world, deeply yearn. "The Latter-day Saints," he said,

> are trying to do the work that Israel failed to do; and that the former Saints did not accomplish, and we can only do it by becoming one even as the Father and the Son are one, and this in order that the world may believe that we are sent of God. We have got to be perfect, and come to the measure of the stature of Christ Jesus, in order that the world may know that Jesus has sent and commissioned His Apostles, and restored the holy Priesthood. If we have division in our midst; if we be divided either spiritually or temporally, we never can be the people that God designs us to become, nor can we ever become instruments in His hands of making the world believe that the holy Priesthood has been restored, and that we have the everlasting Gospel.[35]

---

34 Wilford Woodruff, DWW, 126.
35 Lorenzo Snow, JD, 23:341.

CHAPTER 20

THE INFLUENCE OF SATAN

"There are two influences in the world today," said George Albert Smith, during a great worldwide conflict,

> and have been from the beginning. One is an influence that is constructive, that radiates happiness and builds character. The other influence is one that destroys, turns men into demons, tears down and discourages. We are all susceptible to both. The one comes from our Heavenly Father, and the other comes from the source of evil that has been in the world from the beginning, seeking to bring about the destruction of the human family. The war that is being waged today is being fought by people who have not had the inspiration of the Almighty. It has been forced upon the world by those who have listened to the tempter, who would destroy all happiness in this life and in the life to come.[1]

Is God unable to put an end to this? Can he not make the world so that temptation, evil, and corruption have no place in it? The answer given by the prophets and apostles of the modern era has always been that, yes, he can, but that he cannot do it without thwarting his own plan and taking away the freedom of his children. "For it must needs be," said the ancient prophet Lehi to his son Jacob, "that there is an opposition in all things. If not so, my first-born in the wilderness, righteousness could not be brought to pass, neither wickedness, neither holiness nor misery, neither good nor bad."[2] Only freely chosen righteousness is real righteousness.

THE BATTLE OVER AGENCY

The costs of our freedom, it is true, are high. Many have failed in mortality, and many more will do so before the process runs its full course. There has been great suffering. But it was the judgment of our all-merciful and all-knowing Father in Heaven—and eventually it

---

[1] George Albert Smith, SGO, 42.
[2] 2 Nephi 2:11.

was our judgment, as well—that the cost of Lucifer's coercive coun-
terproposal (which would have "saved" us all, but with a "salvation"
that would never, could never, release us from his chains) was even
higher. As Ezra Taft Benson explained,

> In the war in heaven the devil advocated absolute eternal secu-
> rity at the sacrifice of our freedom. Although there is nothing
> more desirable to a Latter-day Saint than eternal security in
> God's presence, and although God knew, as did we, that some
> of us would not achieve this security if we were allowed our
> freedom—yet the very God of heaven, who has more mercy
> than us all, still decreed no guaranteed security except by a
> man's own freedom of choice and individual initiative.[3]

Thus, our struggle with Satan will continue until the end of the
present world order. And even then, when he is bound, Latter-day Saint
theology reveals it will not be because God has stepped in to coerce our
obedience, but because, in the freely chosen obedience of those who
will remain after the great destructions of the last days, Satan has lost
his power to tempt. "There was always," Wilford Woodruff said,

> a war between light and darkness, God and the devil, Saint
> and sinner, correct principles and false doctrines. We ourselves
> have a warfare with the evil propensities of our nature: we
> have already had to meet a warfare outwardly. In some
> instances there has been a physical contest, and our enemies
> have sought our destruction from the beginning. That warfare
> will continue until Satan is bound and iniquity swept from
> the earth. We need not suppose that we shall have peace in
> this conflict, for there will be no peace to the righteous until
> he reigns whose right it is to reign.[4]

In the meantime, Lucifer enjoys perfectly enormous power and
vast influence throughout the earth. As Harold B. Lee noted, "So
powerful was Satan that the Master, you recall, spoke of him as the
prince of this world. Said he, '. . the prince of this world cometh, and
hath nothing in me.' (John 14:30.)"[5]

---

[3] Ezra Taft Benson, CR, October 1961, 71.
[4] Wilford Woodruff, DWW, 239.
[5] Harold B. Lee, CR, October 1965, 128.

OPPOSITION FROM THE FORCES OF EVIL

From the beginning, the devil's power and influence have been directed in an unusually frank way against the prophets of the Lord. Wilford Woodruff knew this from personal experience, as well as from his study of the scriptures. "There is one thing true," he said,

> with regard to the history and travels of the Saints of God in every age of the world—they have had to pass through trials, tribulations and persecutions, and have had to contend with opposition, and this will always be their fate until the power of evil is overcome. This is one of the legacies that is designed from God to the Saints while dwelling in the flesh among a world of devils, for the world is full of them, there are millions and millions—all that were cast out of heaven; they never die, and they never leave the earth, but they dwell here and will continue to do so until Satan is bound.[6]

But Lucifer's fear and enmity became especially obvious when the Lord himself entered mortality in the person of Jesus of Nazareth. As Harold B. Lee remarked, "His coming as the Son of God seemed to have intensified the hatred of the forces of evil."[7] George Albert Smith, too, reflected upon this aspect of the New Testament record. "As we are now able to view things," he said,

> without personalities entering into our consideration, it seems incredible that Jesus, going about "doing good" and blessing the people, should have been subjected to such persecution and finally crucifixion at the hands of those who should have been his friends. Satan saw in the coming of Jesus the establishment of a movement that would ultimately mean destruction of his power in the earth. Therefore, he put into the hearts of the selfish spiritual leaders of the people, whom the people were quick to follow, the desire to oppose Jesus and his followers so that many may be led away to their destruction. The opposition to Jesus and his followers was motivated by Satan, who worked through the spiritual leaders of the people of that day. So has it been in the opposition to the Prophet Joseph Smith,

---

6 Wilford Woodruff, JD, 17:245.
7 Harold B. Lee, CR, October 1965, 128.

to the work established by the Lord in the earth in this last dispensation, and unto those who have accepted his message—such persecutions, drivings, and ultimate killings have seldom been recorded in the history of the world.[8]

As his final hours of liberty approach, and as he sees that his various schemes to thwart the plan of God have failed, Satan will grow increasingly desperate. Accordingly, prophets ancient and modern have unitedly testified that his power will be unleashed to a previously unimaginable degree in the last days. All pretense of subtlety will be cast off. "Even more than in Paul's day," predicted Hugh B. Brown,

> you will wrestle against principalities, powers, the rulers of darkness in this world, and spiritual wickedness in high places. The enemy is well organized, numerous and militant and has fiendish and cunning leadership; of this you should be aware and of this you must beware.[9]

When will this time of increased Satanic power come? It requires no predictive or prophetic gift to discern that we are already entering into it. "This is the great day of Satan's power," declared Bruce R. McConkie.

> It is the day of false Christs, false prophets, false miracles, false religions, false doctrines, false philosophies. It is a day when fables take precedence over facts, when all but the very elect are deceived. Of this day our Lord said: "There shall also arise false Christs, and false prophets, and shall show great signs and wonders, insomuch, that, if possible, they shall deceive the very elect, who are the elect according to the covenant." (Joseph Smith—Matthew 1:22; Revelation 13:13-14.)[10]

FALSE IDEOLOGIES AND TEACHINGS

One of the great ideologies of modern times, an ideology that did in fact deceive many idealistic people and that, with its cousin

---

[8] George Albert Smith, SGO, 42.
[9] Hugh B. Brown, AL, 47.
[10] Bruce R. McConkie, MD, 730.

National Socialism, has led to the deaths of tens of millions, is communism. Modern prophets have warned strongly against it and against all variant forms of it, seeing in it an attempt by Lucifer to impose upon us something of the very plan that he presented in the great antemortal council in heaven and that we rejected there. Hugh B. Brown, for example, testified that "he who is leading the forces of Communism and other isms of that kind is none other than Lucifer, the fallen Son of the Morning, Beelzebub, Satan."[11] And Ezra Taft Benson exhorted the Saints to take an active stand against any form of Satan's reemerging plan. "The fight against godless communism," he said,

> is a very real part of every man's duty who holds the priesthood. It is the fight against slavery, immorality, atheism, terrorism, cruelty, barbarism, deceit, and the destruction of human life through a kind of tyranny unsurpassed by anything in human history. Here is a struggle against the evil, satanical priestcraft of Lucifer. Truly it can be called, "a continuation of the war in heaven."[12]

And, Elder Benson taught, an ideology need not be expressly named *communism* in order to merit opposition from those who are committed to human freedom:

> Today the devil as a wolf in a supposedly new suit of sheep's clothing is enticing some men, both in and out of the Church, to parrot his line by advocating planned government guaranteed security programs at the expense of our liberties. Latterday Saints should be reminded how and why they voted as they did in heaven. If some have decided to change their vote they should repent—throw their support on the side of freedom—and cease promoting this subversion.[13]

Delbert L. Stapley, of the Council of the Twelve, warned what will happen if the righteous fail to participate in political affairs when morally significant issues are involved:

---

11 Hugh B. Brown, AL, 34.
12 Ezra Taft Benson, CR, October 1961, 70–71.
13 Ezra Taft Benson, CR, October 1961, 71.

If wickedness prevails and wicked men rule, then we will be as other nations. We will stand alone without the guiding influence and power of God to sustain us in time of trouble and in meeting the challenge and threat of internal and external Satanic ideologies, also the evil designs and intrigues of men and nations.[14]

Bruce R. McConkie recognized in the world around him important indications that the last days are approaching. Therefore, consistent with earlier prophets, he also testified that, bad as things are, they will get worse before they get better:

The signs of the times include the prevailing apostate darkness in the sects of Christendom and in the religious world in general. False churches, false prophets, false worship—breeding as they do a way of life that runs counter to the divine will—all these are signs of the times. As men's consciences are seared with the hot iron of sin, the Spirit of the Lord ceases to strive with them, sorrow and fear increase in their hearts, and they are prone, increasingly, to do that which is evil—all of which things are signs of the times. Robbery, plunder, murder, and violent crimes of all sorts; many of the strikes and labor disputes in the industrial world; much of the litigation that clogs the courts of the nations; drug abuse and indecent and immoral conduct; the spreading plague of evil abortions; the abominations of incest and homosexuality—all these things are signs of the times. Satan is not dead, and his influence is increasing and shall increase in the world until the end comes.[15]

Wilford Woodruff had detected the same trends, and he implored the Saints, urgently, to increase their efforts to build the kingdom before the floods burst upon it with full force. Speaking of those outside the Church who reject the commandments of God, he said,

I would to God they would repent, that their eyes might be opened to see their condition; but the devil has power over them; he rules the children of men, he holds Babylon in his

---

[14] Delbert L. Stapley, CR, October 1963, 114.
[15] Bruce R. McConkie, MiM, 403.

own hand, and leads the people whithersoever he will. There are changes awaiting us, they are even nigh at our very doors, and I know it by the revelations of Jesus Christ; I know it by the visions of heaven; I know it by the administrations of angels, and I know it by the inspiration of heaven, that is given to all men who seek the Lord; and the hand of God will not stay these things. We have no time to lose.[16]

PEACE TO BE TAKEN FROM THE EARTH

The result of Satan's surging power will be—and we can see it even now—vastly increased violence. Hatred and lack of feeling will, more and more, characterize the personal interactions of those who disdain God and his revelations. As Elder McConkie testified:

> On November 1, 1831, the Lord said: "The hour is not yet, but is nigh at hand, when peace shall be taken from the earth, and the devil shall have power over his own dominion." (D&C 1:35.) Later, Elder George A. Smith left us this apt statement: "Peace is taken from the earth, and wrath and indignation among the people is the result; they care not for anything but to quarrel and destroy each other. The same spirit that dwelt in the breasts of the Nephites during the last battles that were fought by them on this continent, when they continued to fight until they were exterminated, is again on earth and is increasing." (Journal History, Sept. 23, 1855.) Never again will there be peace on earth until the Prince of Peace (returning in power and glory to destroy the warring nations) comes to bring it.[17]

The famous battles and wars of the last days, long predicted by the prophets of the Old and New Testaments, will grow out of Satan's influence. Orson Pratt said of the rebellious wicked that God

> will give them up to the power of the Devil, and he will have power over them, and he will carry them about as chaff before a whirlwind. He will gather up millions upon millions of people into the valleys round about Jerusalem in order to destroy

---

16 Wilford Woodruff, DWW, 229.
17 Bruce R. McConkie, MD, 727–28.

the Jews after they have gathered. How will the Devil do this? He will perform miracles to do it. The Bible says the kings of the earth and the great ones will be deceived by these false miracles. It says there shall be three unclean spirits that shall go forth working miracles, and they are spirits of devils. Where do they go? To the kings of the earth; and what will they do? Gather them up to battle unto the great day of God Almighty. Where? Into the valley of Armageddon.[18]

The Latter-day Saints, too, will be at war, symbolically if not literally. Indeed, they already are. And this comes as no surprise, for they have seen how their leaders, and even their Savior, have been treated by Satan and his ministers. Jesus Christ warned his followers not to expect better treatment than he had received:

> The disciple is not above his master, nor the servant above his lord. It is enough for the disciple that he be as his master, and the servant as his lord. If they have called the master of the house Beelzebub, how much more shall they call them of his household?[19]

The Saints of the nineteenth century experienced this all at first hand, and with unmistakable clarity. Writing with his counsellor, George Q. Cannon, President John Taylor (who bore in his body until the day of his death bullets from the very guns that had martyred the Prophet Joseph Smith) commented:

> If lies could overwhelm the work of God, we should be completely crushed under their weight. It is this great influence upon which Satan depends to thwart the purposes of God and check the spread of truth; and, unfortunately for the world, it appears willing to drink in his spirit and to believe his fabrications. It is this that arouses mobs and causes them to indulge in acts of violence and hostility against unoffending servants of God, and that has incited them to shed the blood of innocent men in the most cruel and barbarous manner.[20]

---

[18] Orson Pratt, JD, 7:189.
[19] Matthew 10:24–25.
[20] John Taylor, George Q. Cannon, MFP, 3:81.

THE PREVALENCE AND ACCEPTANCE
OF FALSEHOODS

"It is verily true," said Wilford Woodruff, "that we have a warfare to engage in, for Satan seeks to engage in one with us, with our children, and with all the rising generation."[21] And, given his own experience, it is doubtful that he imagined that that warfare would always be metaphorical.

Already in the nineteenth century, the Saints knew much of the impact that lies told against them by anti-Mormons could have on outside observers. "Probably at no period in the world's history has Satan had such power over the hearts of the children of men as he appears to wield at the present," wrote John Taylor and George Q. Cannon.

> He has flooded the earth with lies, endeavoring by means of these deceptions to retard the work of God, to destroy its influence, and to make victims of its believers, especially those who have the authority to administer the ordinances of the Gospel. A more striking illustration of his power in this respect has not been furnished us than was witnessed at the meetings which were attended by some of the members of the Grand Army of the Republic who were passing through here. It would be incredible to believe that people could be so deceived by the false statements which were made to them by our enemies who reside here, had it not been witnessed. The most abominable falsehoods, which could be disproved with the greatest ease, were told with an unblushing effrontery that was Satanic; though many of the visitors had opportunities of seeing for themselves, and of mingling with the people, some went away fully imbued with the idea that the Latter-day Saints ought to be exterminated from the face of the earth. But to the credit of humanity be it said, others became thoroughly disgusted with the proceedings, and denounced unsparingly the folly and wrong of condemning a people affording so many evidences of the qualities that go to make excellent citizens, from the one-sided statements of their avowed enemies.[22]

---

21 Wilford Woodruff, JD, 8:270.
22 John Taylor, George Q. Cannon, MFP, 3:81.

But Satan's influence is not effective merely beyond the confines of the Church. Church authorities have recognized how he has directed much of his attention to seducing the Saints themselves. And he has had far more success than he should have. He has sought, as we saw in the previous chapter, to split them up, to turn them into enemies one of another, and, by so doing, to lessen the power they could have as a united body. Again, John Taylor and George Q. Cannon recognized this and warned against it in the nineteenth century:

> Not only has Satan sent forth his lies outside of our society, but he uses his influence in this direction among us. The tendency in our settlements and cities to listen to and believe in every wild and slanderous rumor which may be put in circulation is to be deeply deplored. No matter how unfounded and destitute of even the semblance of truth such reports may be, there are those among us so silly and credulous as to readily believe them. The injury that is thus wrought is not easily measured. Many of the evils from which we have suffered have been greatly aggravated by this disposition on the part of some who call themselves Latter-day Saints. The man who frames a lie is a great sinner; but the one who loves a lie, and who circulates a lie after it is told, is also under condemnation.[23]

And such a person slows the progress of the Church down by lulling its membership into a false state of security, distracting them with temptations and diversions of many kinds. "The devil knows," Ezra Taft Benson said,

> that if the elders of Israel should ever wake up, they could step forth and help preserve freedom and extend the gospel. Therefore the devil has concentrated, and to a large extent successfully, in neutralizing much of the priesthood. He has reduced them to sleeping giants. His arguments are clever.[24]

GOD'S SERVANTS WILL OVERCOME SATAN'S POWER

Nevertheless, although the Saints of God face huge obstacles, those who remain faithful, who hold true to their covenants and dedicate

---

[23] John Taylor, George Q. Cannon, MFP, 3:83.
[24] Ezra Taft Benson, CR, April 1965, 123.

themselves to the building of the kingdom, have a divine promise of victory. The outcome of this struggle is not, and never has been, in doubt. The words of the prophets attest to this fact. "The Lord has planted his Church and kingdom upon the earth in other ages," said Wilford Woodruff,

> but those that undertook to maintain it were soon destroyed, through the power of wicked men and devils. Righteous men were not permitted to live upon the earth. Even the Son of God was not permitted to preach righteousness but a short time before he and his followers were crucified and slain. But the day has now come when he has begun to prepare the way that he may come and take possession of the earth himself, and reign King of nations, as he does now King of Saints. The day of the Devil's power to prevail against the kingdom of God has passed away.[25]

Hugh B. Brown prayed that all the Saints would share this confidence, based on the promises of the Lord found in scripture and given through living oracles:

> God bless us all that we may face these troubled times with faith rather than fear, that we, believing in Christ and God the Father, may not feel that the adversary can overcome us. Ominous though the times are, I say to you that truth will triumph. He who leads the great forces in the name of Israel's God will triumph.[26]

Blessed with the same assurance, Brigham Young savored the coming triumph of the kingdom. "I will out-general the Devil," he said, in a flourish of nineteenth-century bravado that (unlike most) was backed by divine authority,

> and baffle him in every turn, and head him in every nook and corner; and he shall be turned hither and thither as the Lord will. I am determined, in the name of Israel's God, to see the Devil whipped from the earth, and out-generaled and fooled in all his schemes, and whirled about by this Church until he

---

[25] Wilford Woodruff, JD, 6:120.
[26] Hugh B. Brown, AL, 34.

is glad to leave the earth and go to his own place; and then we will see whether or not the Lord God has all things that belong to him.[27]

Wilford Woodruff likewise rejoiced in the absolute confidence of ultimate victory. "I know that the Devil seeks to overthrow this people," he said,

> and it seems that the powers of darkness have to a great extent prevailed in their attempts to control the hearts of the children of men. For many generations the powers of darkness have had almost universal sway; but I thank God that I have lived to see the day when the kingdom of God has been set up on the earth, and that it is no more to be thrown down forever. Men with wicked hearts may seek to pull down the cause of truth, but all their efforts will be in vain, for the blessing of the Almighty is upon his Saints, the inspiration of the heavens is upon his servants, and they will overcome the powers of temptation and of the Adversary.[28]

The victory will not come all at once, and it will not come without high casualties. Many, even in the Church, will fall before Satan's final, furious onslaught. And God's spokesmen in this dispensation have made clear that the definitive triumph over Satan will not actually take place until after the Millennium, after the devil escapes briefly from the captivity that will make possible that thousand-year period of peace, prosperity, and righteousness. John Taylor wrote of this, recalling that

> the spirit of rebellion has gone on ever since the devil and his angels were cast out of heaven. He and they have been making war against the saints, and will continue to do so; but Satan will finally be overcome. Before that, however, Satan will be bound for a thousand years, and during that time we will have a chance to build temples and to be baptized for the dead, and to do a work pertaining to the world that has been, as well as to the world that now is, and to operate under the direction of the Almighty in bringing to pass those

---

27 Brigham Young, JD, 6:198.
28 Wilford Woodruff, JD, 8:270.

designs which he contemplated from the foundation of the world.[29]

THE END OF SATAN'S INFLUENCE

Joseph Fielding Smith further explained that

> when the thousand years are ended, Satan shall be loosed for a little season and wickedness shall return to the earth. Satan shall gather his forces and in anger attempt a vain effort to wrest the earth from Christ. Michael, the great prince, the archangel, who once graced the earth and was known as Adam, the father of the human family, shall fight the battles of the just and shall overcome.[30]

The probationary period will finally be brought to an end, however. When the purposes of God are complete, he will call off the process. Humankind will be tested, but not infinitely or indefinitely. Satan will not be permitted to assault and re-assault those who have already rebuffed his blandishments, and those who delight to serve him will be removed. President John Taylor wrote eloquently of the final triumph of good, and the final ending of Lucifer's reign of murder, ugliness, and immorality, and it is fitting that we close with his testimony:

> This state of things, then, is merely permitted for a season, to develop the designs and influences of Satan, and their effects; to develop the weakness of man, and his incompetency to rule and govern himself without God; to manifest the mercy of God, in bearing with man, in the midst of his rebellion; to show man his ingratitude, and the depth of his depravity, in order that he may appreciate more fully the mercy and long-suffering of God, and the purity and holiness that reign in the eternal world. Man has tasted the misery of sin and rebellion, and drunk of the cup of sorrow, in order that he may appreciate more fully the joy and happiness that spring from obedience to God, and his laws. But to think for a moment that man here will always be permitted to subvert the designs of

---

[29] John Taylor, GK, 174.
[30] Joseph Fielding Smith, DS, 3:66.

God, and the world be for ever under the dominion of Satan, is the height of folly, and only develops more fully the pride, littleness, and emptiness of man. For notwithstanding man is a weak creature, in comparison to God, yet he has within him the germs of greatness and immortality. God is his Father, and though now wandering in darkness, sunk, degraded, and fallen, he is destined, in the purposes of God, to be great, dignified, and exalted; to occupy a glorious position in the eternal world, and to fulfil the object of his creation. Will this design be frustrated by the powers of darkness, or the influence of wicked and ungodly men? Verily, no. To suppose such a thing, manifests the greatest absurdity, which can only be equalled by the weakness and ignorance from whence it springs. What! God, the author of the universe, and of all created good, suffer his plans to be frustrated by the powers of the Devil? Shall this beautiful world, and all its inhabitants, become a prey to Satan and his influences, and those celestial, pure principles that exist in the eternal world, be for ever banished? Shall the earth still be defiled under the inhabitants thereof, when God is our Father? Shall iniquity, corruption, and depravity always spread their contaminating influences, and this earth, that ought to have been a paradise, be a desolate miserable wreck? Shall tyranny, oppression, and iniquity for ever rule? Shall the neck of the righteous always be under the feet of the ungodly? No, says every principle of reason, for the Almighty God is its maker. No, echoes the voice of all the prophets, there shall be a restitution of all things. No say the Scriptures of all truth, "The earth shall become as the Garden of Eden," the wicked shall be rooted out of it; the time shall come when the Saints shall possess the kingdom, and the earth shall become as the garden of the Lord. No, responds the voice of all the dead Saints, we died in the hope of better things.[31]

---

[31] John Taylor, GG, 70–71.

INDEX

ABOUT THE AUTHOR

A native of southern California, Daniel C. Peterson received a bachelor's degree in Greek and philosophy from BYU and, after several years of study in Jerusalem and Cairo, earned his Ph.D. in Near Eastern Languages and Cultures from the University of California at Los Angeles (UCLA).

Dr. Peterson currently teaches at BYU, where he is an associate professor of Islamic Studies and Arabic and was just released as a member of the Jerusalem Academic Coordinating Committee, which oversees academic programs at BYU's Jerusalem Center for Near Eastern Studies. He is the managing editor of the new Islamic Translation Series, which publishes dual-language editions of classical works of medieval Arabic and Persian philosophy.

Dr. Peterson served in the Switzerland Zürich Mission, and, for approximately eight years, on the Gospel Doctrine writing committee for The Church of Jesus Christ of Latter-day Saints. At the present time, he is a member of a BYU campus bishopric. He is chairman of the Board of Trustees of the Foundation for Ancient Research and Mormon Studies (FARMS), and edits the *FARMS Review of Books*.

Dr. Peterson is married to the former Deborah Stephens, of Lakewood, Colorado, and they are the parents of three boys.